Saint Mary's Press®
Essential Guide to Biblical Life and Times

Martin C. Albl, PhD

D1616945

saint mary's press

The publishing team included Brian Singer-Towns, development editor; The Crosiers / Gene Plaisted, OSC, cover image; prepress and manufacturing coordinated by the production departments of Saint Mary's Press.

Printed in the United States of America

4345

ISBN 978-0-88489-898-6

Library of Congress Cataloging-in-Publication Data

Albl, Martin C.
Saint Mary's Press essential guide to biblical life and times / Martin C. Albl.
    p. cm.
Includes bibliographical references and index.
ISBN 978-0-88489-898-6 (pbk.)
    1. Sociology, Biblical. 2. Palestine—Social life and customs—To 70 AD.
3. Bible—Antiquities. I. Title. II. Title: Essential guide to biblical life and times.
BS670.A45 2009
220.9'5—dc22

                                                                    2009015763

Dedication

This work is dedicated to my wife, Judy, who shares with me a love of the Bible as well as a curiosity about the cultures that produced it. Her support made this book possible.

Author Acknowledgments

I wish to thank my editor, Brian Singer-Towns, for his helpful suggestions, flexibility, and patience in working with me. Thanks are due also to the rest of the Saint Mary's Press team who helped to see this project to completion.

Acknowledgments

Contents

List of Articles

Introduction

God's Word Written by Human Authors

A basic Christian belief is that the Bible is the Word of God. Because God is eternal and unchanging, it seems very reasonable to assume that the Bible, as God's Word, would be eternal and unchanging as well.

But we need to consider this assumption carefully. In addition to understanding the Bible as God's Word, Christians also believe that the Bible was written by human authors. As the Second Vatican Council taught, "God speaks in Sacred Scripture through men in human fashion" (*Dei Verbum,* no. 12). This is clear from the title of many of the books themselves, such as the Gospel According to Luke and Paul's Letter to the Romans. And as we know, human beings are far from being eternal and unchanging—we are all formed and limited by our particular culture and society.

Christians also believe that the biblical authors were inspired by the Holy Spirit. If this is true, then isn't it possible that God took away any and all human limitations and allowed the authors to record his perfect and unchanging Word?

The best way to answer this question is to consider the writings of the biblical authors themselves. When we read the letters of Paul, for example, we do not get the impression that God is dictating to him word for word. Many of Paul's statements are very ordinary and personal: "I, Paul, write this in my own hand" (Phlm v. 19). "When you come, bring the cloak I left with Carpus in Troas" (2 Tm 4:13). The author of the Gospel of Luke tells us that he wrote by investigating and arranging eyewitness accounts about Jesus (see 1:1–4). In other words, Luke worked very much like any other human historian.

The Human Author Shaped by Society and Culture

If we wish to understand the Bible, we must take seriously the fact that all human beings are shaped by particular societies and cultures. There is no such thing as a generic human being; an individual human being must belong to at least one social and cultural group. As the council taught, to understand a biblical author correctly, we must consider how that author was influenced by "the situations of his own time and culture" (*Dei Verbum,* no. 12).

If we wish to understand a person from another culture and society, several things are necessary. Most basically, if he or she speaks another language, we must translate his or her words into English. Yet even if we understand the person's words, we may not understand the particular meaning those words have in his or her society and culture. To really understand this person, we would need to know something about his or her culture.

Let's apply this scenario to the Bible. Not only did the authors write in other languages (Hebrew, Aramaic, and Greek), but they also lived in societies and cultures that are very different from our modern American experiences. Thankfully, we have reliable English translations of those ancient writings. But an accurate translation does not guarantee that we will understand the message of these authors, because the meaning of any message is inescapably influenced by the assumptions and values of the society and culture in which it was written.

To get a concrete sense of just how different biblical societies are from our own, consider a brief list of some cultural and social givens of biblical societies:

- Slavery is a natural and acceptable social institution.
- Marriages are arranged by families. They are based on family needs, not on the romantic interests of the couple.
- Generally, women are under the legal authority of men for their entire lives—first their father's, then their husband's.
- In Israelite society, a range of actions was punishable by death, including practicing sorcery and fortune-telling, or eating the blood of an animal.

This brief list should be sufficient to show just how different many of biblical society's beliefs and customs were. If we wish to understand the Word of God properly, we must try to understand the cultural and social context of the human authors of the Bible.

Approaching the Biblical Societies and Cultures

We begin with two brief definitions. By *society*, I mean the social structures or institutions that are established by a particular people. These institutions include the family (or kinship group), economic institutions, religious institutions, and political institutions. In biblical societies, the dominant structures are kinship and politics: the economy and religion were not separate institutions.

Here is one example from the time of Jesus: The Jewish high priest (religious realm) was appointed by King Herod (political realm) from a select group of high priestly families (kinship realm). In addition to his religious duties, the high priest was responsible for maintaining social order and ensuring that the Jewish people paid their tribute to the Roman authorities. Biblical societies had no sense of our modern separation of church and state.

Culture refers to the basic values, beliefs, and practices that are shared by a social group. Cultural values and beliefs are expressed and activated through the social institutions.

This book is divided into a series of articles devoted to specific social and cultural topics, arranged in alphabetical order. The following major areas are covered:

- *social and political institutions*, including study of the family or kinship system and political structures
- *social customs*, including dance, music, and hair and dress styles
- *general cultural beliefs and values*, including beliefs about human nature, sexuality,

sickness and healing, and beliefs about the structure of the universe (cosmology)
- *religious beliefs and institutions*, including beliefs about purity, sacrifices, sin, and spiritual powers, as well as the synagogue and Temple systems in which these beliefs functioned
- *economic structures*, including professions in agriculture, fishing, and shepherding, as well as a consideration of the money, tax, and debt systems within the context of patron-client structures

Defining Key Cultural Terms

The term *biblical societies* covers a vast amount of space and time. Over a thousand years lies between the patriarchal societies of Abraham, Isaac, and Jacob and the societies of the New Testament. Biblical societies are found in Palestine, Syria, modern-day Turkey, Greece, and Rome. Following are some key terms necessary for understanding some of that cultural variety:

Canaanite. This is the name for a group of Semitic tribes living in Palestine. See the "Canaanite Religion" article.

Diaspora Jews. This refers to Jews living in communities outside Palestine. In New Testament times, Jewish communities were thriving in various Mediterranean cities: Alexandria in Egypt, Ephesus in modern-day Turkey, Corinth in Greece, Rome, and also in the Near Eastern communities, such as Babylon.

Because most Diaspora Jews spoke Greek, they used a Greek translation of the Hebrew Scriptures known as the Septuagint.

Gentiles. The term *Gentile* is a Jewish term that essentially means a "non-Jew." Sometimes Gentiles are simply called "the nations."

New Testament authors sometimes use the term *Greek* to mean "Gentile," as the Greek or Hellenistic culture was the dominant culture in the ancient Mediterranean world. For example, Paul says that the saving power of the Gospel is "for Jew first, and then Greek" (Rom 1:16).

Greco-Roman culture. By the time the New Testament was written, the entire Mediterranean area was part of the Roman Empire. It is therefore appropriate to speak of a Greco-Roman culture, rather than simply a Hellenistic culture.

The effect of Roman culture was felt primarily in the political and military areas. In the Gospels, Jesus encounters Roman military officers (see Mk 8:5–13), discusses paying taxes to Rome (see 12:13–17), is condemned to death by the Roman governor Pontius Pilate, and is crucified by Roman soldiers (see 15:1–39).

In other areas of culture, however, Roman influence was minimal. Even the Roman soldiers and government officials in Palestine and the Diaspora primarily spoke Greek, not Latin. Roman religion and philosophy was itself heavily influenced by Hellenism.

Hebrew. This is a general term for members of the twelve Tribes of Israel, used especially in Exodus and in First Samuel.

Hellenistic culture. The Greek King Alexander the Great (356 to 323 BC) conquered the Middle East, including Palestine, and lands as far away as India. Long after his reign, Greek language and culture continued to dominate these areas. Higher education, for example, often focused on learning the ancient Greek classics (such as Homer or other Greek poets) or on studying various branches of

Greek philosophy (Platonic, Aristotilean, Stoic). The native cultures of these lands, naturally, also continued to have an influence. The blending of Greek and native influences is known as Hellenistic culture (*Hellas* is the Greek term for Greece).

Israelites. This term is used for members of the twelve Tribes of Israel after the time of Exodus. It can refer specifically to members of the northern kingdom of Israel after they split from the southern kingdom of Judah after the death of Solomon (see 2 Chr 13:16). Its most common use, however, is as the self-designation of those Hebrew-speaking people in Palestine who had a covenant with the Lord. Their descendants who lived outside of Palestine and who spoke Greek also called themselves Israelites, especially when referring to the religious aspects of their lives.

Jews (*Ioudaioi,* in Greek). This term was first used by the exiles returning from Babylon, when they first established the Persian province of Yehud (see Ezr 4:12), later known as the Roman province of Judea. Originally it may have referred simply to the people from Yehud or Judea, but soon it was applied to all those who belonged to the covenant people of the Lord and followed his Law, both inside and outside of Palestine. In contrast to the "insider" group term *Israelites* (the name used by the people to refer to themselves), the term *Jews* is generally used by "outsiders," such as Greco-Roman writers, and also by those followers of the Torah who lived outside Palestine, especially in reference to their relationship with non-Israelites.

Mediterranean culture. Beyond these specific cultures, scholars such as Bruce Malina rightly speak of a Mediterranean culture that not only unites these widespread biblical societies but also includes many social groups existing today. Basic Mediterranean cultural values have changed little over the centuries, maintaining the centrality of the kinship group, a group-oriented (rather than individualistic) perspective, patriarchal leadership of social institutions, and the use of honor and shame to reinforce social norms. So in this sense, the articles in this book will also sometimes speak of a general "biblical culture."

Cultures in Cooperation and Conflict

As we saw from the last definition, the various Mediterranean cultures did not exist in isolation from one another. By the time of Jesus, Jews in Palestine had been influenced by Hellenistic culture for three centuries. Although Jesus grew up in the tiny Jewish village of Nazareth (whose population then was no more than five hundred), only about four miles away from Nazareth was the city of Sepphoris, a walled city with a theater that seated three thousand people.

The Apostle Paul is a good example of the blending of cultures. Paul was born in the city of Tarsus (in modern-day Turkey). Tarsus was a Greek city, known for its schools of philosophy and rhetoric. Paul was proud of his hometown. He tells a Roman officer, "I am a Jew, of Tarsus in Cilicia, a citizen of no mean city" (Acts 21:39). Paul also frequently mentioned the fact that he was born a Roman citizen (see 16:37, 22:25–29). He wrote his letters in Greek. Yet Paul was educated as a Pharisee, a strict follower of Jewish laws (see Phil 3:5, Acts 22:3). Even his name is revealing: in Semitic (Hebrew or Aramaic) circles he is called Saul; in a Greco-Roman environment, he goes by Paul.

Sources for the Study of Biblical Societies

In our study of biblical societies, we rely on information from the following major sources:

The Bible. Our main goal is to achieve a better understanding of the Bible, so we refer to specific passages often. We will include such books at First and Second Maccabees and Tobit, which are part of the Old Testament canon accepted by Catholic and Orthodox churches.

Near Eastern literature. Study of Canaanite and Babylonian religions shows how Israel's neighbors sometimes influenced Israel's beliefs.

Second Temple Jewish literature. Second Temple Judaism refers to Judaism from the time of the rebuilding of the Jerusalem Temple after the Babylonian Exile (around 515 BC) to the destruction of the Second Temple by the Romans in AD 70. The most significant sources include:

- *Dead Sea Scrolls.* These are the writings of a Jewish sect that lived in the Judean wilderness. The scrolls include many copies of biblical books as well as community rules, hymns, biblical commentaries, and other writings that shed light on the community's practices.
- *Writings of Philo of Alexandria (20 BC to AD 50).* Philo of Alexandria was a Jewish philosopher and biblical commentator well acquainted with Hellenistic philosophy and culture.
- *Writings of Josephus (AD 37 to ca. 100).* A Jewish religious, political, and military leader who wrote a history of the Jewish people and an account of the Jewish revolt against the Romans (AD 66 to 70).

Rabbinic literature. The writings of later Jewish rabbis often give insight into biblical culture. Most valuable is the Mishnah, a collection of tractates that record rabbinic legal debates and rulings on various questions of ordinary Jewish life. Although written around the year AD 200, it often reflects debates that took place earlier. The Babylonian and Palestinian Talmuds, commentaries on the Mishnah, were compiled many centuries after biblical times but occasionally provide some insight into biblical values and practices.

Archaeological evidence. The physical remains of temples, synagogues, and ritual baths give us insight into ancient religious beliefs and practices; remains of houses and work tools give us insight into daily life.

Social-scientific studies of modern Mediterranean cultures. As mentioned earlier, studies of modern Mediterranean groups provide insight into ancient cultural values. The bibliography shows the studies on which I have relied most. Especially influential on my thinking is the work of Bruce Malina, John Pilch, and their colleagues.

Supplied with these various tools, you are ready for an excursion into the foreign lands of biblical societies. It is my hope that these pages will help to make your reading of the Bible more understandable and more meaningful.

Alphabetical List of Bible Books and Abbreviations

Book	Abbreviation	Book	Abbreviation
Acts	Acts	2 Kings	2 Kgs
Amos	Am	Lamentations	Lam
Baruch	Bar	Leviticus	Lv
1 Chronicles	1 Chr	Luke	Lk
2 Chronicles	2 Chr	1 Maccabees	1 Mc
Colossians	Col	2 Maccabees	2 Mc
1 Corinthians	1 Cor	Malachi	Mal
2 Corinthians	2 Cor	Mark	Mk
Daniel	Dn	Matthew	Mt
Deuteronomy	Dt	Micah	Mi
Ecclesiastes	Eccl	Nahum	Na
Ephesians	Eph	Nehemiah	Neh
Esther	Est	Numbers	Nm
Exodus	Ex	Obadiah	Ob
Ezekiel	Ez	1 Peter	1 Pt
Ezra	Ezr	2 Peter	2 Pt
Galatians	Gal	Philemon	Phlm
Genesis	Gn	Philippians	Phil
Habakkuk	Hb	Proverbs	Prv
Haggai	Hg	Psalms	Ps(s)
Hebrews	Heb	Revelation	Rv
Hosea	Hos	Romans	Rom
Isaiah	Is	Ruth	Ru
James	Jas	1 Samuel	1 Sm
Jeremiah	Jer	2 Samuel	2 Sm
Job	Jb	Sirach	Sir
Joel	Jl	Song of Songs	Song
1 John1	Jn	1 Thessalonians	1 Thes
2 John2	Jn	2 Thessalonians	2 Thes
3 John3	Jn	1 Timothy	1 Tm
John	Jn	2 Timothy	2 Tm
Jonah	Jon	Titus	Ti
Joshua	Jos	Tobit	Tb
Jude	Jude	Wisdom	Wis
Judges	Jgs	Zechariah	Zec
Judith	Jdt	Zephaniah	Zep
1 Kings	1 Kgs		

Afterlife

We all have some ideas about the afterlife. At a funeral, we hear the pastor speak of heaven. We might watch a TV show about angels. But many details about the afterlife are usually not too clear. Does everyone go to heaven, except perhaps mass murderers like Hitler? Does hell, a place filled with devils and eternal fire, really exist, or was that just a concept invented to scare people into behaving properly? What do people look like in heaven? Are they the same age as when they died? Will we recognize our loved ones in heaven?

The Bible does not have a single response to these questions; rather, as we'll see, biblical beliefs about the afterlife changed and developed over time.

In Old Testament times, the primary belief was that at death all people went to Sheol, a sort of shadowy, underworld existence. After the time of the Babylonian Exile, however, the belief in eternal reward and eternal punishment developed in some Jewish circles together with the concept of a final resurrection of the dead. By Jesus' time, some Jews (the Pharisees, for example) believed in the resurrection of the dead while others (the Sadducees, for example) did not.

Sheol

Throughout most of the Old Testament, there is no conception of the Christian ideas of heaven and hell; rather, the common belief was that all of the dead, both the wicked and the good, would go to Sheol, where they existed in a sort of fleeting, shadowy way. The Hebrew word *Sheol* is sometimes translated as "the netherworld."

No one seems to remember God in Sheol: "Turn, Lord, save my life; / in your mercy rescue me. / For who among the dead remembers you? / Who praises you in Sheol?" (Ps 6:6; see also 115:17 and Is 38:18). Yet the psalmist has a sense that God's presence is still there in some way: "If I ascend to the heavens, you are there; / if I lie down in Sheol, you are there too" (Ps 139:8).

In Sheol "there will be no work, nor reason, nor knowledge, nor wisdom" (Eccl 9:10). Job describes Sheol as a place of dust and darkness, corruption and maggots (17:13–16). Sheol can simply be another name for the grave, or death itself: "My life draws near to Sheol" (Ps 88:4).

For both believers in God and non-believers, the ultimate destiny is Sheol. The psalmist is equally sure that "to Sheol the wicked will depart, / all the nations that forget God" (Ps 9:18). When Jacob believed that his son Joseph was dead, he refused to be consoled, insisting, "No, I will go down mourning to my son in the nether world [Sheol]" (Gn 37:35).

Belief in Sheol is closely associated with ancient Hebrew beliefs about human nature. The Hebrews did not share the Greek conception of the human as composed of a fragile physical body and an immortal soul. They thought more holistically of an essential connection between soul and body, and thus had difficulty conceiving of an immortal life apart from the body (see the "Human Nature" article).

The Old Testament does speak of some exceptions to the fate of Sheol: Enoch "walked with God, and he was no longer here, for God took him" (Gn 5:24), and Elijah is carried alive in a flaming chariot up to heaven in a whirlwind (see 2 Kgs 2:11). These events were mysterious exceptions, however, and give no information about the general fate of humans.

In the Septuagint (the Greek translation of the Hebrew Scriptures used by early Christians), the word *Sheol* was translated with the Greek word *Hades*. In Greek mythology, *Hades* refers to the realm of the dead and its ruler, the god Hades (Pluto, in Roman mythology). In general, the ancient Greek ideas about Hades were similar to Hebrew ideas of life in Sheol: all people, good and bad, descended to Hades and existed in a gloomy and shadowy way.

In the New Testament, Hades is thought of as a temporary place for the dead. Even Jesus descended to Hades after death: Peter says that God did not abandon Jesus in the netherworld (*Hades*, in the original Greek), but rather raised him from the dead (Acts 2:31). At the time of the Last Judgment, according to the Book of Revelation, "Hades and Death" will give up their dead, and the dead will then receive either eternal life in heaven or in hell. Revelation says that Death and Hades will then be "thrown into the pool of fire" (20:14)—Hades will have fulfilled its temporary purpose.

Gehenna and Hell

The term *hell* is not used in the NAB translation of the Bible. The belief in a place of eternal punishment of the wicked or unfaithful, however, is clearly found in the New Testament. In the Gospels, the common term used for this eternal punishment is *Gehenna;* the Book of Revelation uses the terms *pool of fire* or *the second death* for this concept.

Gehenna is the name of a valley that runs southwest of Jerusalem. (*Gehenna* is a Greek version of the Hebrew *Ge-hinnom,* which means "Valley of Hinnom.") In Old Testament times, children were offered in this valley as burnt sacrifices to the Canaanite gods Molech and Baal (see Jer 7:31, 2 Chr 28:3). The prophet Jeremiah threatened that God would punish participants in this worship: the valley of Gehenna would be filled with corpses, and it would be called the "Valley of Slaughter" (Jer 19:6).

The valley was associated with fire: at first with the fires of the sacrifices, and then later, when it became a garbage dump, with the huge, continuous fires with which garbage was burned.

Because of the evil reputation of the valley, its name became associated with developing Jewish ideas about eternal punishment. Gehenna's fires symbolized the eternal fire that punished the wicked. The prophet Isaiah mentions this fire in his description of those condemned by God: "Their worm shall not die, / nor their fire be extinguished; / and they shall be abhorrent to all mankind" (Is 66:24); Jesus connects this verse with Gehenna (see Mk 9:48).

In the synoptic Gospels, Jesus often uses the word *Gehenna.* The whole body can be thrown into Gehenna (see Mt 5:29–30, 10:28); Jesus describes it as "a fiery furnace, where there will be wailing and grinding of teeth" (13:42). It is identified as "the eternal fire prepared for the devil and his angels" (25:41), and "eternal punishment" (25:46).

The Book of Revelation has a similar conception: it refers to the Last Judgment of the wicked as the second death, and describes this second death as a "burning pool of fire and sulfur" (21:8, cf. 19:20, 20:14). The devil, "the beast and the false prophet" are also thrown into the pool where they "will be tormented day and night forever and ever" (20:10).

In today's world, we don't often hear much discussion about hell, so these terrible images of eternal suffering seem strange and disturbing. For many people, it is especially surprising that Jesus himself, whom we generally consider to be meek, mild, and forgiving, most clearly speaks about the possibility of eternal punishment for those who do not repent.

We should remember, however, what the biblical language about Gehenna is trying to express. For Christians the essential meaning of hell is life apart from God. In the Christian view, each person decides, through his or her own attitudes, thoughts, and actions, whether he will ultimately choose to accept or reject God—God does not force people to accept him. If a person chooses (with God's help) to accept God, then the person will be eternally in heaven with God. If the person chooses to reject God, then she or he has chosen to place herself or himself in hell—eternal existence apart from God.

Because God is the perfection of everything that is good, life without God can only mean a life that is separated from everything good—joy, peace, love, and honesty. The existence of a person apart from God would be an eternal existence filled with fear, loneliness, hatred, anger—and this life would truly be hell.

Heaven

Whereas modern Christians tend to think of heaven as a spiritual reality only, the biblical writers did not distinguish clearly between the physical reality of the sky and a spiritual heaven. In both the Hebrew Old Testament and the Greek New Testament, the words for *heaven* can refer to either a physical reality (the sky) or to the spiritual idea of the dwelling place of God, or to both. It is not always clear which of the two is meant in particular Bible passages.

Some ancient Hebrews or Christians may have believed that God did literally live in the sky; others clearly took this language metaphorically. King Solomon, for example, asks: "Can it indeed be that God dwells among men on earth? If the heavens and the highest heavens cannot contain you, how much less this temple which I have built!" (1 Kgs 8:27).

Heaven and the Kingdom of God

In the Gospels, the concept of heaven is closely associated with the belief in the Kingdom of God. (Matthew often uses the term *Kingdom of Heaven* where other Gospel writers have *Kingdom of God.*) The concept of the Kingdom itself is somewhat ambiguous, however. Some references seem to indicate a supernatural heaven, as when Jesus taught: "And if your eye causes you to sin, pluck it out. Better for you to enter in the kingdom of God with one eye than with two eyes to be thrown into Gehenna [hell]" (Mk 9:47).

In other passages, however, it is clear that the Kingdom of God takes place on earth. The best known example is in the Lord's Prayer: "Your kingdom come, / your will be done, / on earth as in heaven" (Mt 6:10). Jesus' disciples are to pray that God's Kingdom be established on the earth.

God's Reign connects the two types of passages. God's Kingdom exists wherever God rules—wherever things are done according to God's will. God's will is done in the supernatural realm of heaven, but it is also done when perfect peace, justice, and love are established on earth. Ancient Jews called this future time of perfect peace and justice the

"Age of the Messiah"; the New Testament typically calls it the Kingdom of God. In Jesus' teaching, the Kingdom of God, like a seed, had already been planted on earth, but it would only be fully established at the fulfillment of history (see Mk 4:30–32).

Heaven as God's Throne

A basic principle of Christian theology is that God and eternal spiritual realities such as heaven and hell cannot be described directly in human language because human language is too limited. Our language about heaven, then, must be based on analogies—we compare the inexpressible reality of heaven with earthly realities we can grasp.

A favorite biblical analogy compares God to a king, thus allowing people to get a small glimpse into God's power, wisdom, and authority. The Bible often depicts God sitting on a throne in heaven (Is 6:1; Ez 1:28; Dn 7:9; Rv, ch. 4–5). Although it is natural to picture God enthroned in a heavenly palace, most passages set God's throne in a heavenly temple that corresponds to the earthly Temple in Jerusalem. Isaiah says, "I saw the Lord seated on a high and lofty throne, with the train of his garment filling the temple" (6:1).

Heaven as a Heavenly Tabernacle and Temple

The ancient Hebrews conceived of the Jersualem Temple as an earthly parallel to heaven. Because the Hebrews believed that God was present in a unique way above the cherubim on the Ark

of the Covenant, they often imagined heaven as analogous either to the Tabernacle (the tent that housed the Ark of the Covenant while the Hebrews wandered in the wilderness) or to the Jerusalem Temple itself (whose Holy of Holies was the permanent location of the Ark).

As we saw, Isaiah says explicitly that God's throne is in the Temple (1:1). In Ezekiel's vision, God's throne is set about the "four living creatures" (Ez 1:4-11) who are identified as the Ark's cherubim (Ez 10:20). In the Book of Revelation, John sees the "temple that is the heavenly tent of testimony opened" and angels coming out (15:5). The Letter to the Hebrews says that the Ark of the Covenant and the Tent that held it were "copies of the heavenly things" (9:23).

Related Passages

Sheol: Ps 6:6, 88:4; Eccl 9:10. *Gehenna:* Jer 19:6, Mt 13:42, Mk 9:48. *Pool of fire:* Rv 19:20, 20:10–15, 21:8. *Kingdom of God:* Mt 6:10; Mk 4:30–32, 9:47. *Last Judgment:* Mt 25:31–46. *God's throne and heavenly Temple:* Is 1:1; 6:1; Ez, ch. 1, 10; Dn 7:9; Rv, ch. 4–5, 9:24, 15:5.

See Also

- "Death and Burial Customs"
- "Cosmology"
- "Human Nature"
- "Resurrection"
- "Temple"

Agriculture

Palestine in biblical times was heavily agricultural. In Jesus' time, around 90 percent of the people of Palestine lived in rural areas.

According to the Creation accounts, already in the Garden of Eden a basic task of humans was "to cultivate and care for" the Garden (see Gn 2:15). The close connection between humans and the soil is indicated in the relationship between the Hebrew word for *man (adam)* and the Hebrew word for *ground (adamah;* see v. 7).

Major crops produced in biblical Palestine included wheat, barley, grapes, olives, and figs. The Book of Deuteronomy describes, "For the LORD, your God, is bringing you into a good country, a land with streams of water, with springs and fountains welling up in the hills and valleys, a land of wheat and barley, of vines and fig trees and pomegranates, of olive trees and of honey, a land where you can eat bread without stint and where you will lack nothing" (8:7–9).

This passage from Deuteronomy, however, is rather idealistic. Much of Palestine is hilly and rocky, and land often had to be cleared before it could be farmed (see Is 5:2). Palestine has few natural water sources, so agriculture was heavily dependent on rain. The rainy season is relatively short (October to April), and droughts were common, so Israelite farmers often sought divine help from the Lord, or, in some cases, from Baal, the Canaanite god of rain and fertility. The Lord promised the Israelites "seasonal rain" if they would obey his commandments and keep the covenant (see Dt 11:13–14). Samuel says: "Are we not in the harvest time for wheat? Yet I shall call to the LORD, and

he will send thunder and rain" (1 Sm 12:17).

Before planting, the land was plowed with a wooden frame plow with a metal tip (made of copper, bronze, and later iron). The plow was pulled by animals, usually oxen. Elisha was called as a prophet when he was plowing with twelve yoke of oxen (see 1 Kgs 19:19). Seeds were planted either by broadcasting by hand (as in Jesus' parable of the sower, in Mk 4:3–9) or by a seed drill attached to the plow.

Seeds are planted in the fall, and crops are harvested in the spring.

Allusions to Agricultural Practices

Jesus often uses agricultural images. He compares preaching about the Kingdom of God with sowing seeds (see Mk 4:3–20, Jn 4:35–38). If the people accept, understand, and live out the Word, they produce a good harvest.

In a similar way, the Kingdom of God is compared to a mustard seed that starts out small, but then grows to be a large plant (see Mk 4:31–32).

The Letter of James uses the farmer as an example of patience: "See how the farmer waits for the precious fruit of the earth, being patient with it until it receives the early and the late rains" (Jas 5:7). (The early rains refer to rainfall in October and November; the late rains refer to precipitation in April.)

Even Paul, who grew up, lived, and preached in major urban areas, employs agricultural images. He compares the resurrection body with a seed that "dies," is buried in the ground, and sprouts up again as a new life (see 1 Cor 15:36–38,43–44).

Grains

The most common grains raised in Palestine were wheat and barley, and these were most commonly made into bread. (For more on the role of bread in biblical times, see the "Food and Drink" article.)

The three pilgrimage festivals are all associated with the planting and harvesting of the grain. Passover marks the beginning of barley harvest; the Feast of Weeks (Pentecost) celebrates the end of wheat harvest; Booths marks the beginning of harvest of fruits and the planting of seeds. Ruth (ch. 2) refers to the barley and wheat harvests.

Grains were either pulled out by hand or cut with a sickle: "When you go through your neighbor's grainfield, you may pluck some of the ears with your hand, but do not put a sickle to your neighbor's grain" (Dt 23:26). In the Book of Revelation, angels use sharp sickles in bringing judgment on the earth (14:14–20). The harvest is often used as an image of Last Judgment: "Then at harvest time I will say to the harvesters, 'First collect the weeds and tie them in bundles for burning; but gather the wheat into my barn'" (Mt 13:30). Jesus compares those who preach in his name to harvesters: "Look up and see the fields ripe for the harvest" (Jn 4:35).

The harvested grain was then threshed—the kernels of grained were removed from the stalk. To accomplish this, farmers would beat the grain or use a threshing sledge (planks with rocks or metal attached to the underside that were dragged over the harvested grain by an animal). The Bible often refers to the threshing floor where this was done (see 1 Chr 21:20–25).

To separate wheat from chaff, the farmer then tossed the threshed grain into the air with a winnowing fork; the lighter chaff blew away, while the heavier kernels fell to the ground. The chaff was then gathered up and burned. John the Baptist uses the process as a symbol of divine judgment (see Mt 3:12).

Cultivation of Grapes

Grapes were an important crop in ancient Israel. They were eaten directly, dried to make raisins, and used to make wine.

In Palestine the grape harvest took place in September. The grapes were gathered and placed in a winepress, which was essentially a stone tub with channels cut to allow the grape juice to flow out when the fruit was crushed. One or more men crushed the grapes by treading on them with their feet; the juice then flowed into a basin. Wine was stored in jars (see Jn 2:1–11) or in wineskins made from goatskins (see Mk 2:22).

Vineyards were typically protected by a fence or hedge; families would often build a watchtower on high ground overlooking their vineyard to protect their grapes during the growing and harvest seasons (see Is 5:2, Mk 12:1). Common people owned vineyards that were passed down through the generations. King Ahab and Queen Jezebel show their greed and cruelty in seizing Naboth's family vineyard (see 1 Kgs, ch. 21). Israelite kings typically owned large vineyards (see 1 Chr 27:27).

Symbolism of the Vineyard

In a famous parable in the Book of Isaiah, a vineyard represents the people of Israel; the Lord is the owner (see 5:1–7, 27:2–4). The Lord carefully takes care of the vineyard, but it produces only wild grapes: a symbol of the people's unfaithfulness and corruption. The Lord then allows it to be trampled down and ruined: a symbol of judgment on the people of Israel.

Jesus takes over this same image in his parables (see Mk 12:1–12). In Jesus' version, the tenant farmers are the Jewish religious leaders of his time, and servants sent by the owner to the tenants are the prophets. The beloved son that the owner sends in the end is Jesus himself. The parable reflects the Jewish leaders' rejection of Jesus, and the Lord's giving the vineyard to others symbolizes the giving of the Kingdom to the "new Israel," the followers of Jesus.

Though crushing grapes for wine was a joyful event, the cultural association between the juice bursting from the grapes and blood (see the phrase "blood of grapes" in Gn 49:11, Sir 38:26) together with symbolism of crushing, allows the trampling of the grapes to function as a symbol of God's judgment. Isaiah records God's judgment upon the people of Edom: "I trampled down the peoples in my anger, / I crushed them in my wrath, / and I let their blood run out upon the ground" (63:6). In the New Testament, the image is applied to Christ's judgment: "He himself will tread out in the wine press the wine of the fury and wrath of God the almighty" (Rv 19:15). The image was later taken over in a line from the "Battle Hymn of the Republic."

The grapevine itself often symbolizes Israel: "You brought a vine out of Egypt; / you drove away the nations and planted it" (Ps 80:9). Israel is a luxuriant vine whose fruit matches its growth.

In John's Gospel, Jesus applies this image to himself: "I am the true vine, and my Father is the vine grower" (15:1). He describes his disciples as the branches of the vine. Branches that did not bear fruit would be cut off and burned; those branches that did bear fruit would be pruned so that they would bear more fruit.

For further information on the cultural significance of the wine made from grapes, see the "Food and Drink" article.

Cultivation of Fruit Trees

Ancient Israelites also cultivated fruit trees: the two main products were olives and figs.

Cultivation of Olives

Olives were cultivated mainly for their oil. It was considered an essential agricultural product—God promises to send rain, so that the people will have "grain, wine and oil to gather in" (Dt 11:14). Sirach lists it as one of the necessities of life (see 39:26).

Olive trees grow to twenty feet in height and can live for centuries. They are cultivated in olive groves or orchards (see Ex 23:11, Jos 24:13) and harvested

Olive trees are an important crop in Israel, providing olives and olive oil.

by beating the branches with a stick (see Dt 24:20, Is 24:13).

Gethsemane, where Jesus prayed with his disciples before his Crucifixion, was an olive grove (see Mt 26:36) located on the Mount of Olives near Jerusalem. The name Gethsemane itself means "oil press"—a hollowed out stone and a beam used to crush olives.

Olive oil was used in cooking. It was often mixed with flour to make cakes (see Nm 11:8, Ez 16:13). It was a staple of a common person's diet: a poor widow had only a handful of flour in her jar and a little oil in her jug (see 1 Kgs 17:12). Cakes mixed with oil were commonly offered in the sacrificial rituals (see Lv 7:12).

For further cultural significance of olive oil, see the "Anointing" article.

Cultivation of Figs

Fig trees range in size from a tall tree to a low bush. One of Jesus' parables illustrates how fig trees were grown in orchards and cultivated and fertilized (see Lk 13:6–9). Figs are harvested both in summer and in winter in the Mediterranean region: "When its branch becomes tender and sprouts leaves, you know that summer is near" (Mt 24:32).

Figs were a staple of the common person's diet; they were eaten fresh or pressed into cakes (see 1 Sm 30:12). The fig tree is mentioned already in the description of the Garden of Eden (see Gn 3:7). Owning one's own fig tree was a symbol of security, self-sufficiency, and peace in ancient Israel: "Every man sat under his vine and his fig tree, / with no one to disturb him" (1 Mc 14:12). It was part of the eschatological vision: people "shall beat their swords into plowshares, / and their spears into pruning hooks. . . . Every man shall sit under his own vine / or under his own fig

tree, undisturbed" (Mi 4:3–4; see also Zec 3:10). Thus when Jesus tells Nathanael, "I saw you under the fig tree" (Jn 1:50), he alludes to a rich symbol of peace in the coming age.

The fig tree, by extension, was a symbol of Israel (see Jer 8:13, Jl 1:7, Hos 9:10). When Jesus curses a fig tree and it withers (see Mk 11:12–14,20–25), this can best be understood as a sign of God's judgment on Israel, especially because the story of the fig tree is connected with Jesus' "cleansing" of the Temple (see 11:15–19)—an action that many scholars see as a symbol of the destruction of the Temple and the beginning of the eschatological age.

Related Passages

Common agricultural products: Dt 8:7–9. ***Sowing and harvesting:*** Gn 2:7,15; Dt 8:7–9, 11:13–14, 23:26; 1 Kgs 19:19; 1 Chr 21:20–25; Is 5:2; Mt 13:30, 3:12; Mk 4:3–20,31–32; Jn 4:35–38; 1 Cor 15:36–38,43–44; Jas 5:7; Rv 14:14–20. ***Vineyard and vines:*** Gn 49:11; 1 Kgs, ch. 21; Ps 80:9; Is 5:1–7, 27:2–4, 63:6; Mt 20:1–16; 21:33–46; Mk 2:22, 12:1–12; Jn 2:1–17. ***Olive trees and fig trees:*** Gn 3:7; Ex 23:11; Lv 7:12; Dt 11:14, 24:20; Jos 24:13; 1 Mc 14:12; Sir 39:26; Jer 8:13; Hos 9:10; Jl 1:7; Mi 4:3–4; Zec 3:10; Mt 24:32, 26:36; Mk 11:12–25; Lk 13:6–9; Jn 1:50.

See Also

- "Anointing"
- "Festivals"
- "Food and Drink"
- "Meals"
- "Poverty and Wealth"
- "Torah"

Anointing

The basic action of anointing involves applying olive oil onto a person or object. It was both a common practice and a powerful symbol. Anointing could involve olive oil alone, or oil mixed with perfumes made from spices, myrrh, or other aromatic materials (such a mixture is called an ointment; see Lk 7:38).

In ancient Greco-Roman cultures, olive oil was both a regularly used product and an important symbol of strength, cleanliness, and good health. Athletes rubbed themselves with oil before exercising, and people anointed themselves with oil after bathing. Olive oil was a major export item in the Roman Empire and was often used in daily life for cooking and for illumination in oil lamps.

Thus the psalmist thanks God for "oil to make our faces gleam, / food to build our strength" (Ps 104:15). It is associated with joyful times: "Give them oil of gladness in place of mourning" (Is 61:3). "You set a table before me / as my enemies watch; / You anoint my head with oil; / my cup overflows" (Ps 23:5).

Religious Use of Anointing

In addition to these everyday uses, oil was also employed in religious ceremonies, especially to consecrate (make holy) a person or object. Anointing was part of the consecration ritual for a priest: "Aaron and his sons you shall also anoint and consecrate as my priests" (Ex 30:30). Jacob poured oil on a stone that marked a place at which he had encountered God (see Gn 28:18). Moses "sprinkled some of this oil seven times on the altar, and anointed the al-

tar, with all its appurtenances, and the laver, with its base, thus consecrating them" (Lv 8:11).

A king was anointed also, signifying that God had set him apart, consecrated him, for the task of leading God's Chosen People and carrying out God's will in defeating evil and establishing justice, especially for the poor and defenseless. "Samuel poured oil on Saul's head; he also kissed him, saying: 'The LORD anoints you commander over his heritage'" (1 Sm 10:1). "I have chosen David, my servant; / with my holy oil I have anointed him. / My hand will be with him, / my arm will make him strong" (Ps 89:21–22).

Some prophets were anointed too. God tells the prophet Elijah to anoint

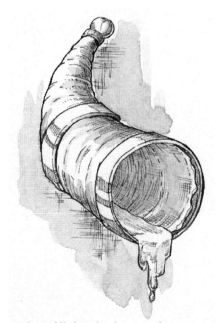

A horn filled with oil was used to anoint some biblical leaders, designating that the person had been chosen by God for a special purpose.

Jehu as king of Israel, and Elisha as prophet to succeed himself (see 1 Kgs 19:16).

Oil and Healing

Olive oil was also used for medicinal purposes throughout the ancient Mediterranean world. Greek medical writings often mention it as a remedy for various ills, as did Jewish culture. When he comes upon the traveler who was beaten by robbers, the Good Samaritan "poured oil and wine over his wounds and bandaged them" (Lk 10:34).

Early Christians also used oil to heal. When Jesus sent out his disciples to the Galilean villages, "they anointed with oil many who were sick and cured them" (Mk 6:13). When a person in the church community is sick, the Letter of James instructs the person to "summon the presbyters of the church, and they should pray over him and anoint [him] with oil in the name of the Lord" (Jas 5:14).

Anointing and Jesus the Messiah

The Hebrew word *messiah* literally means "one who is anointed." As a biblical title, the term refers primarily to Israelite kings who were often described in a highly idealized manner: "He shall judge the poor with justice / . . . and with the breath of his lips he shall slay the wicked" (Is 11:4). Eventually, the belief developed that at the climax of history, an ideal king ("messiah") would come and establish the perfect Reign of God's Peace and Justice on earth ("the age of the Messiah"); a peace that would extend to nature as well: "Then the wolf shall be a guest of the lamb, / and the leopard shall lie down with the kid; / The calf and the young lion shall browse together, / with a little child to guide them" (Is 11:6).

In the Gospels, Jesus identifies himself as the expected Messiah (see Mk 8:27–30, 14:61). The Greek translation of *messiah* is *Christos*. Thus, the name Jesus Christ is actually a title meaning "Jesus, the Messiah" or "Jesus, the anointed one."

Related Passages

Anointing and health: Ps 23:5, 104:15; Mk 6:13; Lk 10:34; Jas 5:14. *Anointing of kings and prophets:* 1 Sm 10:1, 1 Kgs 19:16. *Age of the messiah:* Is 11:1–9. *Jesus the Messiah:* Mk 8:27–30, 14:61.

See Also

• "Agriculture"

Atonement

One of the most well-known biblical beliefs is that "Christ died for our sins" (1 Cor 15:3). In more technical terms, Christians say that Jesus' death makes *atonement* for sins—it "takes away" or "pays for" our sins so that they are forgiven. But how can this belief make sense in today's world? What does dying have to do with forgiveness of sins? Even if Jesus' death is somehow related to forgiveness, how could the death of one person affect the sins of another? These are reasonable questions. To help answer them, we will need to turn to the cultural background of the Scriptures.

The essential idea behind atonement is the belief that one must "make up" for doing some wrong. We are actually quite familiar with this concept in our everyday experience. For example, let's say Kathleen and Claudia have been best friends since they were children. One day they have a huge disagreement, and Kathleen makes some cutting remarks that hurt Claudia deeply. The girls don't speak to each other for several days. At that point, however, they are ready to talk again. But Kathleen realizes that just telling Claudia she's sorry will not be enough. She feels a need to make it up to Claudia by doing something special, something good and positive for her. So perhaps she'll take Claudia out to supper or do some other act of kindness or thoughtfulness.

The concept seems to involve a sense of balance: if a wrong is done, something good must then be done to make up for that wrong.

Atonement and Sacrifice

The concept of atonement was prevalent in ancient religions and was closely connected with sacrifices offered to the gods. In Greek and Roman religions, animals were sacrificed; human sacrifices occurred in the Aztec and Canaanite religions. Sacrifices were not always done to make up for a sin—they might be given in thanksgiving or in an effort to appease the anger of a god. The need to offer something personal or precious as a sacrifice, however, is a common theme across many ancient cultures.

The biblical concept of atonements is most clearly in the "sin offering"—if a person broke one of God's commandments, he or she would need to offer a sacrifice to atone for the sin (see Lv 12:6, 14:18–20). The ancient Hebrew concept of sin, however, was much broader than our modern concept of intentionally doing something morally wrong—it included breaking laws of purity, either intentionally or unintentionally (see the "Purity," "Sacrifices and Offerings," and "Sin" articles).

The Book of Leviticus connects the idea of atonement with blood: "Since the life of a living body is in its blood, I have made you put it on the altar, so that atonement may thereby be made for your own lives, because it is the blood, as the seat of life, that makes atonement" (Lv 17:11).

The idea seems to be that humans must offer something precious to the divine powers, especially when atoning for sin. The blood of animals is especially important, because it is symbolic of life, the most precious gift a human has. It is possible that animals were thought to represent their human owners. So instead of a person's paying for his sin with her or his own life, it is possible that the ancient Hebrews (at least originally) believed that God would allow the person to pay, or atone, for sin with the life of one of her or his animals. This may be the point in the story in Genesis 22:1–19. At the last moment, God allows Abraham to substitute the sacrifice of a ram for the sacrifice of his son Isaac. A similar custom allowed the Israelites to pay a ransom for the firstborn child (see Nm 18:15; see also 2:40–51).

The Hebrew word usually translated as "atonement" is *kippur*, which literally means "covering." This would imply that the sin must be covered so that it is no longer offensive to God.

Why Doesn't God Forgive and Forget?

If God is just and merciful, why doesn't God simply forgive our sins without demanding some kind of atonement? The idea that God could just "forgive and forget" sounds reasonable at first, but if we consider the idea in more depth, we'll find some difficulties.

Let's take a theoretical example of a serial killer—a man who had kidnapped, tortured, and killed several people, simply at random. Let's imagine that after a year in prison, he had a complete and genuine change of heart. He truly repented his deeds and resolved to start a new life.

But would it be right to simply forgive and forget what he had done? Doesn't our sense of justice demand that this man do something to make up, or atone, for his crimes, that he not be forgiven so easily? We might even have the sense that it's impossible for him to be forgiven because his crimes were so horrible.

So too the Bible reflects this need to cleanse a wrongdoing by making up for it through offering a sacrifice.

Christ's Atoning Death

So if animal sacrifices were acceptable in Old Testament times to atone for sin, why would the death of Jesus be necessary? Again, some cultural background helps us answer the question.

In addition to animal sacrifices, ancient Greek and Roman writings are filled with references to great heroes sacrificing their lives for their countries. The Roman statesman Cato, for example, spoke of offering his life as a "ransom" to atone for the sins of his people.

In the Old Testament, the prophet Isaiah announces that a figure known simply as the Lord's servant will atone for his people through his suffering:

But he was pierced for our offenses,
crushed for our sins,
Upon him was the chastisement that
makes us whole,
by his stripes we were healed
We had all gone astray like sheep,
each following his own way;
But the Lord laid upon him the guilt
of all.
(53:5–6)

A clear belief that the death of martyrs can be a "'ransom" for the sins of the people is also found in the Second Temple writing 4 Maccabees.

New Testament writers applied these concepts to Jesus' death. The Letter to the Hebrews teaches that Jesus' sacrifice takes away the need for any further animal sacrifices: "He entered once for all into the sanctuary, not with the blood of goats and calves but with his own blood, thus obtaining eternal redemption" (9:12). Paul teaches that Jesus was "set forth as an expiation, through faith, by his blood" (Rom 3:25).

The Gospels record that this was Jesus' own understanding of his death: "Then he took a cup, gave thanks, and gave it to them, saying, 'Drink from it, all of you, for this is my blood of the covenant, which will be shed on behalf of many for the forgiveness of sins'" (Mt 26:27).

To fully grasp the significance of Jesus' words, we need to recall ancient Jewish beliefs about how the messiah, as the representative of the Chosen People, would initiate the Kingdom of God on earth—a Kingdom that would include the final forgiveness of sin. Thus, what happened to Jesus as the representative of the people affected all the people.

Is God a Bloodthirsty Tyrant?

Some Christians are troubled by the doctrine of the atonement because it can make God appear as a bloodthirsty tyrant who demands the death of his Son in order to make up for sins. Such an interpretation is a misunderstanding, however, for several reasons.

As we have seen, the concept of atonement is not arbitrary but rather reflects a fundamental human belief that wrongdoing must be made up for. Virtually all ancient religions believed that it was necessary to offer the life of an animal in order to atone for sin, and virtually all ancient cultures believed that a person could offer his or her own life as a kind of atoning sacrifice for the people. Finally, the point of the doctrine is not that God punishes his Son for the sins of others. The point is that God's Son freely chose to offer himself, out of love, in order to make atonement: "I will lay down my life for my sheep. . . . No one takes it from me, but I lay it down on my own" (Jn 10:15–18).

Related Passages

Atoning sacrifices: Lv 12:6, 14:18–20, 17:11. *Atoning death in the Old Testament:* Is 52:13—53:12. *Christ's atoning death:* Mt 26:27; Rom 3:25; 1 Cor 15:3; Heb, ch. 9–10.

See Also

- "Purity"
- "Sacrifices and Offerings"
- "Sin"

Canaanite Religion

Canaanites is a general name for the ancient native tribes who lived in the land of Palestine alongside the Israelites. We often encounter their distinctive religious beliefs in the Old Testament.

Canaan and Canaanites

Canaan is an ancient name for the land that now includes the modern nations of Israel, Palestine, parts of southern Lebanon, and parts of southwestern Syria (see Nm 34:2–13). In general, it refers to the lands between the Egyptian empire in the south and the Mesopotamian empires (Assyrian, Babylonian) to the north and east.

Canaanite peoples never formed a political unity but shared a common language (Northwest Semitic) and religion. Canaanite tribes included the Phoenicians, Amorites, and Horites (Hurrians). The Canaanites were also related to other Semitic groups—the Edomites, Moabites, Ammonites, Philistines, and Israelites. They were active traders, especially known for their exports of purple-dyed textiles (the names Canaan and Phoenicia are related to the word *purple*). The Phoenicians are credited with developing the first alphabet.

Canaanite Gods and Goddesses

A primary focus of Canaanite worship was fertility. Rituals petitioned the gods for both the fertility of the soil in order to grow crops and human fertility in order to have children.

The Canaanites worshiped many gods: El was known as the father of the gods, while his companion, Asherah, was known as the mother of the gods.

In Semitic languages, *el* can mean simply "the divine" or "god;" the plural form *elohim* means gods. In Canaanite texts, however, if often refers specifically to the father of the gods, El. This god had many titles: El-Elyon (meaning "God Most High," see Gn 14:18–20); El-Berith (meaning "God of the Covenant," see Jgs 9:46), El-Shaddai (translated as "God the Almighty," although possibly meaning "God of the Mountain," see Ex 6:3).

The biblical authors systematically took the names of El and applied them to the Lord (Yahweh). For example, the Canaanite priest Melchizedek worshiped El-Elyon, (God Most High), but Abraham assumed that God Most High and the Lord are the same: the one God who created the heavens and the earth (see Gn 14:18–22). We see a similar process of identification in Exodus 6:3: "As God the Almighty I appeared to Abraham, Isaac and Jacob, but my name, Lord, I did not make known to them."

In Canaanite religion, El is often portrayed as head of the divine council or court. This image of El seems to have influenced the numerous biblical accounts of the Lord (Yahweh) as the leader of the divine council (see the "Spiritual Powers" article).

Baal is perhaps the most important Canaanite god. In Semitic languages, the word *baal* means "lord" or "master" but, like the word *el,* is often used to signify one specific god. Baal was the god of storms and vegetation; worshipers called on him to send the rain needed to grow their crops. Because Canaan had frequent droughts and was highly dependent on rain for agriculture, the worship of Baal was very popular.

Like the name El, the name Baal is often connected with special titles, such as Baal-zebub (which may mean "Lord of the flies," see 2 Kgs 1:2) or Baal-peor (Peor is the place of Baal's shrine; see Nm 25:3). The Old Testament thus sometimes refers to the worship of "the Baals" (see Jgs 2:11). The name Beelzebul, used for Satan in the New Testament (see Mt 12:24–27), is apparently based on this variation of Baal's name.

In one Canaanite myth, Baal defeats the forces of chaos, represented by "Prince Sea." This myth (along with the Babylonian epic *Enuma Elish*) seems to have influenced some descriptions of God's victory over the forces of dragons and chaotic waters (see Ps 74:12–15).

Asherah is the goddess of love and fertility (see 1 Kgs 15:13) and mother of the gods. Sacred wooden poles used in her worship ceremonies are known as *asherot* (singular: *ashera*).

The goddess Astarte, also known as Ashtoreth, is the companion of Baal (see 1 Kgs 11:5). Her name is also found in the plural Ashtaroth (see Jgs 2:13), again referring to the fact that she was worshiped at different places. Her worship was widespread throughout the Near East, where she was known as a goddess of war as well as a goddess of love and fertility.

The Canaanite god Molech seems to have been a god of the dead. He is associated with sacrifices of children (see Lv 18:21, Dt 18:10). Jeremiah adds that children were also sacrificed to Baal (see 19:5). The ritual apparently involved killing children and burning their bodies (see Ez 16:20–21). The practice is especially connected with the Valley of Hinnom (*Ge-hinnom,* in Hebrew), south of Jerusalem (see Jer 7:31, 32:35). Because of its association with this practice, the name of the valley was adapted as Gehenna—the name for hell in the Gospels (see Mt 5:22).

Canaanite Worship

Canaanites worshiped their gods in temples (King Ahab built a temple to Baal in Samaria, see 1 Kgs 16:32; the Philistines had a temple of Astarte, see 1 Sm 31:10). They also worshiped at open-air altars built on hills and by tree groves. Here they erected stone pillars, associated with the worship of Baal, as well as sacred poles, associated with the worship of Astarte (see Ex 34:13). A summary statement says, "They, too, built for themselves high places, pillars, and sacred poles, upon every high hill and under every green tree" (1 Kgs 14:23).

The high place was one of the earliest places of worship for the ancient Canaanites. Located on a hill, it would usually have an altar and often a sacred grove of trees.

Fertility rituals involving sexual intercourse ("sacred prostitution") apparently formed part of the worship rituals (see 1 Kgs 14:24, 2 Kgs 23:7). Judah mistakenly thought Tamar was one of these "temple prostitutes" (see Gn 38:21–22).

Canaanite Worship and Israel: Attraction and Rejection

The Bible warns frequently that association with the Canaanite people will lead to a worship of their gods (see Ex 34:11–13, Dt 7:1–5). Deuteronomy goes so far as to call for the destruction of the Canaanite people.

The frequent warnings imply that many Israelites were in fact attracted to the worship of the Canaanite gods. Already in the time of Moses, some Israelites were worshiping Baal-Peor (see Nm, ch. 25). During the time of the judges, Gideon destroyed his father's altar to Baal and cut down the sacred pole (see Jgs 6:25).

Even kings of Israel and Judah worshiped the Canaanite gods. Solomon worshiped Astarte (see 1 Kgs 11:5). Ahab, King of Israel, married Jezebel, a woman from the Canaanite city of Sidon, and built a temple to Baal in his capital of Samaria (see 1 Kgs 16:31–33). Jezebel fed 450 prophets of Baal and four hundred prophets of Asherah at her table (see 1 Kgs 18:19). King Manasseh of Judah erected altars to Baal and sacred poles in the Jerusalem Temple itself (see 2 Kgs 21:3–7).

This last example shows that many Israelites did not reject the worship of the Lord in favor of Canaanite gods, but rather combined the two. Inscriptions found in the Sinai Peninsula even refer to "Yahweh and his Asherah."

The Bible records many conflicts between worshipers of the Canaanite gods and those dedicated to the worship of the Lord alone. Queen Jezebel persecuted and killed the prophets of the Lord (see 1 Kgs 18:13). The prophet Elijah had a contest with some prophets of Baal, designed to discover which god was stronger; Elijah won the contest and killed the prophets (see vv. 21–40). Other prophets verbally attacked the worship of Baal (see Hos 2:15; Jer 2:8, 23:13).

Certain kings tried to stamp out the Canaanite influence. Jehu destroyed the temple of Baal in Samaria, slaughtering all the worshipers (see 2 Kgs 10:18–27). Hezekiah attacked the cultic sites (see 18:4). Josiah carried out the definitive attack on Canaanite worship (see 23:4–20), including removing the objects used to worship "Baal, Asherah, and the whole host of heaven" (23:4) from the Temple and defiling the site of Molech worship in the valley on Ben-hinnom (see 23:10).

References to Canaanite worship: Gn 38:21–22; Ex 34:11–13; Nm, ch. 25; Dt 7:1–5; Jgs 2:10–13, 6:25; 1 Sm 31:10; 1 Kgs 11:5–8, 14:23–24, 15:13, 16:31–33, 18:13,19,21–40; 2 Kgs 21:3–7, 23:7; Jer 2:8, 23:13; Hos 2:15. *Child sacrifices to Molech:* Lv 18:21; Dt 18:10; Jer 7:31; 32:35; Ez 16:20 –21. *Israelite attacks on Canaanite worship:* Dt 7:1–5; 1 Kgs 18:21–40; 2 Kgs 10:18–27, 18:4, 23:4–20.

Related Passages

The Lord and El: Gn 14:18–22, Ex 6:3, Jgs 9:46. *Elijah and the prophets of Baal:* 1 Kgs 16:31–33, 18:21–40.

See Also

- "Afterlife"
- "Creation"
- "Spiritual Powers"

Chosen People

The Jewish people are sometimes known as God's Chosen People. But does it make sense to claim that God would have a Chosen People? After all, isn't God the God of all people? Why would God play favorites—choosing one nation over another?

The One God and the Many Gods

To understand the concept, we must first remember that in ancient times, every nation worshiped its own gods. The ancient Greeks worshiped Zeus, god of lightning and thunder; Apollo, god of the sun; Athena, goddess of wisdom; along with countless other gods and goddesses. The Romans worshiped their own gods and goddesses, as did the Egyptians and every other ancient people.

At first then, the God of Israel was understood as just one of the many gods of the nations. Eventually, how-ever, the Israelites came to believe that the Lord was not simply a local god but the Creator of all: "I am God, there is no other" (Is 46:9). Closely connected with this development was the belief that it was Israel's task to proclaim this belief in one God to all other nations: "It is too little, he says, for you to be my servant, / to raise up the tribes of Jacob, / and restore the survivors of Israel; / I will make you a light to the nations, / that my salvation may reach to the ends of the earth" (49:6; see also Gn 12:2–3). The Lord first chose Israel, but eventually God's Word would be proclaimed to all nations.

As a sign of God's faithfulness in choosing Israel, God enters into a covenant—an agreement, an exchange of promises—with the people. God promises to bless the people, and the people remain in his blessings as long as they obey the commandments of the Torah (see the "Covenant" article).

If the Israelites are God's Chosen People, this does not mean they are stronger or "better" than any other nation. It simply means God chose them for a certain task: to reveal to the other nations that there is only one God, and to teach the ethical laws of this one God to all nations.

God's Surprising Choices

Why did God choose Israel and not some other nation? "It was not because you are the largest of all nations that the Lord set his heart on you and chose you, for you are really the smallest of all nations" (Dt 7:7).

Looking closely, we see a pattern of God's surprising choices throughout the whole Bible. God often calls upon people who consider themselves unworthy or whom other people see as weak and powerless.

We see this pattern from the beginning. When God calls Abraham to become the father of the new Chosen People (see Gn 12:1–3), no particular reason is given. Abraham is not especially wise, intelligent, or a great leader.

Later God chooses Jacob, and not Isaac's firstborn son, Esau, to continue the line of the Chosen People (see ch. 27). In ancient Hebrew society, the eldest son was in a favored position, receiving a double portion of the father's inheritance (see Dt 21:17). In making these choices, God goes against the Israelite culture's rules and expectations.

Choosing the Weak

Consider also Moses' reaction when God chooses him to lead the people out of Egypt: "I have never been eloquent, neither in the past, nor recently, nor now that you have spoken to your servant; but I am slow of speech and tongue" (Ex 4:10). Jeremiah reacts in a similar way when God calls on him to be a prophet: "'Ah Lord GOD!' I said, / 'I know not how to speak; I am too young'" (Jer 1:5).

But the Lord accepts neither the excuses of Moses nor of Jeremiah. The Lord has a plan, and he chooses people who fulfill it, even when the ones chosen, or others, consider them unworthy.

In New Testament times, God continues the same pattern. Paul reminds the church members of Corinth that "not many of you were wise by human standards, not many were powerful, not many were of noble birth" (1 Cor 1:26).

God's preference for the weak and lowly goes hand in hand with "the message of the cross" (v. 18), the Christian message that proclaims "Christ crucified" (v. 23)—the power of God displayed in the weakness of a crucified man.

There is no reason to doubt that the same pattern continues today. God continues to choose people, and God continues to make surprising choices. In the eyes of the world today, many people are looked upon as unpopular, even as losers. But, as the Bible shows us very clearly, it's precisely these people for whom God often has a very specific plan. God sees goodness, talent, and potential where the world, and often we ourselves, do not.

The Chosen People and the Torah

Any cultural group reinforces the identity of its members by emphasizing shared beliefs and practices. Thus, Americans reinforce their shared political identity by reciting the Pledge of Allegiance in public schools, or in singing the National Anthem at a sporting event.

For ancient Israelites, the Torah was the great shaper of identity. It made them who they were—it gave them their identity. A Jew could simply be identified as someone who followed God's Torah. When the males were circumcised, this was a physical sign and reminder that God has set them apart as a special people. When the people followed the food laws on a daily basis, or observed the Sabbath rest on a weekly basis, they were continually reminded that God had set them apart for a special task.

Jews and Gentiles

Israel's status as the Chosen People set them apart from all other nations. Only Israel worshiped the Lord (Yahweh); only Israel followed the Torah. In the Bible, all other nations are thus grouped under the label "Gentiles" (the Bible also frequently refers to them simply as "the nations").

Parts of the Old Testament teach a harsh and uncompromising attitude toward the Gentiles. Israel is warned not to associate with them, lest they be led astray into worshiping their gods instead of the Lord. "You shall not intermarry with them, neither giving your daughters to their sons not taking their daughters for your sons. For they would turn your sons from following me to serving other gods. . . ." (Dt 7:3–4; see also the prohibitions against marrying Gentiles in Ez, ch. 9–10; Neh 13:23–30; and the criticism of Solomon for marrying foreign women and worshiping their gods in 1 Kgs 11:1–10). The Book of Deuteronomy goes so far as to command the Israelites to destroy the Gentile nations who lived in the land of Canaan (see Dt, ch. 7).

Yet there is also an openness to the Gentiles within the Old Testament. In Jonah, for example, God sends Jonah to preach repentance to the Gentile people of Nineveh. The Book of Ruth shares this more open attitude. Ruth is a Gentile resident of Moab who marries an Israelite. After her husband's death, she returns to Israel with her mother-in-law, accepts the God of Israel, remarries an Israelite, and becomes part of Israel. In fact, Ruth was the great-grandmother of the greatest of the kings of Israel, David. Finally, we can mention the belief that Israel was to be a "light to the nations" (Is 49:6) by proclaiming the belief in the one God to them.

This tension between a closed and more open attitude toward outsiders is characteristic of any cultural group. At times Israel displayed a closed attitude to avoid losing its own religious beliefs and identity; at other times, Israel was more confident in interacting with other nations, believing that it had a message to share with them.

The Church as the Chosen People

The earliest followers of Jesus were all Jews. They thought of themselves simply as members of the Chosen People who believed that Jesus was the Messiah.

Yet inevitably followers of Jesus came to regard themselves as separate from other Jews. Several factors were involved in this transition. One essential factor was a changed attitude toward the Torah: a decision was made that Gentiles could become followers of Jesus without obeying all the commandments of the Torah (see Acts, ch. 15; Gal, ch. 2). When this crucial step was taken, the Jesus movement began to take on a separate identity. The Book of Acts of the Apostles reports that Gentiles began to join the church in Antioch, "and it was in Antioch that the disciples were first called Christians" (11:26).

A further factor was that the Christian belief in the divinity of Jesus came to be seen as a contradiction of traditional Jewish beliefs in the oneness of God.

The early Christian communities were called churches. In Greek the word is *ekklesia*, which literally means "the ones who are called out." It thus refers specifically to the idea that church members, Christians, are those whom God has called out of the general population to join a distinct group. The First Letter of Peter calls Christians "a chosen race, a royal priesthood, a holy nation, a people of his own" (2:9). Instead of the laws of the Torah, churches soon developed their own distinctive beliefs and practices that reinforced their own Christian group identity. The rituals of Baptism and the Lord's Supper are two central practices.

Related Passages

God's choices: Gen 12:2–3; Dt, ch. 28; Is 49:6; Rom 1:19–20. ***God's choice of the weak:*** Gn 12:1–3, 21:1–8, ch. 27; Ex 4:10; Dt 7:7, 21:17; Jer 1:5; 1 Cor 1:18,23,26. ***Separation from the Gentiles:*** Dt, ch. 7; 1 Kgs 11:1–10; Ez, ch. 9–10; Neh 13:23–30. ***Openness to the Gentiles:*** Is 49:6, Ruth, Jonah. ***Gentiles and Torah:*** Acts 11:26, ch. 15; Gal, ch. 2; 1 Pt 2:9.

See Also

- "Covenant"
- "Torah"

Cosmology

Cosmology refers to any culture's overall understanding of the universe and its laws. In interpreting the Bible, we must remember that the ancient Hebrews did not have access to modern scientific information. For example, they did not realize that the earth is a tiny speck in the vast universe, but shared the common ancient view that the earth was the center of all reality (sometimes known as the Ptolomaic view, named after the Greek astronomer Ptolemy).

The ancient Hebrews thought of the sky as a sort of dome-shaped covering over the earth that separated the waters below it (seas, rivers, lakes) from the water above it (see Gn 1:6–8). Above the sky, the Israelites pictured storehouses or chambers filled with snow and hail (see Jb 38:22). Some biblical texts refer to windows in the dome. When these windows were open, the water above the dome fell as rain (see Gn 7:11). The sun, moon, and stars are set into the dome (see 1:14–18).

The earth itself is flat, supported by pillars above a watery abyss (see 1:2), as shown in the following passages: "For God founded it [the earth] on the seas (Ps 24:2); "He shakes the earth out of its place, and the pillars beneath it tremble" (Jb 9:6). Sheol, the realm of the dead, is pictured as under the earth: "Ask for a sign from the Lord your God; let it be deep as the nether world [Sheol] or high as the sky" (Is 7:11).

Hellenistic beliefs (reflected in the New Testament) see earth as a sphere in the middle of the universe. Around the earth revolve the sun, moon, and the five visible planets known to the ancient world (Mercury, Venus, Mars, Jupiter, and Saturn), each at its own heavenly level. There are thus seven levels of heaven, or simply "seven heavens." Other ancient cosmologies speak of only three levels of heaven (see 2 Cor 12:2). In all cosmologies, however, each level increases in light and glory, until one comes to God at the highest level.

Living Stars

Ancient Greek philosophers such as Plato and ancient Jewish thinkers such as Philo believed that the planets and stars were living beings, or at least that these heavenly bodies were inhabited by spiritual powers. The Bible often associates such beliefs with non-Israelite religions: priests "burned incense to Baal, to the sun, moon, and signs of the Zodiac, and to the whole host of heaven" (2 Kgs 23:5; see also Zep 1:5, Am 5:26).

Several biblical passages also assume that stars are living, spiritual forces. Some seem to be angelic powers allied with God. In the Book of Judges we read, "From the heavens the stars, too, fought" (5:20), and Job describes how "the morning stars sang in chorus" (38:7). A star falling from the sky to the earth is identified as an angel (see Rv 9:1). The term *hosts of Heaven* refers to angelic armies, but also to stars (see Neh 9:6, Ps 33:6).

Other passages, however, refer to stars who are opposed to the Lord: Jude alludes to rebellious stars who are punished (see v. 13); Isaiah records that on "that day the LORD will punish / the host of the heavens" (24:21).

Heaven as a Mirror of Earth

Many ancient cultures also believed that events in the sky mirrored events on the earth. The Roman historian Tacitus commented that the appearance of a comet meant a change in emperors. A new star was said to appear at the birth of Emperor Alexander Severus.

Matthew associates a special star with Jesus' birth. The magi (learned men with special knowledge about the stars) "saw his star at its rising" (Mt 2:2) and followed it to the place where the child was.

The Book of Revelation presents a scene of God's throne room in heaven. In his heavenly vision, John sees a scroll opened, representing future events that are "written" in God's plan. As the scroll is opened, events such as war and famine are unleashed upon the earth (see ch. 5–6).

Heavenly Signs of the End Times

Signs in the sky are especially associated with the end times, the Last Judgment. The prophet Joel gives a typical description: "I will work wonders in the heavens and on the earth, / blood, fire, and columns of smoke. / The sun will be turned to darkness, / and the moon to blood, / at the coming of the day of the LORD, / the great and terrible day" (3:3–4).

In Matthew, Jesus' disciples ask him, "what sign will there be of your coming, and of the end of the age?" (24:3). After describing various disturbances on earth, Jesus describes the heavenly signs, using the typical language of the Old Testament: "Immediately after the tribulation of those days, / the sun will be darkened, / and the moon will not give its light, / and the stars will fall from the sky, / and the powers of the heavens will be shaken" (v. 29). Notice the close connection between the disturbance of the heavenly bodies and the fact that the (spiritual) powers of heaven will be shaken.

These heavenly signs were not always understood literally. Primarily, they function symbolically to express the connections between heavenly events and earthly events. The great wars and struggles on earth reflect struggles in the spiritual realm.

Related Passages

Creation: Gn 17:11; Jb 9:6, 38:22; Ps 24:2; Is 7:11. *Levels of heaven:* 2 Cor 12:1–10. *Stars:* Jgs 5:20, 38:7; Mt 2:1–12; Jude, v. 13; Rv 9:1. *Correspondence of heaven and earth:* Mt 2:1,9; 24:3–31; Rv, ch. 5–6.

See Also

- "Afterlife"
- "Creation"

Covenant

A covenant is essentially an agreement between two people or groups, involving promises and commitments on both sides. At the individual level, Jonathan, for example, entered into a covenant (*berith*, in Hebrew) with David, giving David his military uniform, sword, and bow as symbols of his loyalty to David (see 1 Sm 18:1–4). A covenant is typically an arrangement between a patron, a person with greater social status and prestige, and a client. The patron offers the client protection or other benefits; the client commits to offering loyalty and concrete services to the patron.

The main biblical sense of covenant refers to the patron-client relationship between God and his people. The New Testament refers to the renewed relationship between God and his people through Christ as a New Covenant.

In the Old Testament, we see two general types of covenants—those involving God's promises to the people, and those emphasizing the people's duties to God.

Covenants Involving God's Promises to the People

In Genesis, chapter 12, the Lord calls Abraham out of his own country, promising to bless Abraham and make of him a great nation. Furthermore, God promises that "all the communities of the earth / shall find blessing in you" (Gn 12:1–3; see 15:5). In Genesis, chapter 17, God promises that Abraham will become father to a "host of nations" (v. 4).

Later, the Apostle Paul picks up on this promise of blessing to all the communities of the earth, arguing that God's promise of blessing applies to the Gentiles as well as the Jewish people (Gal 3:8).

God also promises the land of Canaan to Abraham and his descendants (Gn 15:7, 17:8). In return, Abraham, his household, and all his male descendants were to be circumcised as a "sign of the covenant" (17:11).

Similarly, God promises to King David that his descendants would always be on his throne: "I will make his royal throne firm forever. . . . Your house and your kingdom shall endure forever before me; your throne shall stand firm forever" (2 Sm 7:13–16).

In cultural context, these passages portray God as a great Near Eastern king: a patron who grants land or other privileges to his clients. The purpose of the promises always involves the strengthening or the stability of the clients: God promises that the people will be a prosperous nation, that they will own the land, and that they shall always have the leadership of the descendants of the great King David. In return, the people promise loyalty to their patron by following the patron's commandments. We notice that this theme of the success and health of the covenant people also has a broader aspect to it: all the nations will be blessed through Israel (see Gn 12:3; see the "Chosen People" article).

The Noahide Covenant

The concept of a more universal covenant is found already, in the covenant God established with Noah (see Gn 9:9). God promises that "never again shall all bodily creatures be destroyed by the waters of a flood; there shall not be another flood to devastate the earth" (v. 11). The sign of this covenant was a rainbow.

In later Jewish tradition, the rabbis called this the Noahide Covenant, and identified seven laws connected with it, including "Do not murder," "Do not steal," "Do not worship idols," "Do not eat an animal while it is still living," and "Do not commit sexual immorality." In rabbinic interpretations, these seven commandments applied to all people on earth; the Jewish people alone were given the further commandments in the Torah revealed to Moses. When the early followers of Jesus debated whether Gentiles who joined their community would also have to follow the commandments of the Torah, a council of leaders (led by James, the brother of Jesus) decided that such Gentiles would only be required "to abstain from meat sacrificed to idols, from blood, from meats of strangled animals, and from unlawful marriage" (Acts 15:29)—an apparent reference to some version of the Noahide Covenant.

Covenant and the Understanding of God

The belief that the Lord enters into covenants with his people significantly influenced the Hebrew understanding of God. Generally, in the worldview of the ancient non-Israelite religions of the Near East, the gods were considered arbitrary and capricious. They might bless or curse the people, depending on unforeseeable circumstances. When the God of Israel entered into a covenant with Israel, however, God became more predictable—God bound himself (in a sense) to his promises. Thus the Bible often refers to God's faithfulness, especially his faithfulness to the covenant promises.

The Hebrew word *hesed* is often used to describe God's covenant-based faithfulness and loyalty to his people. The word is often translated as "steadfast love" or simply "loving kindness." A related word is *aman*, which is often translated as "faithfulness." "Understand, then, that the LORD, your God, is God indeed, the faithful God who keeps his merciful covenant down to the thousandth generation toward those who love him and keep his commandments" (Dt 7:9).

Covenants Stressing the Duties of the People

A second type of covenant emphasizes the duties of the people in grateful response to God's past help and promise of future blessing. Again, the cultural background to this concept can be found in ancient treaties between a strong king and his vassal, or client-ruler. Ancient Hittite treaties between the king and his clients, for example, contain the following elements:

- An introduction describes the "great king" who is making the treaty.
- A summary of the favors that the "great king" has done for his client-ruler in the past.
- A list of the duties of the client king.
- A list of the witnesses to the treaty.
- A list of blessings / rewards that the client king will receive for obeying the covenant requirements, and a list of curses that will fall upon him if he fails to obey.

We can see the general outline of this pattern in Exodus, chapter 20. There the Lord proclaims himself as "I, the LORD, am your God, who brought you out of the land of Egypt, that place of slavery" (v. 2). The "duties" of the Hebrew people are spelled out in the Ten Commandments, and in the rest of the commandments of Torah. Lists of blessings for obeying and curses for not obeying are found in Leviticus, chapter 26, and Deuteronomy, chapter 28.

Covenant and Ritual

A covenant agreement was often marked with some kind of ritual action: circumcision as a reminder of the covenant (see Gn 17:11), or walking in between the two parts of sacrificed animals split in two (see 15:9–10). (This last custom may have served as a warning to the parties of the agreement of their fate if they broke the terms of the covenant.) After the people had agreed to follow the commandments of Torah, Moses sprinkled them with blood from some sacrificed bulls, saying, "This is the blood of the covenant which the LORD has made with you in accordance with all these words of his" (Ex 24:8).

The New Covenant

The prophet Jeremiah proclaimed that a new covenant would characterize the new relationship between God and God's people in the messianic age: "The days are coming, says the LORD, when I will make a new covenant with the house of Israel and the house of Judah. . . . I will place my law within them, and write it upon their hearts; I will be their God, and they shall be my people" (Jer 31:31–33).

In his Last Supper with his disciples, Jesus picks up on language from Exodus 24:8 when he says, "This cup is the new covenant in my blood, which will be shed for you" (Lk 22:20). This reflects Jesus' belief that his death would be a key in fully bringing in the messianic age. The cup of wine was a dramatic symbol of his blood, his willingness to give up his life on behalf of his people (see the "Atonement" article).

The Letter to the Hebrews also regards Jesus' death as the beginning of the New Covenant: "When he speaks of a 'new' covenant, he declares the first one is obsolete" (Heb 8:13). Jesus' death is the perfect atonement for sins that takes away the need for the sacrifices of the old covenant (Heb 9:1–15).

Creation

The Bible has two main ways of understanding God's creation of the universe: (1) creation by bringing order to disorder and chaos, and (2) creation from nothing. Most Christians today assume that God created the universe from nothing: God created all things, and so logically nothing could have existed before God began to create. We will see, however, that the concept of God's creating the universe from nothing didn't develop until the later stages of biblical thought.

Creation in the Book of Genesis: Order out of Disorder

Many ancient Near Eastern cultures imagined the creation of the world as the victory of powers of order over disorder. In the ancient Babylonian epic the *Enuma Elish*, Creation is described as a battle between the god Marduk and the dragon goddess Tiamat. Canaanite texts speak of a battle between the god Baal Haddu and the forces of chaos and death. These destructive forces are often characterized either as water itself ("Prince Sea" in the Canaanite accounts) or as some type of sea monster or serpent. These same ideas and images are also reflected in the Old Testament. Consider the opening words of the Bi-

ble: "In the beginning, when God created the heavens and the earth, the earth was a formless wasteland, and darkness covered the abyss, while a mighty wind swept over the waters" (Gn 1:1–2). Notice that something is already present when God created: the formless wasteland, the abyss, waters. God's Creation brings order to this dark and watery chaos.

Throughout the six days of Creation, God creates by his speech: "Then God said, 'Let there be light,' and there was light" (v. 3). Notice that the created light must be carefully set apart from the forces of darkness, chaos, and destruction that threaten them: "God then separated the light from the darkness" (v. 4). The author describes God's creation of the sun, moon, and stars in a similar fashion: "Then God said: 'Let there be lights in the dome of the sky, to separate day from night. Let them mark the fixed times, the days and the years'" (v. 14). Here the sense of time—days and years—is understood as an ordering of timeless chaos. God also brings order to the watery chaos: "'Let there be a dome in the middle of the waters, to separate one body of water from the other.' . . . Then God said, 'Let the water under the sky be gathered into a single basin, so that the dry land may appear'" (vv. 6,9).

Creation in the Psalms: God's Defeat of Chaos and Disorder

In many of the Psalms, we can catch glimpses, reminiscent of Marduk and Tiamat, of the image of God as a warrior defeating the forces of watery chaos and disorder:

> The voice of the LORD is over the waters; / the God of glory thunders, the LORD, over the mighty waters. . . . The LORD sits enthroned above the flood! (Ps 29:3,10)

The psalmist praised the Lord for his defeat of the Rahab the sea monster:

> You rule the raging sea; / you still its swelling waves. / You crushed Rahab with a mortal blow; / your strong arm scattered your foes. / Yours are the heavens, yours the earth; / you founded the world and everything in it. (Ps 89:10–12)

The following Psalm shows the connection between God's victories over the sea monsters and his placing the sun and the moon in order:

> Yet you, God, are my king from of old, / winning victories throughout the earth. / You stirred up the sea in your might; / you smashed the heads of the dragons on the waters. / You crushed the heads of Leviathan, / tossed him for food to the sharks. / You opened up springs and torrents, / brought dry land out of the primeval waters. / Yours the day and yours the night; / you set the moon and sun in place. / You fixed all the limits of the earth; / summer and winter

you made. (74:12–17; see also Jb 26:10–13, Is 51:9–10)

In the biblical view, forces of chaos and destruction were not simply defeated once and for all in the Creation: they are a constant threat. The prophet Daniel, for example, envisions the four great empires that conquered and oppressed the Jewish people as beasts that arise from the chaotic "great sea" (see Dn 7:2). The related vision in Revelation also speaks of the Satanic beast arising from the sea (see 13:1).

Creation, Order, and God's Wisdom

Think for a minute of the "laws of nature." We call gravity, for example, a law of nature—if we drop an object, it is a "law" that it will fall to the ground because of gravity. In the same way, laws of nature keep the planets revolving around the sun, spring following winter, and plants growing from seeds. The laws of nature make our world orderly and predictable: we would lead very insecure lives if we had to worry each night when we went to bed whether the sun would rise in the morning.

As we've seen, the Bible shares this same sense of God's bringing order into the universe by his Creation. In certain passages, the Bible expresses this idea with a specific claim: God creates through his Wisdom or through his Word. This claim is very similar to our concept of the "laws of nature." In ancient Greek philosophy, the term Word (logos, in Greek) refers to a divine power of reason that keeps all things in the universe together in an orderly way.

In the Book of Proverbs, God's Wisdom is portrayed in an imaginative way as speaking about her work with God.

Notice again how Creation is described as bringing order to the chaotic waters:

> *When he established the heavens I [Wisdom] was there, / when he marked out the vault over the face of the deep; / When he made firm the skies above, / when he fixed fast the foundations of the earth; / When he set for the sea its limit, / so that the waters should not transgress his command; / Then was I beside him as his craftsman. . . . (Prv 8:27–29)*

The Gospel of John uses the Greek philosophical term *Word (logos)* to express this same idea: "In the beginning was the Word, / and the Word was with God, / and the Word was God. / . . . All things came to be through him" (1:1–3).

Creation from Nothing

The later biblical tradition is influenced by a more abstract, philosophical way of looking at Creation. It makes a great story to say that God defeated the sea monsters and brought order to the chaotic sea when he was creating the earth, but the logical question is this: How did the sea, not to mention the monsters, get there in the first place?

Logically, nothing can exist by itself: everything must have a cause that first brought it into existence. The only exception is the very first thing that ever existed: by definition, it *cannot* have a previous cause, otherwise it wouldn't be the *first* thing. So the Christian philosophical tradition (as expressed, for example, by Saint Thomas Aquinas) refers to God as the First Cause: the eternal cause of all other things that was itself not caused.

So this philosophical point of view accepts the basic point of the creation stories about seas and monsters (God creates by bringing order), but it denies that the stories are literally true. Logically, God, the First Cause, must have created the world out of nothing. (The Latin phrase for "creation out of nothing"—*creatio ex nihilo*—is worth remembering.) In the beginning, there can only have been God.

This philosophical position exists already in the later Old Testament, in the Second Book of Maccabees. A mother encourages her son, "I beg you, child, to look at the heavens and the earth and see all that is in them; then you will know that God did not make them out of existing things; and in the same way the human race came into existence" (7:28).

The same sense is reflected in the Letter to the Hebrews: "By faith we understand that the universe was ordered by the word of God, so that what is visible came into being through the invisible" (11:3).

The New Creation

At the end of Revelation, after the forces of chaos and evil are defeated once and for all, and the new heavens and the new earth are established, John says simply, "The sea was no more" (Rv 21:1). John's description of the new heavens and the new earth at the end of time reminds us that the Bible imagines the end times (God's Last Judgment of good and evil) as similar to the beginning. Heaven will be a kind of renewed creation: John's description of the New Jerusalem includes a reference to the "tree of life," last seen in the Garden of Eden (Rv 22:2).

When Isaiah describes the Day of Judgment (the "Day of the Lord"), he uses the same creation symbolism we discussed earlier: "On that day, / The LORD will punish with his sword / that is cruel, great, and strong, / Leviathan the fleeing serpent, / Leviathan the coiled serpent; / and he will slay the dragon that is in the sea" (Is 27:1).

Related Passages

Creation as bringing order to chaos: Gn, ch. 1; Jb 26:10; Ps 74:12–17, 89:10–12, 29:3,10; Is 51:9–10. *Cre-ation and wisdom:* 2 Mc 7:28, Prv 8:27–29, Jn 1:1–3, Heb 11:3. *Creation from nothing:* 2 Mc 7:28, Heb 11:3. *New Creation:* Is 27:1; Rv 21:1, 22:2.

See Also

- "Afterlife"
- "Cosmology"

Crucifixion

Most people today associate crucifixion with Jesus' death. The cross on which Jesus died has become a major symbol of Christianity.

In the ancient world, however, crucifixion was used as a punishment in many societies. Living victims of this punishment were nailed or tied to crosses, trees, or stakes; sometimes the dead bodies of criminals were treated in this way. The cruel practice was found among the Persians, Greeks, Romans, and other peoples. Jesus was just one of thousands of people killed by crucifixion in the ancient world.

In the Roman method of crucifixion, the victim was tied or nailed to a wooden cross. The victim often remained alive for several days, all the while enduring terrible pain. The actual cause of death was often asphyxiation; when the victim no longer had the strength to hold up his body, he would slump down and his breathing would be cut off. The Gospels report the Roman custom of breaking the victim's legs (ensuring that the victim could no longer hold up his body) in order to speed up death. Jesus' legs were not broken, as he was already dead when the Roman soldiers came (see Jn 19:31–33).

The purpose of crucifixion was twofold—to torture the victim as long as possible before death, as a cruel pun-

Jesus was mocked and tortured before his Crucifixion, when Roman soldiers pressed a crown made of thorns into his scalp.

ishment, and to serve as a warning to others. Therefore, crucifixions often took place in public places, such as the crossroads of busy highways, on hilltops, and even in theaters. Often rebels who revolted against a government were publicly crucified to deter others. Six thousand slaves were crucified along the Appian Way, a major highway leading into Rome, after the slave revolt led by Spartacus was crushed.

The Roman practice also shamed and humiliated the victim in every way. The victim was often tortured first and then stripped naked before crucifixion. The Gospels record how the Roman soldiers tortured Jesus, mocked him, and then stripped off his clothes before crucifying him (see Mk 15:15–20).

In Roman society, the penalty was reserved mainly for criminals, rebels, and slaves; the Roman statesman Cicero simply calls it the "slaves' punishment." Cicero also writes that Roman citizens should not even spend time thinking about crucifixion, as it was such a degrading and unworthy way of dying.

Another Roman practice was to attach to the top of the cross a sign indicating the alleged crime of the victim. The inscription on Jesus' cross read, "Jesus the Nazorean, the King of the Jews," written in Hebrew, Latin, and Greek (Jn 19:19–20). This refers to the fact that Jesus was crucified as the Messiah, one who claimed to be the king sent by God to rule over the Jewish people. Today you might see "INRI" at the top of a crucifix: these letters represent the Latin translation of the inscription *Iesous Nazarenus Rex Iudaeorum* ("Jesus of Nazareth, King of the Jews").

Crucifixion in the Roman Empire was thus understood as a great source of shame, a punishment given only to the lowest criminals and slaves. So when the early Christians taught that their Lord and Savior had been crucified, most people must have thought that the Christians were crazy for worshiping a man who had been shamed in this way. The Apostle Paul writes, "We proclaim Christ crucified, a stumbling block to the Jews and foolishness to the Gentiles" (1 Cor 1:23). It was a stumbling block for most Jews, because a common Jewish expectation of the messiah is that he would be a great king who would drive out the Roman oppressors—it was in-conceivable that God's chosen messiah would be crucified. The Gentiles too would have had a very difficult time believing that any kind of savior or honored religious figure would be crucified.

The followers of Jesus, however, transformed the negative and shameful connotations of the cross into a life-giving teaching. Jesus himself insisted that his follower "must deny himself, take up his cross, and follow me. For whoever wishes to save his life will lose it, but whoever loses his life for my sake and that of the gospel will save it" (Mk 8:34–35). Thus, the cross symbolizes the followers' willingness to accept the hardships involved in following Jesus, but this acceptance leads to saving one's life. Paul similarly taught that it is through death that our new life is attained: "We were indeed buried with him through baptism into death, so that, just as Christ was raised from the dead by the glory of the Father, we too might live in newness of life" (Rom 6:4).

Related Passages

Jesus' Crucifixion: Mt 27:27–56, Jn 19:17–37. *Symbolism of the cross:* Mk 8:34–35, Rom 6:1–11, 1 Cor 1:18–25.

See Also

- "Atonement"
- "Punishment"

Dance and Music

Music can help us to express our deepest emotions: from the deepest sadness to the most intense joy. It played this same broad role in biblical societies.

The importance of music is evident already in the first chapters of Genesis where a musician is listed as one of the key ancestors of humanity: Jubal, "ancestor of all who play the lyre and the pipe" (Gn 4:21).

Simple Melodies

Middle Eastern music is characterized by relatively simple melodic patterns; the skill of the musician is shown in producing variations of these patterns. Many of the Psalms begin with musical instructions, including what melody to use. The instruction "For the leader; according to 'The deer of the dawn'" (Ps 22:1) is equivalent to a modern song leader's telling his singers to sing along to the tune of "Row, Row, Row Your Boat."

The simple, repeated melodies can have a hypnotic effect on listeners. King Saul meets a band of prophets "in a prophetic state, coming down from the high place preceded by lyres, tambourines, flutes and harps" (1 Sm 10:5). It is possible that these prophets attained this "prophetic state" (apparently an altered state of consciousness in which they received messages from God) at least partly through listening to the hypnotic beat of the musical instruments (see also 2 Kgs 3:15).

Occasions for Music

Music sometimes expressed sorrow, as we see in the Psalms of lament (such as Psalms 3–7), and the entire Book of Lamentations. The psalmist is not ashamed to let all his emotions show: "All night long tears drench my bed" (Ps 6:7); "Look upon me, have pity on me, / for I am alone and afflicted" (25:16). At times he even feels forsaken by God: "My God, my God, why have you abandoned me? / Why so far from my call for help, / from my cries of anguish?" (22:2).

Music helped to mourn a loss: flute players played after the death of a little girl (see Mt 9:23). Women were hired as professional mourners at funerals: they would compose and chant lamentations. Jeremiah says, "Tell the wailing women to come, / summon the best of them; / Let them come quickly / and intone a dirge for us, / That our eyes may be wet with weeping, / our cheeks run with tears" (Jer 9:16–17). Ezekiel records, "This is a dirge, and it shall be sung: the daughters of the nations shall chant it" (Ez 32:16).

Emotions of joy were also expressed through music. "Is anyone in good spirits? He should sing praise" (Jas 5:13). When Saul was depressed, David's playing on the harp cheered him up (see 1 Sm 16:16–23). Individuals composed songs of thanksgiving for God's blessings (see 1 Sm 2:1–10, Lk 1:46–55). The Psalms are filled with these joyous expressions too: "Hallelujah! / Praise the Lord, my soul; / I shall praise the Lord all my life, / sing praise to my God while I live" (146:1–2).

Music also expressed the joy of Israel's public celebrations. Women greeted Saul and David's victorious return from battle, singing songs and dancing, with tambourines (see 1 Sm 18:6–7; see also Jgs, ch. 5; Ex, ch. 15). A king's coronation was marked with horns and trumpets (see 2 Chr 23:13, 1 Kgs 1:39).

David entered Jerusalem with the Ark of the Covenant, "dancing before the Lord with abandon" (2 Sm 6:14). The great religious festivals of Israel included music: the Hallel Psalms (113–118) were associated with the Feasts of Passover and of Booths. The hymn that Jesus and his disciples sang after the Last Supper (see Mk 14:26) was most likely one of the Hallel psalms.

Music was also part of the feasts in private homes (see Is 5:12, Lk 15:25).

Women and Music

Women are closely associated with music in the Bible. Women chanted at funerals (see Jer 9:16–17) and celebrated national victories with singing and dancing (see 1 Sm 18:6–7; see also Jgs, ch. 5, 11:34; Ex, ch. 15; Jdt 16:1–17). Great songs of remembrance and praise are associated with women: Miriam's song (see Ex, ch. 15), Deborah's song (see Jgs, ch. 5), Hannah's song (see 1 Sm 2:1–10), Judith's song (see Jdt 16:1–17), and Mary's song (see Lk 1:46–55). Ezra and Nehemiah mention female singers (see Ezr 2:65, Neh 7:67).

Music in the Temple Service

The Book of Psalms records the sacred hymns of Israel sung in the Jerusalem Temple. In Second Temple times, the Levites, assistants to Israel's priests, served as the Temple singers (see 1 Chr 6:16–33, ch. 25). Names of Levitical singers are also attached to various Psalms: Psalms of Asaph (see 50, 73–83) and Psalms of "the Korahites" (see 42–49, 84–85, 87–88), for example.

According to the Mishnah, Levites sung the fifteen Psalms of Ascent (Psalms 120–134) on the fifteen steps leading from the Court of the Women to the Court of the Israelites in the Jerusalem Temple.

Heavenly Music

The music of the Temple service was understood as a reflection of the heavenly worship of God. Isaiah sees God seated on his throne in the Temple, with six-winged angels known as seraphim around him, crying out, "Holy, holy, holy is the LORD of hosts!" (Is 6:1–3).

This heavenly worship is portrayed in detail in the Book of Revelation. Before God's heavenly throne, four living creatures and twenty-four elders holding harps sing praises (see 4:8–11, 5:8–10). The creatures and elders are joined by countless angels and finally "every creature in heaven and on earth and under the earth and in the sea, everything in the universe" (5:11–13; see also 7:9–10). Revelation also refers to the chosen 144,000 singing a "new hymn" before God's throne (14:3).

Music in Early Christian Worship

In one of the earliest non-Christian references to Christian worship, Pliny the Younger (ca. 61–112), a Roman official in Asia Minor, writes of Christians in his district who gather together before dawn to sing hymns to Christ as to a god (see also 1 Cor 14:26).

Paul encourages his community to address "one another [in] psalms and hymns and spiritual songs, singing and playing to the Lord in your hearts" (Eph 5:19; see also Col 3:16). Basic theological beliefs about Jesus were also expressed through song; scholars note that several New Testament passages were originally hymns (for example, Phil 2:6–11, 1 Tm 3:16; perhaps Jn 1:1–14).

Although musical instruments were used in the Temple service, they were not allowed in the Jewish synagogues. Early Christian worship seems to have followed synagogue practice by restricting musical worship to singing (see 1 Cor 14:26, Eph 5:19–20, Col 3:16).

Instruments

In ancient Israel, trumpets or horns were blown to gather the whole community or their leaders together (see Nm 10:3–4). They were used especially for military purposes, such as sounding an alarm to prepare for war (see v.9, Jgs 3:27). Trumpets are also associated with the eschatological age. In the Old Testament, with the Day of the Lord (see Is 27:13, Jl 2:1); in the New Testament, with Christ's return, "For the Lord himself, with a word of command, with the voice of an archangel and with the trumpet of God, will come down from heaven" (1 Thes 4:16; see Mt 24:31). The shofar, or ram's horn, was blown to indicate the beginning of the Day of Atonement (see Lv 25:9), and also as a warning of coming war (see Jer 6:1).

Other popular instruments included a kind of rattle (translated as "*sistrum,*" see 2 Sm 6:5), cymbals (see Neh 12:27), the harp (see 1 Sm 16:23), and the lyre, pipes, and flutes. These were used in joyful processions, as when David brought the Ark into Jerusalem (see 2 Sm 6:3–5). The *tof,* translated as "tambourine" and often associated with women such as Miriam (see Ex 15:20; see also Jgs 11:34, 1 Sm 18:6) was actually more of a small drum made of animal hide stretched over a wooden frame.

Dance

Dancing is a common biblical expression of joy; Ecclesiastes speaks of "a time to weep, and a time to laugh; / a time to mourn, and a time to dance" (3:4). David danced before the Ark of the Covenant (see 2 Sm 6:14). Dancing was a part of private celebrations: the return of a lost son was celebrated with music and dancing (see Lk 15:25).

The daughter of Queen Herodias performed a dance at a great feast on Herod Agrippa's birthday (see Mk 6:22); probably this was similar to the so-called belly dance that is familiar in Middle Eastern cultures.

Women sang and danced as they greeted Saul and David, who are returning successfully from battle (1 Sm 18:6–7); the women of Israel dance in honor of Judith (see Jdt 15:12); Jeremiah alludes to women dancing joyfully when Israel returns from exile (see 31:4,13).

Related Passages

Biblical books of songs: Psalms, Lamentations. *Women's songs of praise:* Ex, ch. 15; Jgs, ch. 5; 1 Sm 2:1–10; Jdt 16:1–17; Lk 2:46–55. *Trumpets and horns:* Jl 2:1, Lv 25:9. *Professional mourners:* Jer 9:16–17, Mt 9:23. *Celebration and procession songs:* 1 Sm 18:6–7, 2 Sm 6:5–16, 1 Chr 16:8–36. *New Testament hymns:* Mk 14:26, Phil 2:6–11, Eph 5:19–20, Col 3:16. *Heavenly hymns and praises:* Is 6:1–3; Rv 4:8–11, 5:8–13, 7:9–10, 14:31. *Temple singers:* 1 Chr 6:16–33, ch. 25.

See Also

- "Death and Burial Customs"
- "Priests and Levites"
- "Temple"
- "Women"

Death and Burial Customs

Biblical cultures were very open about expressing emotions, including grief. After hearing of his son Absalom's death, David "said as he wept, 'My son Absalom! My son, my son Absalom! If only I had died instead of you, Absalom, my son, my son!'" (2 Sm 19:1). Mourners also expressed their grief through certain ritualized actions: "Then Jacob rent his clothes, put sackcloth on his loins, and mourned his son many days" (Gn 37:34). (Sackcloth was a type of rough cloth, usually made from goat's hair.) Other mourning customs were fasting for seven days (see 1 Sm 31:13), beating one's chest (see Lk 23:48), shaving one's head and beard (see Is 15:2), and sitting in the dust on the ground (see Jb 2:12–13).

Professional mourners would be hired for funerals: "Attention! tell the wailing women to come, / summon the best of them; / Let them come quickly / and intone a dirge for us, / That our eyes may be wet with weeping, / our cheeks run with tears" (Jer 9:16–17). Songs of lamentation were composed: "Jeremiah also composed a lamentation over Josiah, which is recited to this day by all the male and female singers" (2 Chr 35:25; see Mt 9:23).

Burial Customs

For a body to be left unburied was one of the greatest curses: "If he is deprived of burial, of this man I proclaim that the child born dead is more fortunate than he" (Eccl 6:3). It is the sign of a righteous person that he or she is concerned with giving the dead a proper burial—chapters 1 and 2 of the Book of Tobit describe this virtue.

After death, the body was washed and anointed, and the eyes were closed (see Acts 9:37). Spices were sometimes used to anoint the body: "When the sabbath was over, Mary Magdalene, Mary, the mother of James, and Salome bought spices so that they might go and anoint him" (Mk 16:1; see Jn 19:39–40). The purpose of this anointing may have been to control the stench of the decaying body, as mourners entered cave tombs frequently to bring in new bodies (see discussion below). In Palestine the hands and feet of the dead body were wrapped with linen cloth. The head was wrapped separately. Lazarus was "tied hand and foot with burial bands, and his face was wrapped in a cloth" (Jn 11:44; see also 20:7).

The burial took place soon after death. Even the body of an executed criminal "shall not remain on the tree overnight. You shall bury it the same day" (Dt 21:23). The body was put on a bier and carried to the tomb for burial (see Lk 7:11–14).

Touching a dead body made a person impure for seven days; the person

Mourners in biblical times often wore sackcloth, a rough fabric woven from goat or camel hair.

had to bathe ritually, with water mixed with the ashes of a red heifer, to become clean again. If an impure person touched another object, it too became unclean, and could transmit uncleanness to anyone else who touched it (see Nm 19:11–22). Priests followed especially strict purity laws: they were allowed to come near the bodies of close relatives only, and the high priest was forbidden to come into contact with any corpse at all, even his father or mother (see Lv 21:1–12).

In Palestine wealthy people were buried in family tombs cut into rock; these tombs usually had several chambers. Bodies were placed into niches, about the size of a body, cut into the rock walls. When all the niches were full and more space was needed for burials, the bones would be removed and placed in stone boxes known as ossuaries.

The centrality of the family was reflected in the practice of family burial places. Abraham and Sarah, Isaac and Rebekah, and Jacob and Leah were buried in a family tomb purchased by Abraham (see Gn 23:1–20, 49:29–32). David buried the bones of Saul and his son Jonathan in the tomb of Saul's father (see 2 Sm 21:14). Jacob instructed his sons: "Do not let me be buried in Egypt. When I lie with my ancestors, have me taken out of Egypt and buried in their burial place" (Gn 47:29–30). The phrases "taken to his kinsmen" and "rested with his ancestors" (25:8; 2 Kgs 21:18) are often used to describe a person's death—they may refer to the custom of the family tomb, or simply to the idea of a common gathering in Sheol.

Jesus was buried in a rock tomb because one of his followers, Joseph of Arimathea, was wealthy and placed Jesus' body in his own tomb (see Mt 27:57–60). Jews who could not afford a rock tomb buried their dead in trenches dug into the ground, in a way similar to today's customs.

The poor would be placed in a common graveyard (see 2 Kgs 23:6, Jer 26:23). Such graveyards were typically outside of cities and villages, but kings of Judah were buried inside Jerusalem.

Related Passages

Mourning customs: Gn 37:34, 1 Sm 31:13, Jb 2:12–13, Is 15:2. *Professional lamenters:* Jer 9:16–19, Mt 9:23. *Proper burial as a religious obligation:* Tb, ch. 1–2. *Burial customs:* Gn 23:1–19, 49:29–32; Mt 27:57–60; Lk 7:11–14; Jn 11:1–44; Acts 9:37. *Corpse impurity:* Lv 21:1–12, Nm 19:11–22.

See Also

- "Afterlife"
- "Dance and Music"
- "Family"
- "Purity"

Dress and Hair

Common Dress: Tunic and Cloak

The two most common articles of clothing in biblical societies, for both men and women, were the tunic and the cloak.

The tunic was a kind of shirt worn next to the skin. It was usually made of wool; linen clothing was worn by wealthier people and by priests. The tunic was made of two rectangular pieces of cloth, sewn together at one end to leave room for one's head. It might be sleeveless, or have short or long sleeves. When Jesus sent his disciples out to preach and heal in the villages, he told them not to bring a second tunic (see Mt 10:10). Some older translations described Jacob's gift to his son Joseph as a "coat of many colors" (cf. Gn 37:3), but a more correct translation identifies it as a tunic with long sleeves. The tunic was often decorated with stripes.

The tunic was usually fastened with a belt. John the Baptist, for example, wore a leather belt (see Mt 3:4). A money pouch (see 6:8) or a sword (see 1 Sm 25:13) could be hung from the belt. When Jesus tells his disciples to "gird your loins" (see Lk 12:35), he is referring to the image of a man gathering up his long clothes with a belt so that he could walk or run more freely. In other words: "Be ready for action!" The Israelites also had their "loins girt" when they were preparing to flee slavery in Egypt (see Ex 12:11).

Over the shirt or tunic, a person would usually wear a loose-fitting cloak (or mantle) made of wool or goat's hair. (John the Baptist wore clothing of camel's hair [see Mt 3:4].) Jesus tells his disciples, "If anyone wants to go to law with you over your tunic, hand him your cloak as well" (5:40). The disciple Tabitha (also called Dorcas) made both tunics and cloaks (see Acts 9:39). Cloaks were also decorated with stripes and notched bands (for men) and L-shaped stripes (for women). Both tunics and cloaks were dyed; dying was more common for women's clothing, and for the clothing of the wealthy.

The cloak was often used for a blanket at night. The Torah thus requires that if someone takes a person's cloak as collateral for a loan, the cloak must be returned to the owner before nightfall, "for this cloak of his is the only covering he has for his body. What else has he to sleep in?" (Ex 22:26). Cloaks also served other purposes: the Hebrews used cloaks to carry their kneading bowls filled with unleavened bread when they fled from Egypt (see 12:34), and Boaz filled Ruth's cloak with six measures of barley, which she then carried home (see Ru 3:15).

As a head covering, a man might wear a turban (see Jb 29:14, Ez 24:17); the high priest wore an elaborate miter on his head (see Ex 29:6).

Women would wear a head covering or veil, especially when they were in the presence of strangers (see Gn 24:65, Song 4:1, Is 47:2). There is no clear evidence, however, that in Jesus' time women in ancient Palestine wore a separate veil in public. A woman could pull up part of her cloak to cover her head at culturally appropriate times (such as during worship; see 1 Cor 11:5–6).

Women, especially the wealthy, wore bracelets, anklets, and rings, including nose rings (see Gn 24:22,47; Is 3:18–21; Ez 16:11–12).

The most common footwear was sandals worn without socks. The sandal was a piece of leather or wood attached to the foot with a strap or thong. They were worn by both men and women (see Song 7:2). Moses is told to remove the sandals from his feet as a sign of reverence for God's holiness (see Ex 3:5). John the Baptist says of the coming Messiah, "I am not worthy to stoop and loosen the thongs of his sandals" (Mk 1:8).

Symbolic Uses of Clothing

Walking barefoot was a sign of grief: when David had to flee Jerusalem because of the rebellion of his son Absalom, he went barefoot (see 2 Sm 15:30). Among traditional Jews today, going barefoot is still part of the mourning ritual for the loss of a loved one. Mourners would also wear sackcloth—a rough cloth usually made from goat's hair (see Gn 37:34, Jon 3:5–8).

The Torah forbids a person to wear clothing made from wool and linen woven together (see Dt 22:11). The basic idea behind this is symbolic. Wool is from animals, and linen from plants; thus, the two realms should be separate, reinforcing the purity concept that all things must remain within their proper boundaries and in their proper categories.

Special dyes were valued, especially the colors violet, purple, and scarlet, which were used in making the garments of the high priest (see Ex 28:6,15,33). Purple dye was especially valued; the names Canaan and Phoenicia mean "purple," referring to the expertise of the people in making purple dyes. Dying was a major industry in the ancient Mediterranean.

The Christian convert Lydia was a dealer in purple cloth (see Acts 16:14). Purple clothes were worn by royalty, and the wealthy imitated them by wearing purple. Luke describes a rich man "who dressed in purple garments and fine linen and dined sumptuously each day" (16:19). Roman senators wore togas with a broad purple stripe.

Men were to wear tassels (or fringes) on their cloaks, tied with a violet cord (see Nm 15:38, Dt 22:12). The tassels were to serve as a reminder of the Commandments (see Nm 15:39–40). A woman suffering from hemorrhages wished only to touch a tassel of Jesus' cloak (see Mt 9:20); Jesus criticizes the Pharisees for wearing especially long fringes so as to be noticed (see 23:5). Men also wore phylacteries: small boxes containing scriptural verses strapped onto the arms or forehead (see Dt 6:4–8, Mt 23:5).

Hair

In the purity system of ancient Israel, keeping clear boundaries between categories was a primary concern, including distinctions between genders. Hairstyles functioned to make those distinctions: Paul insists that women should wear their hair long, and men should wear their hair short (see 1 Cor 11:14–15). The Romans valued the short hairstyle for men, and first-century Jews were influenced by this fashion. Men thus generally wore their hair short and were clean shaven; if they had a beard, it was neatly trimmed. Ancient Jewish philosophers linked male long hair with homosexual behavior, which they considered to be an unnatural blurring of gender lines that would harm the order of society.

Women usually covered their hair with a net or cloth. Upper-class women often had elaborately braided hair (see 1 Tm 2:9).

Shaving one's hair could be a sign of mourning (Is 22:12).

Hair and Nazirites

Hair length had additional cultural meaning in the case of the Nazirites. The word *Nazirite* comes from the Hebrew verb *nazir,* which means "to set apart as sacred, dedicate." A Nazirite set himself or herself apart with a vow for a certain fixed time in dedication to some special service to God. During this time, the Nazirite was to drink no alcohol, avoid contact with a corpse, and not cut his or her hair (see Nm 6:1–8). When the time of the vow was completed, the Nazirite would offer sacrifices, shave his or her hair, and burn it along with the sacrifice.

Sampson was dedicated to the Nazirite vow from his birth (see Jgs 13:4–7).

According to the account in Judges, the Spirit of the Lord would come upon the dedicated Samson, enabling him to tear apart a lion with his bare hands and kill a thousand men with the jawbone of a donkey (see 14:6, 15:15). Samson's strength was associated with his hair: when it was cut (symbolizing the end of his vow), he lost his extraordinary strength (see 16:17–19,22).

The prophet Samuel had also been dedicated by his mother before his birth (see 1 Sm 1:11). Paul had taken a Nazirite vow that ended when he cut his hair (see Acts 18:18; see also 21:23–26). John the Baptist's life is similar to that of the Nazirite (Lk 1:15: "He will drink neither wine nor strong drink").

Related Passages

Joseph's tunic: Gn 37:3. ***Cloak and essential shelter:*** Ex 22:26. ***Women's jewelry:*** Is 3:18–21, Ez 16:11–12. ***Sackcloth:*** Gn 37:34, Jon 3:5–8. ***Purple clothing:*** Lk 16:19, Acts 16:14. ***Fringes on clothing:*** Nm 15:38; Mt 9:30, 23:5. ***Hair and Nazirite vows:*** Nm 6:1–8; Jgs, ch. 13–16; Acts 21:23–26. ***Women's hair:*** 1 Cor 11:3–16, 1 Tm 2:9.

See Also

- "Poverty and Wealth"
- "Purity"
- "Women"

Dwellings

Tents

One of the first-named ancestors of the human race is Jabal, "the ancestor of all who dwell in tents and keep cattle" (Gn 4:20). Abraham, the first patriarch, lived in a tent (see 18:1). The Israelites lived in tents during their journey through the wilderness after escaping slavery in Egypt; that time is commemorated in the Feast of Booths (also known as Tabernacles). During the Feast of Booths, the people temporarily live in tents, often on the roofs of their homes. The most famous tent in the Bible is the Tent of the Meeting or the Tabernacle (translated simply as "the Dwelling" in the New American Bible) which housed the Ark of the Covenant (see Ex, ch. 40, for a description).

Tents are typically made from black haircloth made from goat's hair (see Song 1:5) and supported by poles and ropes. Strips of cloth, woven on a loom, were sewn together. The floor of the tent was covered with mats or rugs,

and the simple furniture might consist of chests for storage and a low table. Paul, along with his coworkers Priscilla and Aquila, was a tentmaker (see Acts 18:2–3).

Tents became a common metaphor for the temporary nature of earthly life. Paul says, "For we know that if our earthly dwelling, a tent, should be destroyed, we have a building from God, a dwelling not made with hands, eternal in heaven" (2 Cor 5:1). In the Gospel of John's reference to Christ's earthly life, "And the Word became flesh, / and made his dwelling among us" (1:14), the Greek verb used literally means "to pitch a tent."

Homes

A typical house in an Israelite village was constructed from sun-baked bricks. Floors were often hard-packed earth; some families used cobblestones or stone chippings mixed with lime. Roofs were flat, formed by beams laid across the tops of the walls. A mat of reeds or thorn bushes was laid across the beams; over this a coating of dirt or clay, mixed with sand or pebbles. When some men could not get through a crowd to bring a paralyzed man to Jesus, they dug through the roof and lowered him down (see Mk 2:4).

To escape the heat, often people would sleep on their roofs. One couple made a little room on their roof where the prophet Elijah stayed during his visits (see 2 Kgs 4:9–10).

Grass would sprout from these roofs after the spring rains but then quickly wither in the summer heat. The psalmist thus prays that the enemies of Israel may be "like grass on the rooftops / withered in early growth" (Ps 129:6). One of commandments of the Torah orders that a person building a new house put a low wall (parapet) around the roof to prevent people from falling off (see Dt 22:8). The roof could also be used for storage: Rahab dried some flax stalks there (see Jos 2:6).

A typical house in biblical Palestine was divided into three or four rooms. A courtyard, often at the center of the house, was also common. Some rooms were used for storing food (wheat stored in stone jars, for example) or for stabling animals. Wealthier homes were segregated according to gender; certain rooms were the women's quarters (see Est 2:13) and might even have a separate entrance. In the homes of the common people, rooms or spaces in the courtyard were reserved for women at certain times of the day, when the women would gather to spin, weave, or prepare food. Women and children ate separately from the men; women would then serve the men (see Mk 1:31).

Related Passages

"The Dwelling" (Tabernacle): Ex, ch. 40. *Feast of Booths:* Dt 16:13–17. *Tentmakers:* Acts 18:2–3. *The roof:* 2 Kgs 4:9–10, Dt 22:8, Mk 2:1–12.

See Also

- "Family"
- "Marriage"
- "Women"

Family

The family was the central social institution of biblical times. Family ties shaped economic relations: a son would typically take the trade of his father; a few wealthy families often owned the majority of land in a given society. Family ties were central to religion: priests could be drawn from Levitical families only, and high priests from certain elite families only. Families strongly influenced politics. Sons followed their fathers as kings, and the Roman Senate was open to a few powerful, aristocratic families only.

Loyalty to one's family was the essential value in biblical cultures. Ideally, even marriages took place within the same family (endogamous marriages). Unions between cousins were preferred: Jacob married the daughters of his uncle Laban (see Gn 28:2; see also Gn 24:4, Tb 1:9). In this way, the values and loyalties of the family would remain intact.

The Extended Family

In modern Western society, we tend to think of the family as consisting of a father, mother, and their children. The biblical concept of family, however, generally envisioned an extended family. A few generations commonly lived together under one roof—the father, mother, and children were joined by grandparents and married children.

A man could have more than one wife. In addition, servants or slaves of the family, or even an unrelated person living with the family, were considered to be part of the household. This extended sense of family is apparent in one of the Ten Commandments: "No work may be done then either by you, or your son or daughter, or your male or female slave, or your beast, or by the alien who lives with you" (Ex 20:10). When Jacob's family moved to Egypt, "his direct descendants, not counting the wives of Jacob's sons—numbered sixty-six persons in all" (Gn 46:26).

The Patriarchal Family

Within the extended family, each person had a clearly defined social role within a hierarchical structure. The wife managed the household, and the husband earned a living for the family. The father was the head of the household: a wife was subordinate to her husband, children obeyed their parents, and slaves obeyed their masters (see Ex 20:12, Eph 5:21—6:9). The husband protected the honor of his family by ensuring that each person properly fulfilled his or her social role.

A primary duty of the father was to pass down the teachings of the Torah to his children (see Ex 12:26–27, Dt 6:7); he is to raise them "with the training and instruction of the Lord" (Eph 6:4).

The mother, however, also has a significant role: "Hear, my son, your father's instruction, / and reject not your mother's teaching" (Prv 1:8; see 6:20).

Sons often followed in the same trade as their fathers. James and John fished with their father, Zebedee (see Mk 1:19); Joseph the carpenter passed on this trade to Jesus (see Mt 13:55, Mk 6:3).

The father's role was to provide for and protect his family. Thus, widows and orphans were the two most vulnerable groups in ancient Israelite society, for they had no husband or father. Biblical law and prophecy often stresses the need to protect them. Sirach says that God "is not deaf to the wail of the orphan, / nor to the widow when she pours out her complaint" (35:14). This is also carried over in the New Testament: "Religion that is pure and undefiled before God and the Father is this: to care for orphans and widows in their affliction" (Jas 1:27).

Lines of descent are traced through the father, so generally only fathers and sons are listed in the genealogies (lists of ancestors) (see Mt 1:1–17, Lk 3:23–38). After marriage the couple would typically move into the home or neighborhood of the husband's family. Israelite society developed many different social customs to ensure that a man would produce offspring, including polygyny, keeping concubines, and the "Levirate marriage" (see the "Marriage" article).

A father's sons would inherit his property, the eldest son inheriting a double portion (see Dt 21:17). Girls could inherit property if there were no sons (see Nm 27:8).

Family and the Land

The identity of a family is closely identified with its ownership of land. When

King Ahab wishes to buy Naboth's vineyard, Naboth replies, "The LORD forbid . . . that I should give you my ancestral heritage" (1 Kgs 21:3). If a man has to sell his land because of financial need, his nearest relative is obligated to buy it back (see Lv 25:25, Ru 4:1–6). The Jubilee laws mandated that every fifty years, "every one of you shall return to his own property, every one to his own family estate" (Lv 25:10).

Group and Individual Identity

As a general rule in biblical times, a person's identity and worth was determined more by his or her contribution to the family or wider social group (clan, tribe) than by individual achievement. Thus, for instance, marriages were arranged according to the needs of the family, rather than individual preference or attraction. Abraham, for example, sends his servant to find a wife for his son Isaac (see Gn 24:2–4).

Members of a household were in some respects considered an extension of the head of the household. Thus, when Lydia, a dealer in purple cloth, was converted by Paul to become a follower of Christ, "she and her household" were baptized (Acts 16:15). After the Philippian jailer converted, "he and all his family were baptized at once" (16:33). It's clear that the family members (which may have included spouses, children, and servants) did not make individual decisions to follow Christ, but rather were baptized because of their social roles as part of the family.

This understanding of the individual as part of the family group helps to explain a passage found in the Ten Commandments: "For I, the Lord, your God, am a jealous God, inflicting punishment for their fathers' wickedness of the children of those who hate me, down to the third and fourth generation" (Ex 20:5). In this passage, the children are understood as an extension of the family, thus naturally bearing the punishment of the fathers. We should note, however, that biblical passages written at a later date show an awareness of the independence of the individual. The prophet Ezekiel says explicitly, "The son shall not be charged with the guilt of his father, nor shall the father be charged with the guilt of his son" (Ez 18:20).

The Family and the Kingdom of God

Although Jesus was a caring and obedient son (see Lk 2:51, Jn 19:26–27), his vision of the Kingdom of God was a challenge to first-century family-centered social values. Jesus insisted that loyalty to God and God's Kingdom was the highest value: if there was a conflict between loyalty to God and loyalty to the family, one's loyalty to God was more important (see Mk 3:20–35). Jesus taught, "If anyone comes to me without hating his father and mother, wife and children, brothers and sisters, and even his own life, he cannot be my disciple" (Lk 14:26). Jesus' point was not that a person should actively hate his own family, but rather that not even family ties and obligations should prevent a person from doing God's will (see 9:59–62).

Jesus taught that his followers formed a new family, based not on blood and marriage relations, but on a common belief: "Here are my mother and my brothers. [For] whoever does the will of God is my brother and sister and mother" (Mk 3:34–35). Members of Christian churches thus referred to one another as "brothers" and "sisters" (see Rom 16:1, 1 Cor 15:1, Jas 1:2); forming what sociologists call a "fictive kin" group. In this new family, traditional hierarchical authority was redefined: "Whoever wishes to be first among you will be the slave of all" (Mk 10:44).

Blending Patriarchal and Kingdom Values

Later New Testament writings show that Christian groups did accept the basic patriarchal hierarchical structure of the family. So-called household codes explain how order is to be maintained in the household by each person respecting hierarchical authority: the wife is to be subordinate to the husband, children should obey their parents, and slaves should obey their masters (see Eph 5:21—6:9, Col 3:18—4:1, 1 Pt 3:1–7). Nevertheless, these hierarchical relations are qualified by particularly Christian emphases: husbands should "love their wives as their own bodies" (Eph 5:28);

fathers should not provoke their children to anger (see 6:4); masters should not bully their slaves (see v. 9).

Related Passages

Endogamous marriages: Gn 24:4; 28:2, Tb 1:9. *Extended family:* Ex 20:10, Gn 46:26. *Patriarchal and hierarchical structure:* Ex 20:12, Eph 5:21—6:9. *Patriarchal descent:* Lk 3:23–38. *Passing traditions on to children:* Ex 12:26–27, Dt 6:7, Prv 1:8. *Family and land:* 1 Kgs, ch. 21; Lv 25:8–55. *Group identity:* Ex 20:5; Acts 16:15,33. *Family and Kingdom values:* Mk 3:20–35, 10:42–45; Lk 9:59–62, 14:26; Eph 5:21–6:9; Col 3:18—4:1.

See Also

- "Honor and Shame"
- "Marriage"
- "Poverty and Wealth"
- "Women"

Festivals

Holidays and festivals are special times when we take time out from our regular routines to celebrate events of particular significance in our lives.

In the United States, our major holidays include Christmas, Thanksgiving, and the Fourth of July. Notice that these days have a religious significance (celebrating the birth of Jesus, thanking God for the harvest) and historical and political significance (celebrating the Declaration of Independence, remembering the cooperation between the Pilgrim settlers and the Wampanoag Indians at the Plymouth settlement in 1621). So too Israel's festivals had (and have) both religious and historical meaning.

Three of the Israel's major festivals—the Feast of Passover, the Feast of Weeks, and the Feast of Booths (Tabernacles)—were known as pilgrimage festivals, because Israelites were supposed to travel to the Jerusalem Temple to celebrate them. All three combine agricultural and historical significance.

Passover

Originally, Passover (*Pesach,* in Hebrew) and the Feast of Unleavened Bread were two separate festivals. By the time of Jesus, however, they tended to be thought of as a single event.

Passover was observed in spring at the beginning of the barley harvest (see Lv 23:10). It celebrates the return of spring and the growing season.

Historically, the festival also recalls the Exodus of the Israelite slaves from Egypt (see Ex, ch. 12). A lamb was sacrificed and its blood applied to the doorposts of each house as a sign that the Lord would "pass over" that house during the slaughter of all the firstborn of the Egyptians—the last of the plagues sent on Egypt because Pharaoh refused to release the Hebrews (see Ex 12:12–13).

In remembrance of this event, Israelites of later generations continued to sacrifice a lamb, offer other sacrifices, and eat unleavened bread for a week. This bread symbolizes the haste of the people when they left Egypt: they did not have time to allow the bread to rise (see Dt 16:3). Bitter herbs were also eaten; today it is a reminder of the bitterness of slavery (see Ex 12:8).

Shortly before his death, Jesus and his disciples came with thousands of other pilgrims to Jerusalem to celebrate the Passover (see Mk 14:12–16). According to the synoptic Gospels, Jesus' Last Supper with his disciples was a Passover meal (see Mt 26:17–18), but John reports that the supper was eaten the day before the Passover (see Jn 13:1).

Today the Jewish celebration of Passover often falls around the same time as the Christian Holy Week.

Feast of Weeks

The Feast of Weeks (*Shavuot,* in Hebrew; also known as Pentecost) is celebrated in late spring or early summer—fifty days (seven weeks) after Passover. This marks the beginning of the wheat harvest. The "first fruits" of that harvest were made into loaves of bread and offered along with other sacrifices (see Lv 23:15–21). Later the festival became associated with Moses' receiving the Torah from God on Mount Sinai. Today selections from the Book of Ruth (which speaks of barley and wheat harvests in chapters 2–3) are read in synagogue celebrations.

It was at the time of Pentecost, when the disciples were gathered together in Jerusalem after Jesus' Ascension, that the Holy Spirit came upon them, enabling them to speak in many different languages (see Acts 2:1–4). This marked the beginning of the spread of the Christian faith outside of the small community of Jesus' original disciples, so Christians continue to celebrate Pentecost today as the beginning of the universal Church.

Feast of Tabernacles

This feast, also known as the Feast of Booths (*Sukkot,* in Hebrew), is celebrated in fall, the final harvest festival of the year, and so is similar to the celebration

The Israelites marked the lintel and doorposts of their homes with the blood from a slaughtered lamb so the Lord would pass over and not destroy their firstborn.

of Thanksgiving. "You shall celebrate the feast of Booths for seven days, when you have gathered in the produce from your threshing floor and wine press" (Dt 16:13). The Feast of Tabernacles also serves as a reminder of the people's wandering in the desert after the Exodus from Egypt (see Lv 23:43). During these seven days, the people would live in "tabernacles" or "booths"—temporary shelters made from tree branches (see 23:40–43)—as a reminder of when Israelites lived in tents in the wilderness. Numerous sacrifices were offered at this time (see Num 29:13–39). Individuals were to bring to the Temple a basket filled with the "first fruits" of their harvest (Dt 26:1–11).

Every seventh year, the Torah was to be read in the presence of the people (see Dt 31:10–13; see also Neh 8:14–18) during the festival.

In the eschatological vision of Zechariah, all the nations of the earth would gather together with Israel to worship the Lord at the Feast of Booths (see Zec 14:16–19).

Day of Atonement

This is a major feast focused on the atonement, or cleansing, of sin. Although individual sins could be atoned at any time through offering sacrifices and repentance, the Day of Atonement (*Yom Kippur,* in Hebrew) was a special occasion on which the high priest atoned for his own sins, those of his family, and those of the whole nation (see Lv, ch. 16).

During the atonement ceremonies, the high priest would enter the Holy of Holies where the Ark of the Covenant was located. This was the only day of the year when entry was permitted to anyone.

Two goats were involved in the celebration; one was sacrificed. The high priest would lay his hands on the head of the second goat, confessing the sins of the people on it. The goat was then driven off into the wilderness (see Lv 16:20–22). The term *scapegoat* comes from this practice—blaming an innocent person for the faults of others. On this day, the people would also fast (see v. 29).

Today *Yom Kippur* is celebrated together with *Rosh Hashanah,* the Jewish New Year (see 23:23–25). Together these two festivals form the High Holy Days in Judaism.

Hanukkah (Festival of Lights)

This feast is sometimes spelled *Chanukah.* The different spelling is simply a different way to indicate the pronunciation of the Hebrew word. This feast celebrates the Maccabees' rededication of the Jerusalem Temple, after they had recaptured it from the Syrian armies. The leader of the Maccabean army, Judas, declared that an eight-day celebration should be observed for future generations (see 1 Mc 4:59).

Related Passages

Passover: Ex, ch. 12–16, Mk 14:12–26. *Feast of Weeks:* Lv 23:15–21; Ru, ch. 2–3; Acts 2:1–4. *Feast of Tabernacles (Booths):* Lv 23:33–43, Zech 14:16–19. *Day of Atonement:* Lv, ch. 16. *Hanukkah:* 1 Mc 4:36–61. *Festivals in general:* Lv, ch. 23; Dt, ch. 16.

See Also

- "Agriculture"
- "Holiness"
- "Sacrifices and Offerings"
- "Temple"

Fishing

In ancient Israel, popular places for fishing were in the Mediterranean Sea or in the Sea of Galilee. At least four of Jesus' disciples were fishermen: Simon Peter and his brother Andrew, and John and his brother James (Mk 1:16–20).

At the time of Jesus, fishing was a government-controlled industry that functioned as part of the client-patron social system. Local rulers (such as Herod Antipas, tetrarch of Galilee) granted fishing rights to brokers (called tax collectors or publicans in most New Testament translations), who in turn contracted with the fishermen. The brokers would often supply the boats and nets for the fishermen; thus, the fishermen were indebted to the brokers. Because the tax collector Matthew (also known as Levi) had his "customs post" at the fishing center of Capernaum (see Mt 9:9, Mk 2:14), it is quite likely he was such a broker to those who fished the Sea of Galilee.

The actual fishing was generally done by fishing families and cooperatives. James and John fished with their father; no doubt Peter and Andrew also belonged to a fishing family (see Mk 1:16–20). We are told that Simon Peter had his own boat (see Lk 5:3) and that he worked in partnership with others, including James and John (see vv. 7, 10). The fishermen themselves would also hire workers who earned a daily wage (see Mk 1:19–20).

Fishing with a line and hook is mentioned in the Gospels (see Mt 17:27), but the primary method of fishing in Galilee was the use of nets. Two types of nets were used. The casting net, round, and about 15 feet in diameter, was thrown from a boat or the shore (see 4:18). The dragnet could be up to hundreds of feet in length and eight feet wide (see 13:47; Jn 21:8). Sometimes the dragnet was stretched between two boats.

After each fishing outing, the nets would have to be mended, washed, dried, and folded (see Mk 1:19). Nets were made from flax, a material woven from plant fibers.

The catch would be sold at a market. From there, the fish would be salted, pickled, or dried for preservation and transport.

Some of the Galilean fishing boats were quite large. One ancient fishing boat, discovered at the Sea of Galilee and dating from approximately the time of Jesus, was nearly 27 feet long and 7½ feet wide. This boat had a sail and room for four oarsmen and a tillerman. In addition to the crew, it could hold ten passengers, or over one ton of cargo (see Mk 4:35–41).

Fish was part of the daily staple diet of the Galilean people, as is evident in several Gospel stories. When the crowds following Jesus need something to eat, the disciples collect loaves of bread and fish (see 6:38). After his Resurrection, Jesus ate baked fish (see Lk 24:42) and processed fish (see Jn 21:13).

Related Passages

Fishing families and cooperatives: Mk 1:16–20, Lk 5:1–11. **Fishing and the patronage system:** Mk 2:13–14. **Methods of fishing:** Mt 4:18, 13:47–48, 17:27; Jn 21:8. **Fishing boats:** Mk 4:35–41. **Eating fish:** Mk 6:38, Lk 24:42, Jn 21:13.

See Also

- "Agriculture"
- "Food and Drink"
- "Poverty and Wealth"

Food and Drink

Food and drink are obviously essential for our physical survival. But in every society, certain foods are closely associated with the cultural identity of the people. Just think of the cultural pride associated with the special ethnic dishes that every culture serves at holidays or on other special occasions. So too in ancient Israel and the Mediterranean world, certain foods had powerful cultural significance.

Bread

In Mediterranean society, bread was made primarily from cereal grains, such as wheat and barley.

Bread was a staple food that provided most of the nutrition (especially proteins and carbohydrates) for the general population. In biblical cultures, bread was so basic that the word was often used to represent all food. God calls on the people to "shar[e] your bread with the hungry" (Is 58:7), and Jesus instructs his disciples to pray for their "daily bread" (Mt 6:11).

Similarly, the phrase "breaking bread" came to mean simply eating a meal: "They will not break bread with the bereaved" (Jer 16:7). The phrase refers to the custom of breaking the loaf of bread into pieces with one's hands rather than using a knife to slice it. When the sacrament of the Eucharist became established, the phrase "breaking bread" could also refer to that particular sacrament: "On the first day of the week when we gathered to break bread" (Acts 20:7).

Wheat was generally more expensive than barley (see 2 Kgs 7:1), so it was often too expensive for the average Israelite. Notice that the boy in the crowd who gathered around Jesus had barley bread (see Jn 6:9).

The production of bread (including grinding the grain into meal or flour, adding water or leaven, and baking) was a primary task for women in biblical cultures, although men were also involved at times (see Gn 19:3). In Jerusalem during Second Temple times, in fact, a certain part of town was known as the baker's district (see Jer 37:21).

For grinding the grain, a millstone or a mortar and pestle were used: "The people would grind it between millstones or pound it in a mortar" (Nm 11:8; see also Mt 24:41, Rv 18:22). Enough flour was ground for each day's bread, as we see reflected in the petition of the Lord's Prayer, "Give us today our daily bread" (Mt 6:11). Both small, hand-turned millstones and large ones turned by a donkey or an old horse were used (see Jesus' reference to a great millstone that might be hung around a person's neck, in Mt 18:6; the captive Samson was forced to turn a large millstone in Jgs 16:21).

Water was added to the flour to make dough, which was then shaped and baked, usually at a community village oven fueled by dried dung. Leaven might be added before baking to raise the bread and make it less dense. Loaves of bread in Jesus' time were smaller than modern loaves, more like a roll or bun. Jesus compares the Kingdom of God to "yeast that a woman took and mixed [in] with three measures of wheat flour until the whole batch of dough was leavened" (Lk 13:21); he also warns of the "leaven of the Pharisees" (Mk 8:15). Paul asks, "Do you not know that a little yeast leavens all the dough?" (1 Cor 5:6, Gal 5:9).

Bread in the Sacrifices

In addition to its use in everyday life, bread was used in specifically religious contexts.

The ancient Israelites offered sacrifices of both leavened (see Lv 7:13) and unleavened bread (see Ex 29:2). During the Feast of Unleavened Bread (after Passover), fine flour was offered to God along with the sacrifice of the Passover lamb, and the people ate only unleavened bread (see Lv 23:6–13). At the Feast of Weeks, two loaves of leavened bread were offered as part of the "first fruits" of the harvest (see 23:17).

The Bread of the Presence was twelve loaves of bread made from fine flour that the high priest set out every Sabbath on the golden table that stood directly before the Holy of Holies in the Temple; the previous week's bread was eaten by the priests in the Temple area (see Lv 24:5–9, 1 Kgs 7:48). The location of this ritual near the Holy of Holies reveals its importance.

Jesus as the Bread of Life

While the Israelites were wandering in the wilderness after their escape from slavery, God fed them with manna, a kind of bread that fell from heaven (see Ex, ch. 16). The rabbis and Philo saw the manna as a symbol for the Torah—God's law that was sent down from heaven to feed the people. In the Gospel of John, Jesus compares himself with this heavenly bread. "I am the living bread that came down from heaven; whoever eats this bread will live forever; and the bread that I will give is my flesh for the life of the world" (6:51).

For Christians the metaphorical understanding of bread culminates in Jesus' words at the Last Supper. "Jesus

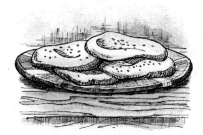

Unleavened bread was used in some of the sacrifices and religious ceremonies of the Israelites.

took bread, said the blessing, broke it, and giving it to his disciples said, 'Take and eat; this is my body'" (Mt 26:26, 1 Cor 11:23–26). This action would have had many levels of cultural significance: bread was the basic food of the people, it had religious significance as an offering in the Temple, and it had a long history as a symbol of God's teaching to his people.

Wine

Wine was made from the fermented juice of grapes and occasionally also from dates or other fruits. It is listed as one of the Lord's blessings: "the grain, the wine, and the oil, / the sheep and the oxen" (Jer 31:12). Sirach includes it as one of the necessities of life, along with water, salt, wheat, milk and honey, and oil (39:26). The Lord is praised for "bring[ing] bread from the earth, / and wine to gladden our hearts" (Ps 104:14–15).

Because water is relatively scarce in Palestine (there are few perennial streams and limited rainfall) and milk quickly turned sour without modern refrigeration, wine was a drink of choice in ancient times. It was drunk at daily meals (see Gn 27:25); a traveler would carry bread and wine as provisions (see Jgs 19:19). John the Baptist was considered strange because he drank no wine (see Lk 7:33); the vow of a Nazirite to drink no wine set him apart as unusual (see Nm 6:1–8, Jgs 13:4). It was also commonly drunk at banquets and feasts, especially higher quality wines: the headwaiter refers to the "good wine" served at the wedding feast at Cana (see Jn 2:10). "Choice wines" will be served at the eschatological banquet (see Is 25:6).

Like bread, wine was also used as an offering, poured out as a libation for the daily offering in the Temple (see Nm 28:7). Libations also accompanied the sacrifice of a lamb at Passover (see Lv 23:13).

Wine was also thought to have medicinal qualities. The "good Samaritan" pours wine on the wounds of a traveler (see Lk 10:34), and the Apostle Paul advises Timothy, "Stop drinking only water, but have a little wine for the sake of your stomach and your frequent illnesses" (1 Tm 5:23).

Beyond the positive uses of wine, the Bible also warns against drinking too much: "Wine is arrogant, strong drink is riotous; none who goes astray for it is wise" (Prv 20:1). "It goes down smoothly; / but in the end it bites like a serpent, / or like a poisonous adder. / Your eyes behold strange sights, / and

Wine—kept in large baked clay or stone jars—was a drink of choice in ancient times because it did not spoil easily.

your heart utters disordered thoughts" (23:31–33). Drunkenness is often associated with immoral behavior: "Let us conduct ourselves properly as in the day, not in orgies and drunkenness" (Rom 13:13).

Wine at the Last Supper

Jesus and his disciples drank wine at the Last Supper. "Then he took a cup, gave thanks, and gave it to them, saying, 'Drink from it, all of you, for this is my blood of the covenant, which will be shed on behalf of many for the forgiveness of sins'" (Mt 26:27–28). Jesus was not the first to associate wine with the symbolism of blood: other passages refer to the "blood of the grape" (Sir 39:26). Jesus also refers to eschatological wine: "I tell you, from now on I shall not drink this fruit of the vine until the day when I drink it with you new in the kingdom of my Father" (Mt 26:29).

The wine at the Last Supper again had several different levels of meaning. As a basic drink, it represents simple nourishment, health, and the community of a family meal. With his reference to shedding his blood, Jesus brought in the symbolism of the wine offering in the sacrifices. With his reference to drinking wine in the Kingdom, Jesus brought in the eschatological dimension of the future Kingdom and the perfection of all things.

Milk and Honey

The Promised Land is often described in the Bible as a land "flowing with milk and honey" (Ex 3:8, Lv 20:24), indicating how these items were associated with health and God's blessings.

Honey made by bees forms the basis of Samson's riddle (see Jgs 14:8–20). The Hebrew word usually translated as "honey" in the phrase "milk and honey," however, does not necessarily mean bee honey. It is a general word referring to various kinds of sweet liquids, such as a syrup made from dates or grapes. Honey can be used metaphorically: the Commandments of the Lord are said to be sweeter than honey (see Ps 19:11).

Goats were the primary source of milk (see Prv 27:27); camels (see Gn 32:16) and sheep (see Dt 32:14) also gave milk. Although cattle were raised, their milk was not used, as it is hard to digest for many people. Because milk soured quickly, it was often eaten in the form of yogurt, butter, or cheese, especially as cheese curds (see Gn 18:8, Is 7:15).

Meat

Meat was generally eaten only by the wealthy or by the average person only on special occasions. A family might keep a specially fed calf that they would slaughter for such occasions. The father in Jesus' parable slaughters the fatted calf when his son returns home (see Lk 15:23); Abraham picks out a choice steer for his guests (see Gn 18:7).

The Torah allows only the meat of clean animals to be eaten (see Lv 11:2–8)—provided that all the blood was drained out first (see 17:14). The meat of certain sacrifices could be eaten by those who offered it (e.g., the flesh of a peace or thanksgiving offering; see 7:15–20). Certain portions, such as the breast and right leg, were reserved for the priest (see 7:29–34). The Passover lamb was eaten by the family (see Ex 12:8, Dt 16:7). Rabbinic sources tell us that the priests actually suffered health problems from eating too much meat.

See the article "Fishing," for more information on fish in the diets of biblical societies.

Grapes

Grapes were an important crop in ancient Israel. They were eaten fresh or dried and as raisins (see 1 Sm 25:18). They were also used to make wine (see the previous section on wine).

In Palestine the grape harvest took place in September. The grapes were gathered and placed in a winepress, essentially a stone tub with channels cut to allow the grape juice to flow out when the grapes were crushed. Wine was stored in jars (see Jn 2:1–11) or in wineskins made from goatskins (see Mk 2:22).

Vegetables

Beans and lentils were the most common vegetables and were an important part of the average person's diet. They were part of David's basic supplies as he fled from his son Absalom (see 2 Sm 17:28). Esau sells Jacob his birthright in exchange for some lentil stew (see Gn 25:27–34).

Grains

As we noted in our discussion of bread, wheat and barley were common grains, along with millet and spelt. Wheat was also eaten in roasted form (see 1 Sm 17:17).

Salt

Sirach lists salt as one of the necessities of life (see 39:26). Salt was abundant in Israel; the salt hills near the Dead Sea were an abundant, major source. Sodom and Gomorrah were likely located at the southern end of the Dead Sea. This is where it is said that Lot's wife was turned into a pillar of salt (see Gn 19:26). Salt was a common seasoning for food and was used as a preservative for items such as fish.

Jesus likened his disciples to salt. "But if salt loses its taste, with what can it be seasoned? It is no longer good for anything but to be thrown out and trampled underfoot" (Mt 5:13; see Mk 9:49–50). The Colossians are advised, "Let your speech be gracious, seasoned with salt" (Col 4:6).

Salt was an important item of trade, and could even be used as money: Roman soldiers received part of their pay in salt (the Latin word for *salt* is the basis for our word *salary*). We can still see the influence of this custom in the saying, "Is this person worth his salt?"

Like oil, salt was often used in religious ceremonies: in cereal offerings (see Lv 2:13), mixed with sacred incense (see Ex 30:35), and in burnt offerings (see Ez 43:24). The phrase "covenant of salt" is used in Leviticus 2:13 and Numbers 18:19 (where it is translated as "inviolable covenant") to describe the covenant between God and Israel. The phrase may refer to the custom of two parties' sealing an agreement by eating the same salt together.

Again like oil, salt is associated with healing and health. Newborn babies were rubbed with salt in the belief that it promoted good heath (see Ez 16:4). The prophet Elisha purifies the unhealthy water of a spring by throwing salt into it (see 2 Kgs 2:19–22).

Related Passages

Feeding miracles: Mk 6:34–44, 8:1–10. *Centrality of bread:* Jer 16:7, Mt 6:11. *Barley:* 2 Kgs 7:1, Jn 6:9. *Making bread:* Mt 24:41, Lk 13:21. *Bread in religious ceremonies:* Ex 13:3–10; Lv 7:13, 24:5–9. *Symbolism of bread and the Last Supper:* Ex, ch. 16; Mt 26:26–30; Jn, ch. 6; 1 Cor 11:23–34. *Centrality of wine:* Gn 27:25, Sir 39:26. *Eschatological wine:* Is 25:6. *Wine in religious ceremonies:* Nm 28:7. *Medicinal properties of wine:* Lk 10:34, 1 Tm 5:23. *Storing wine:* Mk 2:21–22, Jn 2:1–11. *Warnings about drunkenness:* Prv 23:31–33, Rom 13:13. *Wine at the Last Supper:* Mt 26:26–30, 1 Cor 11:23–34. *Milk and honey:* Ex 3:8, Lv 20:24. *Fatted calf:* Gn 18:7, Lk 15:23. *Salt:* Lv 2:13, Sir 39:26, Ez 16:4, Mt 5:13, Mk 9:49–50.

See Also

- "Agriculture"
- "Anointing"
- "Fishing"
- "Food Laws"
- "Meals"
- "Women"

Food Laws

If you know anything about the Jewish religion, you have probably heard about kosher food laws. *Kosher* simply means "okay" or "acceptable." The kosher food laws teach that certain foods (such as the meat of a pig) cannot be eaten at all and that even certain acceptable foods must be prepared or eaten in a certain way (kosher animals must be slaughtered in a certain way; meat and dairy products must be eaten separately). In the Bible, the more common translation of the concept kosher is clean or pure; non-kosher is translated unclean or impure.

Modern Jewish food laws are based not only on scriptural commandments but also on the teachings of the rabbis (teachers) who commented on Scripture. For example, the rule that meat and dairy products must be separated is connected with a rabbinic interpretation of the scriptural commandment, "You shall not boil a kid in its mother's milk" (Ex 23:19). (The practice was apparently a Canaanite ritual; the rabbis judged that it was particularly important, because it is repeated; see 34:26).

We begin with the distinction between clean and unclean animals. Why does the Torah make this distinction?

Clean and Unclean Animals: Possible Reasons for the Distinction

The basic scriptural laws for distinguishing between clean and unclean animals are found in Leviticus, chapter 11, and Deuteronomy 14:3–20. Leviticus asserts that any animal that has a split hoof and chews its cud (for example, a sheep, cow, or goat) is clean, but animals that have only one of these two characteristics (for example, camels and pigs) are unclean and therefore should not be eaten (see Lv 11:2–8). Because Leviticus does not offer an explanation for this distinction, biblical interpreters have developed their own theories.

One school of thought suggests that there is in fact no logical reason. In order to instill in his people a sense of discipline and obedience, God included in the Torah several more or less arbitrary commandments, including these food laws. God's purpose was to teach his people to obey his commandments even when they did not understand them completely.

A second theory suggests that the food laws are symbolic. For example, the commandment to not eat the meat of pigs was a symbolic warning that the people should not behave like pigs (by being dirty or greedy). Philo favored these symbolic (or allegorical) interpretations.

A third suggestion is that the food laws were originally about concern for the health and hygiene of the people. For example, God commanded that pigs should not be eaten because of the health risks of eating pigs' meat (pigs' meat would spoil quickly in the hot climate of the Near East, and pigs carry certain unhealthy bacteria).

Clean and Unclean Within the Concept of Holiness

All three possibilities for the food laws have some merit but in the end are not very convincing. First, they all involve trying to guess God's hidden purpose behind these laws. If God really wanted to teach the people lessons about discipline, morality, or health care, why didn't God just come right out and teach it directly? Second, these explanations are quite broad and often cannot account for the details of the food laws.

We can better understand the food laws by relating them to the Israelite concept of holiness (see the "Holiness" article). An essential aspect of holiness involves the effort to maintain boundaries: anything that keeps within its proper boundaries is kosher, clean, or pure; anything that crosses its proper boundaries is not.

The following chart shows how this concept applies to the details of Leviticus, chapter 11:

Clean	Unclean
Land Animals A "proper" land animal is a creature that has a split hoof and chews the cud (see 11:3). This definition applies to sheep and cattle, animals domesticated by the Hebrews and used for food; these animals were also fit to be used for sacrifices in the Temple.	**Land Animals** Camels chew the cud but don't have hooves. Pigs have split hooves but don't chew the cud (see 11:4–7). They thus blur the boundary lines of the definition.
Water Animals A "proper" water animal is a creature that has fins and scales (see 11:9).	**Water Animals** Unclean water creatures lack either fins or scales (see 11:10–12). Amphibians (land creatures that crawl or swim in the water; see v. 10), blur the boundaries between land and water animals and are thus considered unclean also.
Air Animals A "proper" air animal is a creature that has wings and either flies or hops.	**Air Animals** Winged insects that move on four legs are unclean because they blur the distinction between air and land animals (see v. 20). The winged, four-legged grasshopper, however, is clean, because it uses its legs not to crawl on the ground, but to hop for long distances through the air (see v. 21).
Animals in General In general, animals are considered "proper" if they move in a way that is appropriate to their environment: walking on four legs for land animals, swimming with fins for water animals, flying or hopping through the air for air animals.	**Animals in General** Any creature that "swarms" is unclean (see vv. 41–43). A "swarming" creature is any animal that moves in a manner not appropriate for its particular environment: eels moving through water without fins; snakes moving on the ground without legs (this way of moving is due to God's curse; see Gn 3:14).

This concern for order and proper boundaries is as the heart of the ancient Hebrew concepts of holiness and purity. Both cleanness and holiness center on the concept of wholeness, completeness, and purity. Thus, only a "clean" animal was fit to bring to the holy Temple to be offered as a sacrifice.

The cleanness, or holiness, of the animals directly affected the cleanness or holiness of the people. If the people ate or even touched an unclean animal, they themselves became unclean, and were unfit to approach the holiness of God in his Temple until they had become clean again (see Lv 11:24–26). The food laws of Leviticus end by pointing out this connection: "For I, the Lord, am your God; and you shall make and keep yourselves holy, because

I am holy. You shall not make your-selves unclean, then, by any swarming creature that crawls on the ground. . . . You shall be holy, because I am holy" (vv. 44–45).

New Testament Perspectives on Food Laws

The attitude of the early Christians to-ward the food laws can be understood as only part of their overall understand-ing of the Torah.

What was Jesus' own understand-ing? Jesus himself never rejected the To-rah: "Do not think that I have come to abolish the law or the prophets. I have come not to abolish but to fulfill" (Mt 5:17).

Mark records a debate between Jesus and some "Pharisees and scribes" over purity laws, particularly, washing hands before eating. Jesus tells his disciples, "Do you not realize that everything that goes into a person from outside cannot defile?" (7:18). The Gospel writer then adds the comment, "Thus he declared all foods clean" (v. 19). But this is the writer's interpretation of Jesus' words. It is almost certain that Jesus himself did not declare all foods clean—Jesus' point in the debate with the Pharisees was to emphasize the importance of a person's intention or "heart," not to deny com-pletely the validity of the food laws.

Later Christians, however, did take the final step of declaring that all foods are clean. Peter sees a vision of clean and unclean animals together and is told "what God has made clean you are not to call profane" (Acts 10:15). Paul taught that Gentiles were not required to keep the food laws, though he did not condemn Jews who continued to do so (see Rom 14:1–12; 1 Cor, ch. 8).The Jerusalem Church also taught that food laws did not apply to Gentiles, except for specific rules regarding eating blood and animals, associated with pagan sac-rifices (see Acts 15:22–29).

Christian thought on this issue is closely tied to certain eschatological views. Torah commandments such as the food laws were understood as part of the specific covenant between God and Israel that would no longer apply in the end times. Thus, Paul taught that the Torah was a "disciplinarian" that would be in effect until the age of the Messiah came (see Gal 3:23–25) and that the clear distinctions between Jew (followers of Torah) and Gentile (who did not follow Torah) would no longer apply.

Related Passages

Food laws: Lv, ch. 11; Dt 14:3–20. *New Testament discussion of food laws:* Mk 7:1–23; Acts 10:9—11:18, ch. 15; Rom 14:1–12; 1 Cor, ch. 8.

See Also

- "Chosen People"
- "Holiness"
- "Meals"
- "Purity"
- "Torah"

Holiness

There have been thousands of religions throughout history. They have worshiped different gods, goddesses, or spirits. They have worshiped in different ways, through a variety of prayers, sacrifices, or rituals. Scholars who have studied a variety of the religions, however, identify a basic element common to virtually all of them: the tendency to divide the world into the holy, or sacred, on the one hand, and the ordinary, or profane, on the other.

The realm of the holy is the realm of the supernatural—the reality that is believed to lie beyond the world of everyday experience, beyond the world that we can see, touch, smell, hear, and taste. Every society we know of has believed in the supernatural, although they have imagined it in different ways.

Even people who are not particularly religious maintain some sense of the holy and the ordinary. Many people have a "special" place where they try to get away from the ordinary business of life, whether it is a room in their house or a special spot in the mountains or by the ocean. Certain objects may also have a sense of the sacred, such as a photograph or a special possession from a loved one who has passed away. Certain times will carry a sense of the sacred—memories of Christmas or a special holiday (holy day), or perhaps simply memories of an especially close time spent with family or friends.

The Sacred and Holy Fear

Scholar of religions Rudolf Otto identifies a common element in how religious people think about the sacred: they are at once attracted to it and frightened by it. If that sounds like a contradiction, think about watching a scary movie—we are frightened (at least somewhat), but at the same time we want to see it. And if we actually believed that there was a ghost or supernatural spirit near us, we would be very frightened—and yet fascinated.

In the Scriptures, we see the same combination of attraction and fear in people's reactions to the sacredness—the holiness—of God and of Jesus Christ.

The Old Testament often refers to the "fear of the Lord." "The beginning of wisdom is the fear of the LORD" says the Book of Proverbs (9:10). This "fear" is not a terror that would make one run away but rather is a deep respect and reverence for the holiness of God.

In the presence of God's great holiness, humans often feel very sharply their own limitations, inadequacy, and sin. A great example of this is the call of the prophet Isaiah. The scene is in the holy place of worship, the Jerusalem Temple. The prophet sees a vision of the Lord on his throne, surrounded by angels (known as seraphim), crying, "Holy, holy, holy is the LORD of hosts!" Isaiah's reaction: "Woe is me! I am doomed! For I am a man of unclean lips, living among a people of unclean lips; yet my eyes have seen the King, the LORD of hosts!" (Is 6:1–5).

In the New Testament, Peter has the same reaction to Jesus when he becomes aware of Jesus' supernatural power. Peter "fell at the knees of Jesus and said, 'Depart from me, Lord, for I am a sinful man'" (Luke 5:8).

The sense of human weakness in the presence of God's holiness is also reflected in the belief that a human cannot see God and live. "But my face you cannot see, for no man sees me and still lives"

(Ex 33:20; see also Gn 16:13, 32:31). The sacredness of God is so powerful and holy that a limited, sinful human could not bear to see God in his full reality. God can be seen indirectly only—through God's creation and through God's manifestations on earth.

Holy Places

When we study religions, we see that humans typically encounter supernatural reality in a few specific places. A certain spring or grove of trees might be considered the home of a particular spirit, and thus considered sacred. Sometimes the sacred place was associated with a high hill or mountain. The ancient Greeks believed that the gods lived on Mount Olympus. Traditional Lakota believe that certain buttes are sacred places where the spirits can be encountered. In the Bible, the religious practices of the Canaanites are associated with the "high places" (2 Kgs 12:3, 23:5). Moses received the Ten Commandments on Mount Sinai (see Ex 19:2–3), and Jesus was transfigured and met with holy men from the past (Elijah and Moses) on a mountain (see Mark 9:2–8).

The Ark of the Covenant, kept in the Holy of Holies in the Dwelling Tent and in the Jerusalem Temple, was considered the seat of God's holiness.

Sacred spaces can further be identified with places of worship. Thus the sacred spaces in ancient cities were the temples—the places where the gods were worshiped, and often the places where the gods were thought to be present.

The most sacred place for Jews, of course, was the Jerusalem Temple, where God's presence was found in a unique way. The Temple itself was divided into levels of holiness. The most holy place was the Holy of Holies, the central area of the Temple in which the Ark of the Covenant rested. The Temple itself made the city of Jerusalem holy, as well as the entire land of Israel (see the "Temple" article for details).

Holiness is closely related with the biblical concept of purity. Only those in a state of purity could approach the holiness of the Temple. If an impure person came into contact with the holy, he or she would be destroyed (see Ex 19:21, Nm 18:22). (See the "Purity" article.)

Sacred Time

Ancient religions also divided time into sacred time and ordinary time. Certain times were devoted to the worship of the gods or spirits. We can still identify this custom in our word *holiday*. The word of course originally meant "holy day" and was connected with some type of religious ceremony. In traditional Jewish, Christian, and Muslim societies, the week is divided into six days of ordinary activity, and the seventh is held as sacred (Saturday, Sunday, and Friday, respectively) and devoted to religious observances.

The Jewish year was also marked by special times, holy festivals, usually associated with harvest times. The three most important were the festivals of Passover, Tabernacles (Feast of Booths), and the Feast of Weeks (see the article "Festivals" for details).

A Broad Concept of Holiness

The ancient Hebrew concept of holiness is quite broad; Leviticus, chapter 19, is a good example of its range. The chapter's theme may be summed up by, "Be holy, for I, the LORD, your God, am holy" (v. 2).

Holy actions include what we would call good ethical behavior. "Revere your mother and father" (v. 3); respect the elderly (see v. 32); when harvesting fields or vineyards, leave some for the poor (see vv. 9–10); do not steal or lie (see v. 11), do not mistreat people who are disabled (see v. 14), love your neighbor as yourself (see v. 18), be honest in business dealings (vv. 35–36).

Holiness also included avoiding any sort of religious or spiritual activities outside of the worship of the Lord (see vv. 26–27,31).

Holiness and Order

But consider this commandment, "Do not breed any of your domestic animals with others of a different species; do not sow a field of yours with two different kinds of seed; and do not put on a garment woven with two different kinds of thread" (v. 19). Although this seems to have nothing to do with holiness, anthropologists such as Mary Douglas have shown that we can make sense of such commandments by understanding the connection between holiness and order in traditional cultures.

Religious rituals in many cultures are closely connected with concepts of order and disorder. A ritual often has a symbolic sense of restoring order to a world that is chaotic and unpredictable. Order is thus closely identified with holiness, and disorder and chaos with the realm of the ordinary and profane.

A fundamental belief in ancient Hebrew thought is that God created order in the world by placing everything in its proper categories. We see this concept in the very first chapter of the Bible. In the beginning the earth was a "formless wasteland" (Gn 1:2): in other words, it was chaotic and had no order to it. God creates order by separating things into their proper places. Light is separated from darkness, water from dry land, and so on (see Gn 1:4–18).

The key concept is that order is maintained when everything stays in its proper place. Confusion, conflict, and chaos result if things cross their proper boundaries. In ancient Hebrew thought then, anything that keeps within its proper boundaries is holy and can also be described as kosher, clean, or pure; anything that crosses its proper boundaries is not. The distinction between clean and unclean animals is built on this concept of maintaining clear boundaries between different categories. See the "Food Laws" article for a more detailed discussion.

Holiness and Purity

Another commandment reads, "Do not eat meat with the blood still in it" (Lv 19:26). Again, it's not clear what this commandment has to do with holiness. Yet once we see it in the context of Israelite beliefs concerning purity, we can begin to make sense of it.

Blood was considered the life force of a person or animal. As such, the blood of a sacrifice made atonement for sin (see Lv 17:11; see the "Sacrifices and Offerings" and "Atonement" articles): it cleansed objects or people from sin, restored them to a state of purity. The blood of sacrifices was physically placed on the holy places in order to restore them to a state of holiness (see Lv 4:30,34). Moses sprinkled blood on the people for the same purpose (see Ex 24:8).

The power of the life force must be respected; blood thus could not be treated in an ordinary or profane way by casually eating it.

Holiness and Wholeness

The biblical view of human nature is holistic: there are no sharp distinctions between the physical, mental, and spiritual aspects of a person (see the "Human Nature" article). Holiness is thus associated not only with purity and cleansing of sin but also with the blessings of physical health. Conversely, a close connection exists between sickness, sin, and impurity in the biblical worldview (see the "Sickness and Health" article).

Holiness and the Chosen People

"Be holy, for I, the Lord, your God, am holy" (Lv 19:2). This passage reveals further the essential connection between the sense of God's holiness and the holiness of God's specially chosen covenant people (see the "Chosen People" article).

The holiness of the people was expressed through laws that set the people apart from all other peoples: the food laws, circumcision, the Sabbath rest. Though this sense of holiness could result in an exclusive view that warned against contact with non-Israelites (see Dt 7:1–6), it could also result in the motivation to share the blessings of Israel's relationship with God: the concept of Israel as the "light to the nations" (Is 49:6)

Related Passages

The sacred and holy fear: Ex 19:21, Ex 33:20, Prv 9:10, Is 6:1–5, Lk 5:1–11. *Holy places:* Ex 3:1–6, ch. 19; Mk 9:2–8. *Holy times:* Lv, ch. 23; Dt, ch. 16. *Broad sense of holiness:* Lv, ch. 19. *Holiness and order:* Gn, ch. 1; Lv, ch. 11, 19:19. *Holiness and blood:* Ex 24:8; Lv, ch. 4, 17:11. *Holiness and the Chosen People:* Dt 7:1–6, Is 49:6.

See Also

- "Atonement"
- "Chosen People"
- "Festivals"
- "Food Laws"
- "Purity"
- "Sacrifices and Offerings"
- "Sickness and Health"
- "Sin"
- "Temple"

Honor and Shame

If we are trying to encourage a certain behavior, we often praise a person: "Great job! You should be proud of yourself!" Conversely, if we are trying to discourage a certain behavior, we say things such as, "You know better than that! You ought to be ashamed of yourself!"

These examples show that honor and shame are important in our society. Social scientists who study biblical societies, however, find that these values were not just important but essential to the functioning of those ancient societies. Thus, they are called honor-shame societies. Gaining and maintaining honor is a central activity in such communities, and rules of honor and shame are essential in maintaining the society's social roles and values.

From this social science perspective, honor is defined as a claim to worth that is publicly recognized by one's social group. In other words, honor is a person's public reputation that in turn forms the person's own self-identity. Specifically, a person is honored if he or she follows the social expectations of his or her group.

Shame refers to the lack of honor—it means social humiliation and disgrace. For women, however, it also carries a positive connotation: shame can refer to a woman's ability to guard her honor.

The highly effective role of honor and shame in reinforcing acceptable social behavior is closely related to the group-oriented view of Mediterranean societies. In such communities, the self-identity of an individual is largely formed by the approval (honoring) or rejection (shaming) of the group to which the individual belonged.

Honor, Shame, and Gender Roles

Because honor is a public recognition of a person's claim to social status, it is closely associated with men, as men have the public social role in the patriarchal biblical societies (see the "Family" and "Women" articles). Women have a private social role: their realm is the home, where they raise the children and manage the household.

Shame has a positive connotation for a female: a woman's shame refers to her ability to protect her and her family's honor. She does this primarily through protecting her sexual status as a virgin before her marriage and as a faithful wife throughout her marriage. A woman who fails to protect her sexuality is therefore considered shameless—she brings shame on her family, especially on her father or husband.

Sirach notes that a father must worry constantly about his daughter while she is "unmarried, lest she be seduced, / or, as a wife, lest she prove unfaithful" (42:10). A daughter's shameful behavior shames the father: "Keep a close watch on your daughter, / lest she make you the sport of your enemies, / A byword in the city, a reproach among the people, / an object of derision in public gatherings" (42:11).

The image of the shameless, sexually unchaste woman appears often in the Bible. It is central to the Book of Proverbs, where the young man is warned to avoid the adulteress, who will lead him astray with her "smoothlips" (see Prv 7:4–23, 9:13–18). This adulteress is contrasted with Wisdom, who is personified as an honorable woman (see 9:1–6,11). When the people of Israel go astray from the Lord to worship other gods, they are symbolized as a shameless adulteress or prostitute (see Hos, ch. 1–2; Ez, ch. 16).

Ascribed and Achieved Honor

Social scientists distinguish between ascribed and achieved honor. Ascribed honor is given to a person simply because of his or her birth: a person born into a high priestly Israelite family or a Roman senatorial family had an honored position by default. Achieved honor, in contrast, is earned by one's own personal accomplishments.

Jesus' ascribed honor was low. He was a craftsman, and thus quite low on the social scale. In addition, he came from a common village family. It was for this reason that his fellow villagers "took offense" at him when he returned to the village of Nazareth as a publicly acclaimed teacher and healer (see Mk 6:1–3).

The Gospel writers, however, do try to ascribe family honor to Jesus by recording his genealogy: this shows that he is a descendant of an honorable line that could be traced back to King David (see Mt 1:1–17, Lk 3:23–38). Genealogies are employed frequently in the Bible to illustrate the ascribed honor of an individual or group. (1 Chr 3:1–24 lists descendants of King David; lists in Ezra 2 and 10 establish proper descent from priestly families.)

In an honor-shame society, honor is often acquired as a result of a conflict with another person who has a competing claim to honor. These conflicts often take the form of a challenge-and-response encounter. The Pharisees, an honored group of teachers who were among the ruling elite in Israel, often publicly challenge the authority and honor of Jesus. They challenge Jesus on his teaching regarding divorce: "They were testing him" (Mk 10:2). On his teaching regarding paying taxes, they were trying "to ensnare him in his speech" (12:13). The ruling elite of Jerusalem (chief priests, scribes, and elders) also challenge him: "By what authority are you doing these things?" (11:28). In each case, Jesus answers with a counter-question, challenging the honor of his questioners in return. In these exchanges, Jesus shows himself as the equal of these elite authorities, thus acquiring public honor among the people: "They were utterly amazed at him" (12:17).

Jesus' Challenge to the Kinship System

The honor of the family (in social science terms, the "kinship group") was the central concern in biblical societies. A person married, for example, not because he or she fell in love with someone, but because one family made a marriage arrangement with another family in order to maintain or enhance the family's honor. Politics were dominated by the concern of the ruling elite families (such as the Hasmoneans or Herod's family) to maintain or enhance their honor. A woman's honor was to perform well her role in the family as mother, wife, and manager of the household, while the man's honor was to publicly portray his family's social status. The children's honor was to revere their parents by accepting their authority. "Household codes" (such as the one in Eph 5:21—6:9) illustrate honorable family roles from a Christian perspective.

Jesus' proclamation of the Kingdom of God was a radical challenge to this family-centered value system. When Jesus is told that his family is looking for him, he indicates his followers and says: "Here are my mother and my brothers. [For] whoever does the will of God is my brother and sister and mother" (Mk 3:32–35). In other sayings, Jesus insists that his followers' duty to the Kingdom of God is more important than their duty to their family (see Lk 9:59–62). To make his point absolutely clear, Jesus uses exaggerated language: "If any one comes to me without hating his father and mother, wife and children, brothers and sisters, and even his own life, he cannot be my disciple" (Lk 14:26). The point is that one cannot hold on to the old values in the Kingdom.

Jesus thus pictured the Kingdom of God, which he and his followers were establishing, as a new family, with God as the father, and with new rules for ascribing and achieving honor. It is clear that the early Christian church communities thought of themselves as a new family, referring to fellow church members as brother or sister (see Rom 16:1,17). Even a Christian slave was to be considered a brother (see Phlm, v. 16). In social science terms, Jesus and his followers were establishing fictive kin communities.

Honor, Shame, and Social Hierarchies

The honor-shame system reinforced the carefully defined social hierarchy of biblical societies. One's honor comes from knowing and accepting one's place in that social hierarchy. At a banquet, for example, guests with the highest social status received the best seats. If person sat at a higher level than warranted by his social status, the host might ask the person to move down, thus shaming him (see Lk 14:7–10).

Customs regarding invitations to meals also reflect the honor-shame system. A client might invite his patron to a banquet as a way of honoring him; a patron might invite a client as a way of recognizing the client's services to him. In all cases, an invitation to a banquet required some reciprocal action. If one invites friends, relatives, or wealthy neighbors, it is expected that they "invite you back and you have repayment" (Lk 14:12). In an honor-shame society, even a dinner invitation was a sort of challenge to honor. One had to respond in a socially appropriate way in order to maintain or enhance one's status and honor.

Again, however, Jesus' vision of the Kingdom of God rejects the accepted rules of honor and shame. Jesus advised: "When you hold a banquet, invite the poor, the crippled, the lame, the blind; blessed indeed will you be because of their inability to repay you. For you will be repaid at the resurrection of the righteous" (Lk 14:13–14). Jesus here focuses attention on those with least honor and status in society—those who do not have the means to engage in contests of honor and prestige. The one who invites will not receive the customary honor from the guests, but he will receive honor (blessing) from God.

Related Passages

Honor and gender roles: Ez, ch. 16; Prv, ch. 7–9; Sir 42:9–14; Hos, ch. 1–2. *Honor and family:* Mt 1:1–17; Mk 3:31–35, 6:1–6; Lk 3:23–38, 9:59–62, 14:26. *Honor and challenge and response:* Mk 10:1–12, 11:27–33, 12:13–17. *Honor and meal customs:* Lk 14:7–24.

See Also

- "Family"
- "Poverty and Wealth"
- "Women"

Hospitality

The Greek word for *hospitality* is *philoxenia,* literally, "love *(philos)* of the stranger *(xenos).*" The primary meaning of *xenos* is "strange" or "foreign." In social theory terms, it refers to outsiders or members of the out-group as opposed to one's own social group (the insiders or in-group).

In ancient societies, the in-group had two primary reactions to the stranger. The first was an aggressive rejection or even destruction of the stranger or the alien as a threat to the values or the safety of the in-group. We see this response reflected in one of the meanings of *xenos:* "enemy."

The second reaction was an open welcoming of the stranger in an attempt to socialize him to become part of the in-group and thus no longer a threat. This is the essential social task of hospitality—converting a stranger into a guest, a temporary member of the in-group. This strategy is also reflected in linguistic meaning: in certain contexts, *xenos* can mean "guest." Because guest and host are so closely bound together by rules of hospitality, *xenos* can also be translated as "host."

Hospitality as a Cross-Cultural Value

Traditions involving hospitality for the stranger are known in a wide diversity of cultures. In the harsh desert environment of the Arab Bedouin, protection of the guest—even if the guest is, in other settings, an enemy—is a sacred value. In the ancient Greco-Roman world, the chief god Zeus was known as a protector of the stranger. Those who dared to abuse guests were punished in the underworld.

The value of hospitality was also reinforced through well-known stories about gods' disguising themselves as strangers. In a Greek fable, the disguised gods Zeus and Hermes were denied hospitality by everyone in a certain town, except for an elderly couple, Baucis and Philemon. Zeus destroyed the town because of the people's failure to extend hospitality, having first warned Baucis and Philemon to flee and not look back. We find an echo of this story in Acts of the Apostles, when the citizens of Lystra are convinced that Paul and Barnabas are Zeus and Hermes, gods "come down to us in human form" (14:11–12).

Hospitality to the Stranger in the Old Testament

The memory of their slavery in Egypt is foundational for the Israelites' attitude toward hospitality. "You shall treat the alien who resides with you no differently than the natives born among you; have the same love for him as for yourself; for you too were once aliens in the land of Egypt. I, the LORD, am your God" (Lv 19:34). The stranger should be allowed to participate in the sacred times of Israel: sharing the Sabbath rest (see Ex 20:10) and sacred feasts (see Dt 16:11). With the widow and orphan, the stranger is to share in the benefits from the religious tithes (see 14:29). Legal justice was to be the same for the Israelite and the stranger (see 1:16).

The classic account of biblical hospitality is Abraham's welcoming of strangers who are disguised angels. When Abraham sees three men approaching his tent in the heat of the day, he immediately runs out to greet them, bows to the ground, and begs them to stay. He has water brought to bathe their feet and has them sit in the shade. He has Sarah make bread, slaughters a steer, and serves them curds and milk (see Gn 18:1–8). Later Jewish and Christian tradition regards Abraham's act as the model of hospitality: "Do not neglect hospitality, for through it some have unknowingly entertained angels" (Heb 13:2).

Abraham's story continues when two of the angels visit the house of his nephew Lot in Sodom. When the townspeople demand to have sex with the strangers, Lot protects them, even going to the extent of offering his own daughters to the men in place of the strangers (see Gn 19:1–11). Bruce Malina characterizes Lot's action as "sexual hospitality"—a patriarchal strategy by which a male stranger uses his wife or daughters as a gift to the locals in order to ensure his own safety or the safety of a guest within an alien community (see also Gn 12:10–20, 20:2–18; Jgs 19:22–28). God's ensuing destruction of Sodom is most likely a punishment for the Sodomites' abuse of the laws of hospitality. The account has some striking parallels with the story of Baucis and Philemon.

Another striking variation on this theme occurs in Jesus' parable of the sheep and goats (see Mt 25:31–46). Here a person is saved or condemned based on her or his response to those in need: Did the person visit the sick, clothe the naked, show hospitality to the stranger (see 25:35–36)? At the end of the parable, Jesus reveals that whenever people showed these kindnesses to "these least brothers of mine" (25:40), they really showed the kindnesses to him.

God as a Host

An important biblical metaphor is the understanding of God as a host who shows hospitality to the stranger. As God's Chosen People, the Israelites must imitate God's behavior:

> For the LORD, your God, is the God of gods, the LORD of lords, the great God, mighty and awesome, who has no favorites, accepts no bribes; who executes justice for the orphan and the widow, and befriends the alien, feeding and clothing him. So you too must befriend the alien, for you were once aliens yourselves in the land of Egypt. (Dt 10:17–19)

Similarly, Leviticus portrays God as a host who is the true owner of the land; the Israelites are merely strangers passing through: "You are but aliens who have become my tenants" (Lv 25:23). Israel is to imitate God's values by allowing a poor man opportunities to recover his land if he is forced to sell it (see 25:23–28).

The image of God's people as passing strangers on the earth is repeated elsewhere (see Ps 39:13; 1 Pt 1:1, 2:11). It may well be that the image used in First Peter corresponds to the actual social situation of the readers, who were living as refugees or exiles in foreign lands.

The metaphor of God as a host is consistent with the common biblical image of eschatological salvation as a banquet that God provides as a beneficent host (see Is 25:6–8, Jl 4:17–18). Jesus' parables and stories also portray God as a host inviting people to his banquet (see Mt 8:11, Lk 14:15–24).

Feeding guests was considered a basic requirement of hospitality in Mediterranean cultures.

Early Christian Hospitality Networks

Hospitality was an essential practice in the life of Jesus himself and the early Christian movement. Jesus often relies on hospitality. He eats or lodges at the house of Simon Peter (see Mk 1:29–35), Levi the tax collector (see Lk 5:29), Simon the leper (see Mk 14:3, Lk 7:36), Martha and Mary (see 10:38), and a Pharisee (see 14:1). Jesus shames his host Simon when he points out that Simon failed to provide standard forms of hospitality to him: water to wash his feet, a kiss, oil to anoint his head (see 7:44–46).

In sending out his disciples, Jesus counted on villagers to provide them with hospitality. "Whenever you enter a house, stay there until you leave from there" (Mk 6:10). The disciples as guests offered their hosts the message of the Kingdom of God, expulsion of demons, and healing. In return the hosts provided food and shelter.

Christian prophets and missionaries made regular use of the hospitality network system among fellow believers: Peter stays as a guest at the house of Simon the tanner (see Acts 10:6) and then at the house of Cornelius, a Roman centurion (see 10:49). Paul is a guest in the home of Lydia (see 16:15)

and the Philippian jailer (see 16:34; see also 17:7; 18:2–3; 21:8,16). Gaius hosted Paul (see Rom 16:23); Paul writes to Philemon, to "prepare a guest room for me" (v. 22).

Not surprisingly then, New Testament writers frequently admonish their readers to practice the virtue of hospitality: "Be hospitable to one another without complaining" (1 Pt 4:9; see also Rom 12:13). Hospitality should be a characteristic of Church leaders (see 1 Tm 3:2, 5:10; Ti 1:8).

Christian travelers would often carry letters of recommendation from a trusted authority in order to secure hospitality. Third John is the author's (who is known simply as the Presbyter) recommendation of one of his followers, Demetrius, to his correspondent, Gaius; the author also praises Gaius for his past hospitality. Paul's Letter to the Romans recommends Phoebe, "a minister of the church at Cenchrae," to the Roman congregation (Rom 16:1).

Conflict and Refusal of Hospitality

The Johannine letters show us how hospitality played a role in the social conflicts within early Christian churches. The Presbyter writes to a church community, warning them of a faction that does not share his teaching about Jesus' true humanity: "If anyone comes to you and does not bring this doctrine, do not receive him in your house or even greet him; for whoever greets him shares in his evil works" (2 Jn, vv. 10–11). Diotrephes, a member of Gaius' church, had refused to accept an earlier letter from the Presbyter and refused to extend hospitality to the Presbyter's missionaries (see 3 Jn, vv. 9–10).

Related Passages

Abraham as the model host: Gn 18:1–8. *Abuse of guests:* Gn 19:1–11, Jgs 18:22–28. *Jesus as the stranger:* Mt 25:31–46. *God as a host and the people's duties as hosts:* Dt 10:17–19, Lv 25:23–28. *Christian hospitality networks:* Mk 1:29–35, 6:6–13; Acts 10:6,49; Phlm, v. 22. *Letters of recommendation:* Rom 16:1; 3 Jn, v. 12. *Refusal of hospitality:* 2 Jn, vv. 10–11; 3 Jn, vv. 9–10.

See Also

- "Chosen People"
- "Meals"

Human Nature

How would you describe a human being? Our physical aspects are fairly obvious: we typically have two hands, two arms, two legs, a heart, and a brain, for example. Most people would say we have a mind, although if we ask whether the mind is different from the brain, we might get some differences of opinion. Most people would agree we have a spirit, but again there would be some different views on exactly how to define our spirit. Finally, many people would agree that humans have a soul, but it might not be clear if soul is different from spirit, and, if so, in exactly what way.

This isn't the place to discuss these terms in detail; our point right now is that even today we have different ways of thinking about and describing the precise elements that makes up human nature. Not surprisingly, then, we'll see that there are significant differences between the view of the human nature found in ancient Hebrew culture (reflected mainly in the Old Testament) and the view found in Hellenistic cultures (reflected mainly in the New Testament).

Old Testament View: Body and Living Force

Hebrew thought tends to see the human being holistically: there is not a sharp difference between the physical body and the spirit or soul. The Hebrews did not even have words that we can translate directly as physical and spiritual. They did not think of these two concepts as opposites as most people in modern Western societies do.

Consider this passage from Psalms: "O God, you are my God— / for you I long! / For you my body yearns; / for you my soul thirsts" (63:2). The whole person, in other words, both body and soul, longs for God.

The Hebrew word translated as "body" in the Psalms quotation is *basar*. This same word is translated as "flesh" in some older English biblical translations. It basically refers to what we would call the physical aspect of humans, but it was also used to express the sense that life is short and fragile. Thus, the prophet Isaiah says: "All mankind *(basar)* is grass, / and all their glory like the flower of the field. / The grass withers, the flower wilts" (40:6–7).

The Hebrew word translated as "soul" in the Psalms quotation is *nephesh*. But *nephesh* does not have the same meaning as the modern English word *soul*. We see its sense in the Creation story: "The Lord God formed man out of the clay of the ground and blew into his nostrils the breath of life, and so man became a living being *[nephesh]*" (Gn 2:7). *Nephesh* then, is not really separate from the body *(basar)* of a person. It is simply that aspect of the *basar* that makes the *basar* living. We can then perhaps translate *nephesh* as "life force." The inhabitants of Sheol (the realm of the dead) are never called *nephesh*.

In its verbal form, *nephesh* means "to breathe." *Ruach,* or "breath," is that which distinguishes a dead person from a living person. "When you take away their breath, they perish / and return to the dust from which they came" (Ps 104:29). "If he [God] were to take back his spirit to himself, / withdraw to himself all his breath, / All flesh would perish together, / and man would return to the dust" (Jb 34:14–15). This same word *ruach* can also be translated as "wind" or "spirit." The spirit / breath / wind of God was there from the very beginning of creation: "In the beginning, when God created the heavens and the earth . . . a mighty wind swept over the waters" (Gn 1:2); it is God's breath that gives life to man (see 2:7).

The Hebrew word for *heart, lev,* is closest to what we would call conscience or mind. Abigail advises David not to kill Nabal and his people for insulting him, lest David have this blood on his conscience *(lev)* (see 1 Sm 25:31). Because of his humble request, God grants Solomon a wise heart *(lev)* (see 1 Kgs 3:12).

The holistic Hebrew view of the person is connected with his or her view of the afterlife. The most common Old Testament view of death is that all people, both good and bad, go to Sheol after death, existing in a shadowy sort of way. The Hebrews did not think of a soul or spirit that survived intact after a person's death (see the "Afterlife" article).

New Testament View: Body, Soul, and Spirit

The New Testament is influenced by Greek ideas about human nature. The Greek philosopher Plato, for example, made a sharp distinction between the physical body and the spirit or soul. Whereas the body is weak and changeable, the soul is that part of the human that is eternal and unchanging. Plato actually saw the body as a weight that hindered and dragged down the soul. In this view, physical death could then actually be seen as a blessing, for the eternal soul is finally freed from the body that restricted it.

The Hebrew concept of the weak and fragile nature of the body *(basar)* is carried over in the New Testament Greek word *sarx.* When his disciples are unable to stay awake to keep him company, Jesus tells them, "The spirit is willing but the flesh *[sarx]* is weak" (Mk 14:38). When the Word of God took on the weak human condition, the author uses this word as well: "And the Word became flesh *[sarx]*" (Jn 1:14).

The Apostle Paul uses this word to mean a person's focus on the fleeting, transitory nature of life. Although the *sarx* in itself is not evil, a focus on the things of the *sarx* can lead to forgetting about God. "For the concern of the flesh is hostility toward God" (Rom 8:7).

The Hebrew word *nephesh* corresponds well with the Greek word *psyche* (usually translated as "soul"); basically *psyche* refers to that which gives life to a body, the "life force." At times it can simply mean "life": "For the Son of Man did not come to be served but to serve and to give his life *[psyche]* as a ransom for many" (Mk 10:45). "For whoever wishes to save his life will lose it, but whoever loses his life for my sake and that of the gospel will save it" (8:35). It can also refer to the emotions: "My soul is sorrowful even to death" (14:34).

Paul at one point speaks of a three-part division of the human: "May you entirely, spirit, soul, and body, be preserved blameless for the coming of our Lord Jesus Christ" (1 Thes 5:23). Paul closely associates the spirit (pneuma) with the new spiritual life a person receives when she or he becomes a member of the Body of Christ. The Christian leaves behind the old way of life that focused on the needs of the flesh: "But you are not in the flesh, on the contrary, you are in the spirit, if only the Spirit of God dwells in you" (Rom 8:9). "So whoever is in Christ is a new creation: the old things have passed away; behold, new things have come" (2 Cor 5:17). Paul also contrasts the spiritual (pneumatikos) person and the natural (psychichos) person (see 1 Cor 2:14–15): only the "spiritual" person can understand the things that pertain to God's Spirit.

Despite the contrast between the flesh and the spirit (on the one hand) and the natural soul and the spirit (on the other), the New Testament view of the human is also holistic. It does not accept the Platonic idea that the body is a "prison" for the soul or spirit.

We see the holistic nature of the New Testament view most clearly in Paul's description of the resurrection body. It is not only a person's spirit that is raised from the dead; the body will be raised as well. Paul describes this resurrection body as a spiritual body—meaning a body whose life force is the supernatural spirit, not merely the natural soul. "It is sown a natural body; it is raised a spiritual body" (1 Cor 15:44; compare accounts of Jesus' own resurrection body; for example, Lk 24:36-43).

The life in the resurrection is salvation: the complete healing of all of a person's limitations and sins, and a complete reunion with God. Salvation involves the whole person—not only the soul and spirit are "saved," but also a person's body is renewed and perfected by being made alive through the spirit.

Related Passages

Fragility of the human (basar): Is 40:6–7; Job 34:14–15. **Nephesh, breath, and life force:** Gn 2:7. *Flesh* (sarx) *and spirit* (pneuma): Mk 14:38, Rom 8:1–13. *Psyche as natural life:* Mk 8:35, 10:45. *The spiritual contrasted with the natural:* 1 Cor 2:14–15. *Spiritual body of the resurrection:* 1 Cor 15:35–49, Lk 24:36–43.

See Also

- "Afterlife"
- "Resurrection"

Jewish Sects

Just as Christianity today is divided into different groups (Catholics, Methodists, Lutherans, nondenominational evangelical churches), so too ancient Jewish religion had distinct groups or sects. In Jesus' time in Palestine, three groups were particularly influential. Josephus identifies these groups (he calls them "philosophies"): the Sadducees, the Pharisees, and the Essenes.

We should make clear from the start that only a small minority of people actually belonged to these sects, but their strong influence on Jewish society is undeniable. The Pharisees were the largest of the three, consisting of about six thousand members during the time of Herod the Great (out of a total population of perhaps one million people in Palestine).

These groups can be compared not only to Christian denominations but also to modern political parties. In ancient Judaism, there was no sharp distinction between religion and politics. All three groups were concerned not only with religious behavior but also with the political issues of their day.

Sadducees

The name Sadducees most likely comes from the name Zadok, a priest who anointed David's son Solomon as king (see 1 Kgs 1:32–40). The descendants of Zadok, the Zadokites, were recognized as the only legitimate priests by Ezekiel (see Ez 44:9–31) and the author of the Book of Chronicles. It's likely that the Sadducees were Zadokites who supported the Hasmonean (descendants of the Maccabbees) kings and priests.

The Sadducees were apparently of the elite, wealthy class, and were closely allied with the high priestly families. Josephus says the Sadducees had a following among the rich only, while the Pharisees had a greater following among the common people. In Acts of the Apostles, the Sadducees are associated with the high priest and the Jerusalem Temple (see 4:1–2, 5:17). Josephus names the high priest Ananus as a Sadducee.

In New Testament times, the high priest was appointed by King Herod, the client king of the Romans, then by Herod's son Archelaeus, and later directly by Roman rulers of Judea. With their connections with the high priestly families, the Sadducees were closely tied to Roman rule in Palestine.

Ancient Jews held a variety of different beliefs about the afterlife. Josephus says the Sadducees believed that the soul died along with the body; the Acts of the Apostles reports that "the Sadducees say that there is no resurrection or angels or spirits, while the Pharisees acknowledge all three" (23:8).

Members of the Sadducees tried to show that the belief in resurrection was not logical when they asked Jesus about a hypothetical case in which a woman had married seven men. In the life after resurrection, whose wife would she be? (see Mk 12:18–27). Jesus answered them, "When they rise from the dead, they neither marry nor are given in marriage, but they are like the angels in heaven" (v. 25). In other words, the normal standards of marriage do not apply in the resurrected life.

According to Josephus, the Pharisees and Sadducees were often in conflict. The Pharisees taught many religious rules that were not directly in the Torah; the Sadducees rejected all laws that were not explicitly written in the Torah. Josephus also reports that the Sadducees were harsher in their legal judgments and punishments than were the Pharisees. The rabbinic literature often portrays the Pharisees and Sadducees disagreeing about matters of purity.

Pharisees

It appears that most members of the Pharisees were not priests. They had considerable influence in Israelite society—Josephus reports that at the beginning of the revolt against Rome in AD 66, the leading Pharisees met with the high priests and "men of power" in an attempt to resolve the crisis.

This political influence, however, was indirect. The Pharisees did not hold political offices but rather influenced such leaders as the Hasmonean Queen Salome Alexandra and later Herod the Great. Mark portrays the Pharisees as plotting with the "Herodians" to destroy Jesus (see Mk 3:6, 12:13). They did, however, serve on the council ("Sanhedrin") that advised the high priest (see Acts 5:34; 23:6–9).

Origins of the Pharisees

Many scholars think the Pharisaic party evolved from a group known as the Hasideans, zealous supporters of the Torah who joined the Maccabean revolt: "Then they were joined by a group of Hasideans, valiant Israelites, all of them devout followers of the law" (1 Mc 2:42). The name Hasideans comes from the Hebrew *hasid,* meaning "pious" or "devout."

Most scholars also believe the Pharisaic movement later developed into rabbinic Judaism. This Judaism, based on the Scriptures as interpreted by the Mishnah and Talmud, is the form of the Jewish faith that has survived into modern times. Thus, careful study of early rabbinic documents, such as the Mishnah (ca. AD 200) allows us to gain some insights into the Pharisees' teaching at the time of Jesus.

The Pharisees are often portrayed in the Gospels as hypocritical, concerned more with outward show than with sincere faith, "for they preach but they do not practice" (Mt 23:3–5,25–28). Jesus contrasts the prayers of a self-righteous Pharisee with a humble tax collector; it is the tax collector who goes away justified by God (see Lk 18:9–14). It is not surprising that the Gospel writers tended to focus on negative aspects of the Pharisaic movement, as early Christians and Pharisees were in serious conflict

over basic issues, such as the observance of Torah.

Josephus's portrait is much more positive. He reports that the Pharisees avoided luxury and lived a simple lifestyle. In contrast to the Sadducees, they enjoyed support among the common people.

Pharisees and the Torah

The primary aim of the Pharisees was to apply the details of the Torah to everyday life. Many of the commandments of Torah are vague, and at times they are inconsistent or even contradictory. The Pharisees worked out practical methods to overcome these challenges.

They were well known for "traditions" that they taught as a supplement to, or as an interpretation of, the commandments of the Torah. The synoptic Gospels report that the Pharisees were meticulous about washing their hands and purifying themselves before eating (see Mk 7:3–4)—they apparently applied some priestly purity laws to their own daily meals. Another tradition was the declaration of something as *qorban*—a dedication of a possession to the Temple that allowed a person to continue using it for himself and not sharing it with others (see 7:11).

Josephus reports that the Pharisees were lenient in their judgments about punishments, and we know that some of their traditions allowed Jews to observe the Torah in an easier and more practical manner. For example, strict biblical laws forbade carrying food from house to house on the Sabbath. The Pharasaic tradition of *'eruv* allowed the construction of doorposts and lintels so that several houses could be joined together as one, and families could thus socialize on the Sabbath. The tradition of the *prosbul* allowed a debt to be collected by a community council, even

JEWISH SECTS

during the seventh year, when, according to biblical law (see Dt 15:2), all debts were to be forgiven. This practice made it easier for farmers or craftsmen to get loans when the seventh year was approaching.

Pharisees and Early Christians

Although the Gospels often portray Jesus in conflict with the Pharisees (see Mk 2:23–28, 3:1–6), the relationship between the Pharisees and the early Christian movement was more complex. Followers of Jesus and the Pharisees (in contrast to the Sadducees) shared a belief in the resurrection of the dead and punishment and rewards in the afterlife. The Apostle Paul was a Pharisee (see Phil 3:5, Acts 23:6). Pharisees were also part of the first church community at Jerusalem (see Acts 15:5).

Besides Paul, other notable first-century Pharisees were Gamaliel, an influential member of the Sanhedrin who was "respected by all the people" (5:34), and the priest, general, and historian Josephus.

Essenes

Many scholars identify at least one branch of the Essenes with the community that lived in the desert wilderness at Qumran (although other scholars reject this connection). Qumran is the site on the northwestern end of the Dead Sea at which the so-called Dead Sea Scrolls were found. The Qumran community was governed by a strict hierarchy headed by priests; the so-called Teacher of Righteousness (often mentioned in the scrolls) was apparently the founder of the community.

The community seems to have begun when a group of priests left Jerusalem because of a dispute with the Temple priesthood. They disagreed with the interpretation of Torah practiced by the Jerusalem priests, and especially with interpretation of laws of purity. It is likely that the Qumran community members, with their belief that only a Zadokite should be high priest, rejected the non-Zadokite Hasmonean high priests as illegitimate. The community further disagreed with the Hasmonean adoption of a solar calendar in place of the old lunar one. This dispute was important, as knowing the precise date was essential for keeping the festivals mandated in the Torah.

The Dead Sea Scrolls include many copies of biblical books, commentaries on Scripture, hymns, prayers, and rules for governing the community. One scroll, the "War Scroll," describes a final battle at the end of history in which the Sons of Light (the Qumran community), aided by God, will destroy the powers of darkness (the forces of the community's Jewish opponents as well as Gentiles).

With their withdrawal into the wilderness, their strict lifestyle, and their emphasis on God's coming judgment, the members of the Qumran community are similar to John the Baptist, who preached his apocalyptic message of repentance in the Judean desert. Some scholars, in fact, speculate that John was once a member of the Qumran community. The Gospel writers associate Isaiah's prophecy "A voice of one crying out in the desert: / 'Prepare the way of the Lord, / make straight his paths'" with the John the Baptist (Mk 1:3, see Is 40:3); the Qumran community applied this same prophecy to their own group.

The Essenes thought of themselves as the only faithful remnant of Israel—

they believed their community replaced the Temple as the site of the true, uncorrupted worship of God.

Samaritans

Samaritans are inhabitants of Samaria, a district in central Palestine, between Galilee and Judea.

After the split of Israel into the northern and southern kingdoms after the death of King Solomon, Samaria formed part of the northern kingdom of Israel (see 1 Kgs, ch. 11–12). Its capital was the city of Samaria, constructed by King Omri and his son Ahab in the ninth century (see 16:24). At this time, the people were simply known as Israelites.

The city of Samaria was conquered by the Assyrians in 721 BC, and many of its leading citizens were deported. The Assyrian king settled colonists from Babylon and other cities in the region of Samaria (see 2 Kgs 17:24). The religious rites of the colonists (including worship of the Babylonian god Marduk) were mixed with the worship of the Lord (see vv. 29–33). According to the biblical record, Samaritans in Jesus' time were descendants of these colonists. The Samaritans themselves, however, claimed direct descent from the Israelite tribes of Ephraim and Manasseh. It is after the Babylonian Exile that the people are called Samaritans.

From the time of the return of the Judean exiles from the Babylonian Exile, tensions between Jews and Samaritans arose. The major dispute involved the proper worship of the Lord. The Samaritans were opposed to the rebuilding of Jerusalem and the Temple (see Ezr 4:1–4, Neh 2:18–20), favoring their holy place built on Mount Gerizim in Samaria. The dispute is reflected in the

words of the Samaritan woman to Jesus: "Our ancestors worshiped on this mountain [Mount Gerizim]; but you people say that the place to worship is in Jerusalem" (Jn 4:20).

In addition, Samaritans accept only the first five books, the Pentateuch, of the Old Testament as their Scriptures. Their version of the Pentateuch differs slightly from other ancient Hebrew versions. The most striking difference is the addition of a commandment to build an altar at Mount Gerizim (see Ex 20:17). Samaritans shared with Jews the expectations of a Messiah (see Jn 4:25); Samaritans focused especially on the prophecy that God would raise up another prophet like Moses (see Dt 18:18).

At times the conflict between Jews and Samaritans turned violent. The Hasmonean King John Hyrcanus destroyed the holy place at Gerizim in 128 BC; Samaritans massacred some Jewish pilgrims in AD 52.

Jews in the time of Jesus thus despised Samaritans as foreigners who worshiped the Lord in the wrong way.

Jesus seems to have had some wariness of the Samaritans as well. He warns his disciples, "Do not go into pagan territory or enter a Samaritan town" (Mt 10:5). Yet in other ways, Jesus, as a first-century Jew, had a remarkable openness to Samaritans. His parable of the good Samaritan contrasts a priest and Levite who ignore a man in need with a Samaritan who stops to help (see Lk 10:25–37; see also 17:11–19). This parable would have deeply offended Jesus' Jewish listeners. Most striking is Jesus' conversation with a Samaritan woman at a well (see Jn 4:4–42).

The early followers of Jesus continued his openness. Philip (a member of the first church in Jerusalem), Peter, and John preached about Jesus in Samaria.

As a result, many Samaritans accepted the Gospel and were baptized (see Acts 8:5–25).

Related Passages

Sadducees: Mark 12:18–27; Acts 4:1–2, 5:17–18, 23:7–8. *Pharisees and the Jerusalem Council:* Acts 5:34–39, 23:6–9. *Pharisaic conflicts with Jesus:* Mt, ch. 23; Mk 2:18—3:6, 8:14–21, 10:1–12, 12:13–17. *Pharisaic traditions:* Mk 7:1–23. *Paul as a Pharisee:* Phil 3:5; Acts 23:6. *Samaritans:* Ezr 4:1–4; Neh 2:18–20; Lk 10:25–37, 17:11–19; Jn, ch. 4; Acts 8:5–25.

See Also

- "Afterlife"
- "Priests"

Languages

The Bibles that we read today are English translations of ancient languages. The books of the Old Testament were primarily written in Hebrew, although some parts of Ezra and Daniel were written in Aramaic; Tobit may have been composed in Aramaic. Some of the later books of the Old Testament (such as the Wisdom of Solomon and Second Maccabees) were originally written in Greek or passed down mainly in Greek versions. All the books of the New Testament were originally written in Greek.

Hebrew was the original language of the Israelites. After the time of the Babylonian Exile (after 587 BC), Aramaic was more widely spoken, even among the Jewish people. Aramaic is closely related to Hebrew, and uses the same alphabet. For example, the word for *father* in Hebrew is *Ab;* the word for *father* in Aramaic is *Abba.* Even after Aramaic became more widely spoken, however, Hebrew remained the sacred language used in prayers and, of course, in reading the Scriptures.

Aramaic was the most important spoken language in the Near East for several centuries (ca. 600 BC to AD 700). Aramaic was the main spoken language of Jesus and his disciples.

Although Jesus and his disciples spoke Aramaic, the New Testament was written in Greek. This was primarily because Greek was the most important language in the wider Mediterranean area when the New Testament was written (ca. AD 50 to 130). This was a result of the conquests of Alexander the Great (ca. 300 BC) and the continuing Hellenistic rule and influence in many Mediterranean nations. The Apostle Paul, for example, was a Jew, but he was born outside of the Jewish homeland in Palestine (in Tarsus in modern-day Turkey), so he wrote his letters in Greek.

Greek was an international language in New Testament times: people from different Mediterranean societies were able to communicate with one another in Greek. Greek thus had a role similar to English today; German, Chinese, or Japanese business people are often able to communicate with one another in English.

Because Jesus spoke Aramaic, and the New Testament Gospels are written in Greek, it's obvious that Jesus' words were translated before being written. At certain points in the Gospels (especially in Mark), however, we do catch a glimpse of the original Aramaic expressions of Jesus. In the midst of telling a story about Jesus' healing a young girl, Mark adds the detail that Jesus "took the child by the hand and said to her, '*Talitha koum,*' which means, 'Little girl, I say to you, arise!'" (Mk 5:41). Because Mark is writing for Greek readers, he must translate the Aramaic phrase "*Talitha koum*" for them (see also 7:34 for another Aramaic phrase).

Jesus' prayer in the Garden of Gethsemane before his death also includes the Aramaic word for *father*. Jesus prays, "Abba, Father, all things are possible to you" (14:36).

The land of Israel was ruled by the Roman Empire in the time of Jesus. Although the native language of the Romans was Latin, the Roman government officials in the Eastern Empire (including Israel) usually spoke Greek. The New Testament does have some words that are originally Latin, especially military terms such as *centurion* (see 15:39) and *legion* (see 5:9).

A good example of the multilingual nature of the Mediterranean world is found in the Gospel of John, where we are told that the inscription on the cross on which Jesus was crucified was "written in Hebrew, Latin, and Greek" (Jn 19:20).

Related Passages

Aramaic phrases: Mk 5:41, 7:34, 14:36. *Reference to three languages:* Jn 19:20.

Marriage

Marriage Arrangements

In today's world, marriage is typically a decision made by a couple. Two people fall in love and make the decision to marry and spend their lives together. Marriage in the biblical world, however, was quite different. It was not a decision made by the two individuals but a decision made by the families, and particularly by the fathers as heads of their families. The main consideration was not the love of the couple for each other; rather, it was the interests of the families. This illustrates how the welfare of the family outweighed the welfare of the individual in the ancient Mediterranean worldview.

In Tobit, for example, the father Raguel draws up a contract with Tobiah in which he gives his daughter Sarah to him (see 7:13). Abraham sends his servant to choose a wife for his son Isaac from among his own people (see Gn 24:1–4). Some passages do indicate that the husband had some say in the matter. Isaac sends Jacob to choose for himself one of Laban's daughters—although Jacob's options are clearly limited (see 28:2)!

The Bible does not mention an ideal age for marriage. According to the Talmud, a girl should marry at the age of puberty (around age twelve or thirteen); the Mishnah specifies age eighteen for the male.

Betrothal and Exchange of Goods

The first step in the marriage process is for the two families to make a betrothal—a formal agreement for their children to marry. Joseph and Mary were betrothed when it was found that she was pregnant (see Mt 1:18).

As part of the marriage arrangements, the families exchanged goods and wealth. A father might give his daughter a dowry to help the new couple get a start (see Jos 15:18–19). Some scholars see this as a form of giving a daughter a share of the father's inheritance. On the other hand, the groom or the groom's family might also pay a "bridal price" or "marriage price" to the bride's family (see Gn 34:12, Ex 22:15). Jacob worked seven years for Laban in exchange for his daughter Rachel, and seven years in exchange for his daughter Leah (see Gn 29:15–30). This "bride price" may have been understood as compensation for a family who was losing the help of a daughter.

In any case, these exchanges of goods were a concrete way for the families to establish a mutually beneficial relationship.

The Wedding Celebration

Marriages were celebrated with a great feast (see Gn 29:22, Jn 2:1–12) that would last for several days (see Jgs 14:12, Tb 8:20). Jesus compares this feast to the Kingdom of Heaven (see Mt 22:2, 25:1–13). The couple would be dressed with their finest clothing: John describes the heavenly Jerusalem as "a bride adorned for her husband" (Rv 21:2). Even the guests were to wear a wedding garment (see Mt 22:12).

A bridegroom typically met the bride at her father's house, and then friends and family went in a festive wedding procession from there to the groom's home (often the home of his father), singing, dancing, and playing instruments as they went. If the procession occurred at night, the wedding party had to carry torches or lamps. In Jesus' parable, five foolish young women did not carry extra oil for their lamps and therefore were not prepared to join the procession (see 25:1–13).

Endogamous Marriages

In biblical times, families preferred to marry their children within with the larger extended family—a practice that anthropologists call an endogamous marriage. Abraham made his servant swear that he would find a wife for his son Isaac from within Abraham's own kindred (see Gn 24:4). Tobit says, "When I reached manhood, I married Anna, a woman of our own lineage" (1:9). The ideal marriage was between cousins. Jacob married the daughters of his uncle Laban (see Gn 28:2). This ideal is still reflected in some Middle Eastern societies today. The Bible, however, does prohibit marriages between closer relatives (see Lv 18:6–18).

Endogamous marriages were encouraged for several reasons, including religious harmony and the desire to keep family property within the extended family. Among the socially elite groups, however, marriages outside the family might be contracted for political reasons. Herod the Great married Mariamne, who belonged to the Hasmoneans, the powerful Jewish royal and high priestly family. Kings such as Solomon even married non-Israelite women (Pharaoh's daughter) (see 1 Kgs 3:1). The Bible also records other exceptions to endogamous marriage: Moses marries a Midianite (see Ex 2:21) and Boaz marries Ruth, a woman from Moab (see Ru 4:13).

After the return from the Babylonian Exile, Ezra forbade marriages with foreigners (see Ezr, ch. 9–10), requiring those who had done so to send away their wives and any children from those marriages (see also Neh 13:23–27). Other passages also warn strongly against marriage to foreigners, as this would lead the Israelites to worship foreign gods (see Dt 7:3).

Polygyny, Concubines, and Levirate Marriage

In patriarchal Israelite society, family descent was reckoned through the father (see Lk 3:23–38), so it was imperative for a man to have offspring to continue the family line. Israelite society thus developed many different social customs to ensure that a man would have children.

One custom was polygyny, the custom of allowing a man to marry more than one wife (a woman could have only one husband). Patriarchs such as Jacob (see Gn 29:15–30) practiced polygyny, as did the Hebrew kings; Solomon is said to have had seven hundred wives and three hundred concubines (see 1 Kgs 11:3). By the time of Jesus, the pattern of one husband and one wife, however, seems to be the norm. Jesus' teaching that "a man shall leave his father and mother [and be joined to his wife], and the two shall become one flesh" (Mk 10:7–8) seems to presuppose only one husband and wife. Paul's Letter to Timothy says that a bishop should be "married only once" (1 Tm 3:2). Records in Josephus and the Mishnah, however, show that polygyny was still practiced by some Jews at this time.

The custom of keeping concubines allowed a patriarch to have sexual relations with one or more women who were not his actual wife (or wives) in order to have more children. When Sarah (see Gn 16:2) and Rachel (see 30:1–4) could not bear children, they allowed their husbands to have intercourse with their servants so that they could have children "through them."

Another custom is known as the "Levirate marriage." If a man died childless, his brother was supposed to marry his wife and bring up children in brother's name (see Dt 25:5–10; see also Gn 38:6–10). We see a related custom also in the Book of Ruth, in which Boaz accepts the responsibility of marrying Ruth, a widow who had been married to a relative of Boaz.

Divorce in Mosaic Law

The Torah allowed a man to divorce his wife by giving her a written notice of divorce (see Dt 24:1). Because the Torah does not specify the grounds for divorce, later rabbis debated the issue. The Mishnah records that some rabbis taught that only unfaithfulness was grounds for divorce, while other rabbis allowed a husband to initiate a divorce for a variety of rather minor reasons (for example, if a wife ruined a man's supper, or simply if the man found another woman more attractive than his wife).

An Israelite woman could not initiate a divorce. In Roman societies, however, women did have such rights.

Jesus' Teaching on Divorce and Divorce Today

Jesus' teaching on divorce is radically different. Based on the example of the Book of Genesis, Jesus taught that a married couple was "one flesh" (Mk 10:8, cf. Gn 2:24), and "therefore what God has joined together, no human being must separate" (Mk 10:9). Because that was so, he viewed divorce and remarriage as committing adultery (see vv. 11–12).

The version of Jesus' teaching in the Gospel of Matthew qualifies this strict teaching: Jesus' teaching applies "unless the marriage is unlawful" (5:32). The original Greek of this passage expresses the exception to Jesus' teaching as "except in cases of *porneia*." This Greek word means essentially some kind of sexual sin. Some understand it to mean adultery, while others interpret it to mean marriage between close relatives (see Lv, ch. 18). Such marriages (often allowed in Gentile cultures) would thus be unlawful under the Torah, so the couple could separate.

The Apostle Paul reiterates Jesus' teaching that "a wife should not separate from her husband . . . and a husband should not divorce his wife" (1 Cor 7:10–11). Paul adds the qualification that "if she does separate she must either remain single or become reconciled to her husband" (v. 11). If a Christian spouse is married to a non-Christian, and the non-Christian wishes to divorce, Paul allows a separation (see vv. 15–16).

This strict biblical teaching is a sharp challenge to accepted values in our society, where divorce rates hover around 50 percent. Catholic practice follows Jesus' strict teaching in judging that divorce in a sacramental marriage is impossible—humans do not have the authority to separate what God

has joined. However, in some unions it can be shown that there never was a sacramental marriage. In such a case, the Church can declare the union null, granting the man and woman an "annulment" and freeing them to remarry.

Related Passages

Arranged marriages: Gn 24:1–4, Tb 7:13. *Betrothal:* Mt 1:18. *Dowries / bride price:* Gn 29:15–30, Jos 15:18–19. *Marriage feasts:* Tb 8:20; Mt 22:1–14, 25:1–13; Jn 2:1–12. *Polygyny and concubines:* Gn 16:1–6, ch. 29–30. *Endogamous marriages:* Gn 24:1–4, 28:1–2. *Marriage with non-Israelites:* Ru, ch. 4; Ezr, ch. 9–10; Neh 13:23–27. *Levirate marriage:* Gn 38:6–10; Dt 25:5–10; Ru, ch. 4. *Divorce:* Dt 24:1, Mt 5:31–32, Mk 10:2–12, 1 Cor 7:1–16.

See Also

• "Families"
• "Women"

Meals

In Palestine meals with tables and chairs were often associated with the wealthier classes. In the common homes, the table might be a simple mat on the floor on which the meal was laid out, and those eating sat or squatted around the mat. The meal participants would usually eat out of a common dish placed in the middle of the mat. Jesus says, regarding Judas, "He who has dipped his hand into the dish with me is the one who will betray me" (Mt 26:23).

Under the influence of Roman customs, some Jews at the time of Jesus adopted the custom of eating meals while reclining on couches set up around three

sides of a low table. Guests would lay with the upper part of their body supported by their left arms and cushions behind their backs. In John's account of the Last Supper, the beloved disciple is reclining next to Jesus and leans against Jesus' chest to speak to him privately (see 13:23–25).

In biblical times, a family meal typically began with the father's taking bread, giving thanks to God, breaking it, and distributing it to the family. This was also Jesus' typical pattern of beginning a meal (see Mt 14:19, Mk 14:22).

Generally, in Palestine two meals were eaten. Breakfast was eaten at some point during the morning, and dinner was eaten in the evening.

Eating with the Gods

"Sacred meals" were common in the ancient Hellenistic world. After an animal was sacrificed at a Greek temple, part was burned as a direct offering to the god, part was eaten by the priest, and part was eaten by the worshipers. Dining rooms for these meals were commonly attached to these temples. Plato wrote of worshipers' "associating" with the gods at these sacred meals.

The worshiper also had the option of taking home his or her portion or selling it at the meat market. This latter custom raised a question for Paul: Is it right for a Christian to eat the meat of an animal that had been sacrificed to a god? Paul himself believed that eating the meat of an animal sacrificed to an idol was not harmful; after all, God had created the animal. But if a fellow believer was convinced that such sacrifice made the meat unfit to eat, Paul would respect his or her beliefs and not eat sacrificed meat when he was with such a believer (see Rom 14:2–4; 1 Cor 8:1–13, 10:25–29).

In a similar way, Paul warns members of his Corinthian church to stay away from temple meals. If a person eats one of these meals, she or he shares a unity with the god (Paul calls it a demon) who is worshiped in the meal ritual. At these temples, Paul wrote, they sacrifice "to demons, not to God, and I do not want you to become participants with demons" (1 Cor 10:20).

The Lord's Supper

In the same way, the Christian eating the Lord's Supper associates with Christ:

"The cup of blessing that we bless, is it not a participation in the blood of Christ? The bread that we break, is it not a participation in the body of Christ?" (1 Cor 10:16).

Two meanings of the Lord's Supper overlap for Paul. The eating of the bread associates the believer with Christ—brings the believer into a close union with Christ. But the meal also associates the believers with one another, insofar as they are sharing a meal together. "Because the loaf of bread is one, we, though many, are one body, for we all partake of the one loaf" (v. 17). The image of all church members as one Body of Christ is a central one for Paul (see Rom 12:4–5, 1 Cor 12:12–27).

The ritual sharing of the bread and wine was also connected with a full meal (see 1 Cor 11:20–22). The early Christians called this fuller meal an agape meal (*agape* is one of the Greek words for love) because it was a way of expressing and building up love among the members of a church (see Jude, v. 12).

Meals and Social Status

Eating a meal is not simply a way of getting nourishment. Just think of the junior high or senior high lunchroom. We will most likely find certain groups sitting together to eat defined by common interests, activities, ethnicity, or social status. Meals are used to reinforce group membership, and often young people can be cruel in excluding people who don't "fit in."

Think also of family meals at Christmas or Thanksgiving. They are a time for family and friends to gather, often traveling from a distance. What we value about these occasions is not so much the food itself but the interaction with our loved ones.

So too, in the biblical world, meals had social significance. In the patron-client system of the Mediterranean world, patrons would often hold feasts for their clients, or perhaps a client would host a feast to honor his patron. At these banquets, careful attention was given to the seating arrangements, with the most honored guests receiving the best seats. When Jesus was invited to the home of a leading Pharisee, he noticed "how they were choosing the places of honor at the table" (Lk 14:7). Jesus advises his listeners not to seek out a prestigious seat, because if a more honored guest comes, they might be asked to give it up and thus be shamed (see vv. 8–9).

In the Mediterranean honor-shame system, a guest would be obligated to return the favor to his host. In describing the social system of the Kingdom of God, however, Jesus rejects such concerns about social honor and prestige. "When you hold a lunch or a dinner, do not invite your friends or your brothers or your relatives or your wealthy neighbors, in case they may invite you back and you have repayment" (v. 12).

In Jesus' vision of society, these social competitions would be avoided. "Rather when you hold a banquet, invite the poor, the crippled, the lame, the blind; blessed indeed will you be because of their inability to repay you. For you will be repaid at the resurrection of the righteous" (vv. 13–14).

The fact that Jesus ate with people at the bottom of the Jewish social scale caused comment. "Some scribes that were Pharisees saw that he was eating with sinners and tax collectors and said to his disciples, 'Why does he eat with tax collectors and sinners?'" (Mk 2:16). It's clear that Jesus' customs reflected the values that he expected in the Kingdom of God. "But many who are first will be last, and the last will be first"

(Mt 19:30). Jesus said to the Pharisees, "Tax collectors and prostitutes are entering the kingdom of God before you" (21:31). Participants in the Kingdom would not be socially ranked at certain levels of honor and prestige; all would be seen as social equals under God's rule.

Table fellowship between Jews and Gentiles was also an issue in early Christianity. Because of concerns over purity (especially food laws), Jews would not normally share a meal with Gentiles. Thus, when the Jewish followers of Jesus first began accepting Gentile followers into their churches, tensions arose over sharing meals. Peter at first ate with the Gentiles (see Acts, ch. 10), but then, under pressure from a group who held strictly to the purity laws, refused to share meals with them. Paul publicly condemned Peter as a hypocrite (see Gal 2:11–14).

Messianic Banquet

In the Old Testament, final salvation is pictured as a feast. The prophet Isaiah speaks of the feasting that will take place in messianic age as "a feast of rich food and choice wines, juicy, rich food, and pure, choice wines" (25:6). Jesus describes the Kingdom of Heaven in the same way: "I say to you, many will come from the east and the west and will recline with Abraham, Isaac, and Jacob at the banquet in the kingdom of heaven" (Mt 8:11). Jesus also compares the Kingdom to a wedding feast (see 22:1–14, 25:1–13; see also Lk 14:15–24). Jesus' miracles of feeding people in the wilderness can also be understood as a foreshadowing of the messianic banquet (see Mk 6:34–44, 8:1–10). Jesus connected his own Last Supper with the messianic banquet (see Mt 26:26–29).

Related Passages

Jesus' Last Supper: Mt 26:26–30; Jn 13:23–25; 1 Cor 10:16–17, 11:17–34. *Agape meal:* 1 Cor 11:20–22; Jude, v. 12. *Jesus' feeding the crowds:* Mk 6:34–44, 8:1–10. *Meat sacrificed to other gods:* Rom 14:2–4; 1 Cor 8:1–13, 10:14–23. *Meals and social status:* Lk 14:7–14. *Jesus' eating with social outcasts:* Mk 2:13–17. *Table fellow-ship between Jews and Gentiles:* Gal 2:11–14. *Messianic feast:* Is 25:6; Mt 8:11, 22:1–14, 25:1–13.

See Also

- "Agriculture"
- "Food and Drink"
- "Food Laws"
- "Honor and Shame"

Money

When Abraham bought a piece of land for a burial plot, he weighed out "four hundred shekels of silver" (Gn 23:16). This would have been actual pieces of silver, not coins. The shekel was at first a unit of weight, not of monetary value.

Scales for weighing money were thus an important part of daily life. The Torah frequently demands honesty: "Do not act dishonestly in using measure of length or weight or capacity. You shall have a true scale and true weights" (Lv 19:35–36; see also Ez 45:10–12, Prv 11:1).

The value of a shekel varied in different times and places. Leviticus reports that an unblemished ram was worth two silver shekels (see 5:15).

Not all people used money in biblical times. The primary means of trade, especially in the rural areas, was bartering—people exchanging goods with one another. Taxes and wages were usually paid in kind: a farmer might give up 10 percent of his crop, a shepherd 10 percent of his sheep (see 1 Sm 8:15–17). The king of Moab paid as tribute to the king of Israel 100,000 lambs and the wool of a 100,000 rams (see 2 Kgs 3:4).

Coins

Coins were probably not used in Israelite society until after the Babylonian Exile. The first coins in Israel appear to have been the *yehud* coins struck at Jerusalem shortly after 400 BC, when Judah was under Persian domination. These coins were minted under the authority of the high priests. In later centuries, the Hasmonean rulers struck their own coins, stamped with Jewish symbols, such as the menorah.

Silver was the most common metal used for money exchanges. Abraham purchased a cave with silver (see Gn 23:15–16); Judas was paid thirty pieces of silver for betraying Jesus (see Mt 26:15). Silver was so commonly used that the Hebrew word for *silver* could be used as the general word for *money.*

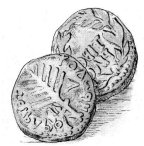

A variety of Jewish, Greek, and Roman coins were used for money during the time of Jesus' earthly life.

Herodian rulers also struck coins, some of which included images of the Roman emperors. Roman procurators such as Pontius Pilate also minted their own coins. Larger silver coins were produced in the imperial mints at Rome and Alexandria. During the Jewish revolt against Roman rule (AD 66 to70), the rebels struck their own coins at Jerusalem.

After Palestine became part of the Roman Empire, Roman coins were introduced. The silver *denarius* was the basic unit of the Roman system, equal to about the daily wage of a laborer (see Mt 20:9–10,13). It bore the image of the Roman emperor and was used for paying taxes to Rome. This was the coin the Pharisees and Herodians showed to Jesus during their debate over paying taxes (see Mk 12:15–17).

Jews were required to pay the Temple tax with a silver shekel minted at Tyre. Because pilgrims came from all over the Mediterranean world with a variety of coins, moneychangers were needed at the Temple to change the pilgrims' money (see Mk 11:15).

The following chart gives information on some common biblical coins:

Jewish Coins		
Name of coin	**Description**	**Biblical passage**
Shekel	Originally a unit of weight, but by New Testament times was a silver coin; worth about four *drachmas*	The thirty pieces of silver paid to Judas were most likely shekels (Mt 27:3).
Greek Coins		
Name of coin	**Description**	**Biblical passage**
Drachma (translated as "coin")	The basic unit of Greek coins, worth about the daily wage of a laborer	Lk 15:8
Didrachma (translated as "Temple tax")	Two-*drachma* coin that was used by Jews to pay the Temple tax	Mt 17:24
Stater (translated as "a coin worth twice as much as the Temple tax")	Four-*drachma* coin	Mt 17:27
Mina (translated as "gold coin")	Coin worth 100 *drachmas*	Lk 19:11–27
Talanton (talent)	Coin varying in worth, but always several thousand *drachmas*	Mt 18:24, 25:15–28

Roman Coins		
Name of coin	**Description**	**Biblical passage**
Denarius	Roman coin, silver, bearing the image of the Roman emperor	Mt 20:9–10, Mk 12:15–17
Assarion (translated as "small coin")	Roman coin, copper, worth one-sixteenth of a silver *denarius*	Mt 10:29, Lk 12:6
Kodrantes, quadrans (translated as "penny")	Roman coin, copper, worth one-fourth of an *assarion*	Mt 5:26
Lepton (translated as a "small coin worth a few cents")	Jewish coin worth half a *quadrans*	Mk 12:42

Related Passages

Paying taxes to the emperor: Mk 12:13–17. *Paying the Temple tax:* Mt 17:24–27. *Parable of the lost coin:* Lk 15:8–10. *Poor widow's contribution:* Mk 12:42–44.

See Also

• "Poverty and Wealth"
• "Temple"

Names

How did you get your name? Perhaps you were named after a relative or after someone your parents admire or simply because your parents liked a particular name. In any case, your name has a deeper significance: it points toward a value outside of yourself.

The Bible often explains names by connecting them with an event at the birth of a child. Both Abraham (at age one hundred) and Sarah (at age ninety) laughed to think that they could still have a child (see Gn 17:17, 18:12, 21:6). Thus, their son was named Isaac, from the Hebrew verb *tsachaq,* which means "to laugh"). Pharoah's daughter drew the baby Moses out of a basket in the Nile, so his name is associated with the similar sounding Hebrew verb *mashah,* "to draw out" (see Ex 2:10).

When Rachel finally bore a child with her husband Jacob, she said, "May the LORD add another son" (Gn 30:24), and so she named him Joseph (in Hebrew, *yoseph* means "may he add"). These and similar Old Testament naming stories are usually not intended to describe actual historical facts about how children were named but are rather imaginative plays on words.

We should note that in the majority of cases in the Old Testament, the mother names the child; neighboring women name Ruth's baby (see Ru 4:17).

Sometimes a person's name is changed due to circumstances later in life. Abram's name is changed to Abraham in connection with God's promise to make him the father of many nations (see Gn 17:5). Sarai's name is changed to Sarah in connection with her giving birth to Isaac (see v. 15). Jacob receives the new name Israel because he struggled with God (see 32:29). Jesus gives his disciple Simon the new name Peter (see Mt 16:18, Jn 1:42), from *petra,* the Greek word for *rock,* because Peter would be the rock on which the foundation of the church would be built (see Mt 16:18).

Names were also formed by using a shortened form of God's name ("El," short for *Elohim,* the Hebrew word for *God;* or "Ya," or "Ja," short for the divine name Yahweh). The name Daniel means "God is my judge." The name Isaiah means "The salvation of Yahweh." Jesus' name, which is a variant of Joshua, is connected with the Hebrew "Yahweh helps" or "Yahweh saves" (see 1:21).

Places are often named after events that occurred there. Jacob names the place where he wrestled with a mysterious "man" Peniel, which is Hebrew for "the face of God," because he saw God "face to face" and lived (see Gn 32:31). Gethsemane means "olive press" because it is an olive grove. Golgotha means "place of the skull" in Aramaic (the Romans carried out their executions there) (see Jn 19:17). *Calvaria* is the Latin word for *skull,* hence the word *Calvary* is sometimes used for this place).

The Power of a Name

In the biblical view, a person's name is not arbitrary but reflects something of a person's true identity. To know a person's name is to have inside knowledge about that person, and perhaps control over him or her. Thus, the strange "man" who wrestles all night with Jacob refuses to tell Jacob his name (see Gn 32:30).

A person's name is closely associated with the power and authority of the person. The disciples heal people "in the name" of Jesus (see Lk 10:17, Acts 3:6; see also Jas 5:14).

Paul relates that after Jesus' death, God greatly exalted him and "bestowed on him the name / that is above every name" (Phil 2:9). This is the divine name Lord that gives Jesus divine power and authority, and thus "at the name of Jesus / every knee should bend, / of those in heaven and on earth and under the earth, / and every tongue confess that / Jesus Christ is Lord" (vv. 10–11).

The Name of God

The name of God is closely associated with God's power and authority. The Hebrew word *Elohim* is generally translated as "God"; it is also the same word used to name the gods of other nations. The name Yahweh, in contrast, is the unique name of the God of Israel, revealed to Moses when God appeared to him at the burning bush (see Ex 3:1–14).

Because of this, the name Yahweh is regarded as especially sacred. (The holy name is sometimes referred to as the *Tetragrammaton,* literally meaning "four letters," referring to the four consonants of the name: YHWH). Pious Jews, in fact, will not pronounce the name as they read the Scriptures aloud, out of respect for its holiness and power. Instead, they will substitute an alternative phrase: "the Name" or "My Lord" (in Greek, *Adonai*). It is for this reason that English translations traditionally use LORD to translate YHWH. Any piece of paper on which the holy name is written must be treated with similar reverence.

This same respect for the name is seen in the commandments of the Torah: "You shall not take the name of the LORD, your God, in vain" (Ex 20:7). "You shall not swear falsely by my name, thus profaning the name of your God" (Lv 19:12). Jesus taught his disciples the same reverence: "Our Father in heaven, / hallowed by your name" (Mt 6:9). This phrase means "Let your name be hallowed" (or be made holy); in other words, it is a prayer that God might reveal his own power and authority.

Related Passages

Names and events at birth: Gn 30:24, Ex 2:10. *Names and life events:* Gn 32:23–33, Mt 16:13–20. *Names formed with the divine name:* Mt 1:21. *Names and authority:* Lk 10:17, Acts 3:6, Phil 2:9–11. *God's revelation of his name:* Ex 3:1–14. *Reverence of God's name:* Ex 20:7, Lv 19:12, Mt 6:9.

See Also

• "Canaanite Religion"

Number Symbolism

The Bible is full of numbers. It records the great ages of people who lived before the Flood (see Gn, ch. 5), it often lists the numbers of soldiers fighting in battles, and one biblical book is even called the Book of Numbers because it begins by recording a detailed census of the tribes of Israel.

Often, however, the numbers of the Bible carry a deeper, more symbolic meaning.

The Symbolism of Twelve

The people of Israel were composed of twelve tribes, each tribe said to be a descendent of one of the twelve sons of Jacob (see Gn 35:23–26).

Politically, the tribes were not strongly unified as one people. In the days before King David, they seemed to form a sort of loose alliance (as we see in the Book of Judges). Although unified under David and his son Solomon, they quickly split: ten of the tribes formed the northern kingdom of Israel, and the tribes of Judah and Benjamin formed the southern kingdom of Judah

(see 1 Kgs, ch. 12). In the time after the northern kingdom was conquered by the Assyrian Empire in 721 BC, the ten tribes gradually disappeared from history. Some were exiled (see 2 Kgs 17:23), and others intermarried with non-Hebrews.

Despite this lack of unity, the number twelve continued to retain a symbolic meaning: it signified the fullness or completeness of the Chosen People Israel. Jews at the time of Jesus expected that in the end days, God would gather the twelve tribes back together.

When Jesus chose a special group of men as his closest followers, he chose the symbolic number twelve (see Mk 3:16–19). With this choice, Jesus signaled his own belief that the end days were coming, when the tribes would be restored and God's Kingdom would be established on earth. Israel would be restored to its fullness, and all the Gentile nations would be saved through Israel. We see the close connection between Israel, the disciples, and eschatological salvation when Jesus tells them that they would "sit on twelve thrones, judging the twelve tribes of Israel" (Mt 19:28).

The early Church took up the symbolism of the twelve Tribes of Israel and applied it to the followers of Jesus. The Letter of James is addressed to "the twelve tribes in the dispersion" (Jas 1:1; see also 1 Pt 1:1). The Book of Revelation makes heavy use of the symbolism of twelve. Those who are chosen by God ("marked with a seal") number 144,000, twelve thousand from each of the twelve Tribes of Israel (see 7:4–8). The number, of course, is not to be taken literally: it represents the fullness or completeness of the Chosen People who follow Jesus. The "new Jerusalem"—a symbol of heaven—has twelve gates, its foundation has twelve courses of stone identified with the twelve tribes, and the city itself is 12,000 *stadia* (a Greek measurement) square (see 21:12–16). In John's vision of God's throne room, he sees twenty-four elders. Most likely, this number symbolically combines the twelve Tribes of Israel and the Twelve Apostles (see Rv 4:4).

The Symbolism of Seven

According to Genesis, God created the heavens and the earth in six days, and rested on the seventh (see 2:2–3). The seventh day is thus recognized and celebrated as the Sabbath, a day of rest (see Ex 20:8–11). The seventh day symbolizes completeness and perfection; the Epistle to the Hebrews understands the Sabbath rest as a symbol of eternal salvation (see 4:1–14).

Many of the commandments of Torah are based on the symbolism of seven. Every seventh year, the Hebrews were to let the land rest (see Lv 25:1–7). Every seven cycles of seven years (i.e., forty-nine years), the Hebrews were to celebrate the Jubilee year: Israelite slaves were to be set free, and land was to be returned to its original owners to ensure that land would not be controlled by a wealthy minority (see vv. 8–55).

Revelation is full of references to seven: John sees Christ standing among seven lampstands, holding seven stars (see 1:12–16). Christ then commands him to write to the seven churches, symbolizing the entire Christian community (see ch. 2). The scroll on which the destiny of the world is written has seven seals (see 5:1); seven angels blow seven trumpets (see 8:2); seven angels unleash seven plagues (see 15:1).

The Symbolism of Six

The number six has a more ambiguous meaning. Positively, the world was created in six days. The glory of the Lord rested on Mount Sinai for six days before the Lord called Moses (see Ex 24:16).

The number 666, however, has satanic associations. It is the "number of the beast," an evil power associated with Satan; the author of Revelation adds that the number "stands for a person" (13:18).

To understand this reference, we must know that ancient languages such as Latin, Greek, and Hebrew did not have separate symbols for numerals—rather, they used letters of the alphabet. You are probably familiar with Roman numerals. The letter I stands for 1, the letter V stands for 5, the letter X stands for 10, and so forth. Thus, every word in these languages has a corresponding number that can be determined by adding up the numerical value of each of its letters. The numerical values of the letters in the name Caesar Nero, written in Hebrew, add up to precisely 666. Thus, many scholars think that John, in a coded way, was identifying the beast with this Roman emperor who was notorious for his persecution of Christians.

The Symbolism of Forty

After Moses led the people out from slavery in Egypt, they wandered in the wilderness for forty years (see Nm 32:13) before finally reaching the Promised Land. This time, which included God's giving of the Torah to Moses at Mount Sinai, is recounted in detail in the Books of Exodus, Leviticus, Numbers, and Deuteronomy. This was a time of trial, testing, and purification in the desert. Thus, the number forty came to symbolize a time of trial. Jesus was tempted in the desert for forty days (see Mt 4:1–11).

The Lord also sent rain for forty days to purify the earth of evil (Gn 7:12). Jonah announced the Lord would destroy Nineveh because of its wickedness in forty days (Jonah 3:4), but the Ninevites repented and thus were saved.

Related Passages

Twelve Tribes of Israel: Gn 35:23–26. *Jesus' Twelve Apostles:* Mk 3:16–19. *Symbolism of twelve:* Rv 4:4, ch. 7, 14:1–5, 21:12–16. *Symbolism of seven:* Gn 2:2–3; Ex 20:8–11; Lv, ch. 25; Heb 4:1–14; Rv 1:12–16, ch. 2–3, 5:1, 8:2, 15:1. *The number of the beast:* Rv 13:11–18. *Symbolism of forty:* Gn 7:12, Nm 32:13, Jon 3:4, Mt 4:1–11.

See Also

• "Chosen People"

Poverty and Wealth

In economic terms, we often think of modern American society as divided into the upper class (the wealthy), the middle class, and the poor, with the majority of Americans considering themselves as part of the middle class.

At the time of Jesus, however, it is more accurate to think of two main economic groups: the elites (those who possess wealth, social status, and / or political power) and the non-elites (the rest of society). In Jesus' time, the entire Mediterranean world was controlled by the Roman Empire, and power and wealth was held by the Roman elite and their supporters throughout the empire.

Elites

In Rome itself, the elites included the emperor and his household, as well as the politically powerful and wealthy orders of senators and equestrians. In Roman provinces such as Galilee and Judea, the elites included Roman rulers (such as Pontius Pilate) as well as native rulers, such as Herod the Great and his sons, who were clients of Rome. Jewish religious authorities such as priests, Sadducees, and some Pharisees also shared this elite status. These religious authorities were not independent of the Roman elite and their clients, however: Herod appointed the high priests and married into the high priestly family of the Hasmoneans.

Although the elites formed only a tiny percentage of the population, they had extraordinary economic and political power in the Roman Empire. Only the elite could hold political office, and thus only their interests were directly represented in the government.

The main source of the elite's wealth was their ownership of land—often vast tracts of land. Pliny the Elder (AD 23–79) claimed that six men owned half of North Africa.

The lifestyle of the elite was one of leisure and plenty. One of Jesus' parables describes "a rich man who dressed in purple garments and fine linen and dined sumptuously each day" (Lk 16:19). In Revelation, John describes the Roman elite (using the code name Babylon to refer to Rome) as "wearing fine linen, purple and scarlet, / adorned [in] gold, precious stones, and pearls" (18:16).

The elite lived almost exclusively in the cities, renting out their rural land to tenant farmers, who paid substantial rents and taxes to the landowners. In Palestine in Jesus' time, more than 90 percent of the population lived in rural areas, and the vast majority of workers were engaged in agriculture.

The Roman economic system was set up to benefit these urban elites. Revenue from taxes was not used for the common good (to build schools or to improve roads); rather, it was used exclusively to further the interests of the elites. Herod the Great used the revenue for such projects as building the Caesaria, a city named in honor of his patron Augustus Caesar and containing a temple dedicated to Augustus.

International trade in Jesus' time also focused on the desires of the elites. The Book of Revelation has an extensive list of luxury items found in the merchant ships that traded with Rome: "gold, silver, precious stones, and pearls; fine linen, purple silk, and scarlet cloth; fragrant wood of every kind, all articles of ivory and all articles of the most expensive wood, bronze, iron, and marble; cinnamon, spice, incense, myrrh, and frankincense; wine, olive oil, fine flour, and wheat; cattle and sheep, horses and chariots, and slaves, that is, human beings" (18:11–13).

Life of the Non-Elites

The non-elites were people who owned little or no land, and thus had to earn their living through their own labor, often working the land as tenants of the wealthy landowners (see Mk 12:1). There were no mechanisms, such as government representation or trade unions, to represent their political or economic interests. The landowners decided which crop to plant, often choosing to plant cash crops, such as vineyards, olives, or wheat, rather than subsistence crops, such as barley, beans, and figs.

The vast majority of rural people in ancient times lived at a subsistence level, constantly in danger of hunger or starvation if their crops failed. There was no "safety net" of Social Security or other government programs. Most farms were too small for farmers to make a comfortable living, and farmers were forced to pay high taxes on what they did earn. When Jesus tells his disciples, "Therefore I tell you, do not worry about your life, what you will eat [or drink], or about your body, what you will wear" (Mt 6:25), the worry about finding enough to eat was a very real one for many.

Some workers did not have steady work but hired themselves out as laborers for a daily wage. One of Jesus' parables tells of a vineyard owner who went down to the marketplace several times during the day to hire daily laborers. With every trip, he found groups in need of work, an indication of the great number of people looking for additional work to survive (see 20:1–16; see also the parable of the prodigal son, Lk 15:11–32).

Old Testament law required land-owners to leave the remnants of the harvest—grains and fruits—for the poor to gather.

The hired worker was not a slave, but at certain times his situation may have been worse than that of a slave. Even if he had no freedom and was treated harshly, the slave could usually depend on food and shelter; the day laborer was never assured of being hired on any particular day and getting the chance to earn his living.

Debts

With a relatively high rate of taxation, farmers and other workers often went into debt. One indication that this happened rather often is the number of times Jesus' parables refer to people who are in debt and are unable to repay their debts (see Mt 18:21–35; Lk 7:41–43, 12:57–59, 16:1–8).

The Roman system of tax collection added to the burden. Taxes were not paid directly to the elite, but rather to brokers who competed for the privilege of collecting taxes in a certain area. The broker kept any profit that he made over and above his targeted amount, which gave him the incentive to collect as much as possible (see the "Taxes and Tithes" article).

The penalties for failure to repay a debt were brutal. A debtor, along with

his family, might be sold as a slave (see Mt 18:25). Philo describes how tax collectors were not above using torture or imprisonment to force other members of debtor's family to pay a debt. One of Jesus' parables refers to a debtor being "handed . . . over to the torturers" until his debt is paid (Mt 18:34).

Jesus' Criticism of the Elite and the Prophetic Tradition

Jesus was critical of the wealthy elite: "It is easier for a camel to pass through [the] eye of [a] needle than for one who is rich to enter the kingdom of God" (Mk 10:25). "But woe to you who are rich, / for you have received your consolation" (Lk 6:24).

We can better understand Jesus' harsh attitude toward the wealthy if we keep in mind the social situation of Jesus' day: the wealth of the elite and their supporters was built on a system that squeezed out maximum taxes and rents from the non-elites. Thus, the prosperity of the rich tended to be built directly on the misery of the poor.

Jesus' criticism of the elite followed a long tradition of Old Testament teaching. The prophets criticized those who built up vast landholdings: "Woe to you who join house to house, / who connect field with field, / Till no room remains" (Is 5:8). "They trample the heads of the weak / into the dust of the earth, / and force the lowly out of the way" (Am 2:7).

Many of the Torah commandments are also designed to avoid ownership by a few large landowners. Deuteronomy says that at the end of every seventh year, all debts owed to fellow Israelites are to be "relaxed" (cf. 15:2). Another law calls for a "Jubilee year" every fifty years in which each person would return to his own property, his family estate. The law is based on the premise that the land cannot be sold to another person permanently, because the real owner of the land is God, and therefore all people are really only tenants on the land (see Lv, ch. 25). Historically, however, it is unclear to what extent such commandments were enforced.

The economic ideal of the Old Testament was that each family should work its own land: "every man sat under his vine and his fig tree, / with no one to disturb him" (1 Mc 14:12; see Mi 4:3–4; Zec 3:10; see the "Family" article).

Economic Status of Jesus and the Early Christians

Jesus is traditionally known as a "carpenter" (Mk 6:3) or the "carpenter's son" (Mt 13:55). Yet the Greek word used here, *tekton,* also has the broader meaning of a builder, including a mason, or a maker of tools for farmers, including plows and yokes. Such workers were paid a daily wage, and had a relatively low social status. Among Jesus' disciples were the very low status Matthew (a tax collector) and relatively low status fishermen. Wealthy women were among Jesus' followers (see Lk 8:1–3).

The economic system in the first church community in Jerusalem after Jesus' death was one of radical equality, a dramatic departure from the system of elite and non-elite. Each person would sell his or her own property and bring the proceeds to the community leaders so that they could distribute them to

the rest of the community members as they had need (see Acts 4:34–36).

Evidence from Paul's letters and Acts of the Apostles itself, however, shows us that the economic system of the Jerusalem Church was not followed in other churches. At Corinth there is a clear division between wealthy and poor church members (see 1 Cor 1:26, 11:22). The same division is apparent among the churches to which James writes (see Jas 2:1–13). Acts of the Apostles often refers to women followers who were wealthy (see 16:14; 17:4,12).

Related Passages

Wealth and lifestyle of the elite: Lk 16:19, Rv 18:11–20. **Day laborers:** Mt 20:1–16. **Tenant farmers:** Mk 12:1–12. **Inability to repay debt:** Mt 18:21–35; Lk 7:41–43, 12:57–59. **Prophetic critique of large landholders:** Is 5:8, Am 2:6–8. **Old Testament laws against large landholders and debt:** Lv 25:8–22, Dt 15:1–11. **Ideal of family ownership of land:** 1 Mc 14:12, Mi 4:3–4. **Jesus' criticism of the elites:** Mk 10:17–31, Lk 6:20–26. **Economic status of Jesus' followers:** Mk 1:16–20, Lk 8:1–3. **Economy of the Jerusalem Church:** Acts 2:42–47, 4:34—5:16. **Economic disparity in early churches:** 1 Cor 1:26, 11:22; Jas 2:1–13. **Role of wealthy women:** Acts 16:14, 17:4,12.

See Also

- "Fishing"
- "Money"
- "Slavery"
- "Taxes and Tithes"

Priests and Levites

In modern times, we think of a priest or a minister as a person who has a special calling or vocation to serve God and God's people. In ancient Judaism, however, the priesthood was hereditary—the tribe of Levi was set aside to serve as priests.

Aaron, Moses' brother, a member of the tribe of Levi, was the first priest, and all his male descendants were priests (see Ex 28:1). The entire tribe of Levi was set apart to oversee the worship of God, at first in the Dwelling that contained the Ark of the Covenant, and later in the Temple (see Nm 1:47–54, 8:5–26; 1 Chr, ch. 24). Male members of the tribe who were not sons of Aaron were known as Levites. They acted primarily as assistants to the priests in conducting the worship of the Lord (see Nm 18:1–5).

Because they had been set aside for this special task, members of the tribe of Levi did not inherit a portion of the land of Israel, nor were they to work the land. Priests and Levites were supported directly through activities of worship. Portions of the sacrifices provided food for the priests and their families, and the Levites were supported by tithes (see vv. 8–21). These tithes were essentially on crops; the Levites in turn were to give a tenth of their tithes to the priests (see vv. 21–32).

Within the priestly families, Zadokite priests (descendants of Zadok, a priest who had anointed and supported King Solomon against his rivals [see 1 Kgs 1:38–39]) held a special position. After the return from the Babylonian Exile, the high priests in Jerusalem were Zadokites and remained so until the time of the Maccabean revolt. After that time, members of the Maccabean family (also known as Hasmoneans), who were non-Zadokites, served as high priests (see 1 Mc 10:18–20). Supporters of the Zadokites objected to this change. One Zadokite priest and his followers fled to Egypt and established a temple there. Another priestly group supporting the Zadokites established their own community in the desert at Qumran. The name Sadducee most likely derives from Zadok—so this Jewish group was probably connected with the Zadokite priesthood too.

Work in the Temple

Priests and Levites were divided into twenty-four divisions (sometimes called courses), meaning that they worked in the Temple for one week out of every twenty-four (see Lk 1:5–10; John the Baptist's father Zechariah belonged to the priestly division of Abijah).

The primary work of the priests at the Temple involved offering sacrifices. They had to inspect the animals for

The breastplate with its twelve gems and the turban-style headdress were worn by the high priest, who was to be a direct descendant of Aaron, Moses' brother.

blemishes, slaughter the animals, skin them, and cut them up for distribution. They would also hear the confessions when a person brought a sin offering. Other tasks included offering incense (see Lk 1:9).

The Levites assisted the priests. Among their tasks were bringing in wood for the sacrifices, slaughtering the animals, and guarding the gates to the Temple. Levites also sang the Psalms during the Temple worship service. Names of some Levitical singers (see 1 Chr 6:16–33) are attached to various Psalms: Asaph (see Ps 50, 73–83), "the sons of Korah" (see 42–49, 84–85, 87–88), Heman (see 88), and Ethan (see 89).

Priests wore special clothes made from linen, not cotton (see Ez 44:17), including undergarments, a tunic, a sash, and a turban (or miter). They most likely worked barefoot.

The high priest wore additional garments, including a type of vest called an *ephod,* a "breastplate," and a crown (see Ex, ch. 28; Lv 8:1–13; Sir 45:8–13). These vestments were made of gold thread, and violet, purple, and scarlet yarn. In two precious stones on the straps of the *ephod* were carved the names of the twelve Tribes of Israel; twelve precious stones also decorated the breastplate. Small golden bells were sewn to the bottom of his tunic.

Priests maintained a higher degree of purity for their work in the Temple; for example, they had special restrictions on coming into contact with a dead body (Lv 21:1–8). Because physical wholeness was closely related to purity and holiness, priests were to have no physical defects (see vv. 16–23).

Only the high priest could enter the Holy of Holies in the Temple, and he could do so only once a year, on the Day of Atonement, *Yom Kippur* (see Lv 16:1–19).

Work Outside of the Temple

The high priest was not a religious leader only; he was also considered a leader of the whole community of Israel. After the Exile in Babylon, the governor of the community in Jerusalem, Zerubbabel, and Joshua, the high priest, are both mentioned as leaders (see Hg 1:1; see also 2 Chr 19:11). Later the Hasmonean rulers were political and military leaders as well as high priests (see 1 Mc 10:19–20).

The title chief priest does not refer to an official position in ancient Judaism; rather, it refers to a group of priests who, due to the fact that they belonged to a few aristocratic, high priestly families, were closely allied with the high priest.

Priests and Levites also served as judges (see Dt 21:5, 2 Chr 19:8–11, Ez 44:24), teachers of the Torah (see Neh 8:5–8, Sir 45:17), and scribes (in the sense of copying texts or writing up legal documents, and also in the sense of teaching the Torah).

Josephus thus says that the priests, led by the high priest and his colleagues, governed Israel by their tasks as interpreters of the Torah, judges, and punishers of wrongdoers.

In the time of Roman rule, the high priest and his council had the primary responsibility for keeping order. If they kept order and made sure that tribute was paid to the Romans, the Romans generally allowed the chief priests a fair amount of freedom to rule. It is likely that the high priest and his council regarded Jesus (with his claims to be the Messiah) as a threat to the Roman rule as well as to their own authority, and thus had him executed.

Sanhedrin

In the Gospel accounts of Jesus' trial, a group known as the Sanhedrin plays a key role. "As soon as morning came, the chief priests with the elders and the scribes, that is, the whole Sanhedrin, held a council" (Mk 15:1). With the urging of the high priest, they condemn Jesus to death (see Mt 26:59, Mk 14:64).

Scholars debate on the exact makeup of the Jerusalem Sanhedrin and the extent of its powers. The Mishna describes the Sanhedrin as composed of seventy-one leaders who met on the Temple Mount to make various judicial and religious decisions.

The name Sanhedrin is derived from the Greek *synedrion,* which is a general word for any gathering or meeting: meetings of city leaders were known as *synedrions.* The Sanhedrin mentioned in the Gospels was most likely the primary council in Jerusalem, led by the high priest and composed of the chief priests and scribes along with non-priestly community leaders.

Scribes

The word *scribe* has a broad range of meanings in the Bible. The general sense of *scribe* is an educated person who knows how to write—similar to the English word *secretary.* The scribe was often a mid-level government official in both ancient Jewish and Hellenistic societies. In the villages, scribes would draw up legal documents (such as marriage agreements or business contracts).

The word *scribe* can also have the sense of one trained in interpreting the law. Ezra, leader of the Jewish community after their return from exile in Babylon, is described as "a scribe, well-versed in the law of Moses" (Ezr 7:6). Ezra was also a priest, which shows that the two roles could overlap.

In the Gospels, the scribes are often associated with Jerusalem and the chief priests (see Mk 14:1), as well as with the Pharisees (see Mt 23:2, Mk 7:1). They have a reputation as teachers of the Law (see Mk 1:22, 9:11).

Related Passages

Priests and Levites as descendants of Aaron: Ex 28:1; Nm 1:47–54, 8:5–26, 18:1–5; 1 Chr, ch. 24. *Assistant role of Levites:* Nm 18:1–7. *Support of priests and Levites through tithes:* Nm 18:8–32. *Vestments of the high priest:* Ex, ch. 28; Sir 45:8–13. *Special purity laws for priests:* Lv, ch. 21. *High priest and the Holy of Holies:* Lv 16:1–19. *Priests as judges and teachers:* Dt 21:5, Sir 45:17. *Sanhedrin:* Mk 14:53–64. *Scribes:* Ezr 7:6; Mk 1:22, 7:1, 9:11, 14:1.

See Also

- "Holiness"
- "Poverty and Wealth"
- "Purity"
- "Sacrifices and Offerings"
- "Temple"

Prophets

In the Bible, a prophet is a person who receives direct messages from God and passes them on to others. Messages are typically received through a vision or a dream and then preached orally.

In the biblical books, a distinction is made between the minor prophets (the twelve books from the Book of Hosea to the Book of Malachi) and the major prophets (the Books of Isaiah, Jeremiah, Ezekiel, and Daniel). The distinction is based primarily on the length of the books: the books of the major prophets are much longer. In the Jewish tradition, the Book of Daniel is not classified with the prophets but with the more general writings.

Figures such as Samuel, Nathan, Elijah, and Elisha (in the Books of Samuel and Kings) are also known as prophets.

Receiving a Message from God

How does a prophet receive a direct message from God? The most common method seems to have been by means of a vision or dream. This is clear from the opening verse of several books of the prophets: "The vision which Isaiah, son of Amoz, had concerning Judah and Jerusalem" (Is 1:1). "The oracle which Habakkuk the prophet received in vision" (Hb 1:1). Ezekiel also asserts, "The heavens opened and I saw divine visions" (Ez 1:1). Daniel speaks of the visions that he saw during the night (see 7:1–2). Jeremiah also describes various visions, saying, "The word of the LORD came to me with the question: What do you see, Jeremiah?"(1:11).

The First Book of Samuel speaks of a "band of prophets," as well as King Saul, falling into a "prophetic state"

because the "spirit of the LORD" had rushed upon them (1 Sm 10:5–6; see also 1 Sm 19:23). This prophetic state involved some kind of altered state of consciousness in which the person was more open to receiving a message from God. This state was often associated with strange behavior. Saul, for example, lay naked all day and night when he was in such a state (see 1 Sm 19:24).

Prophets Within Israelite Society

In the time of the Israelite monarchy, some prophets served as official advisors to the king. These court prophets often flattered the kings and predicted successful outcomes of their wars. The Bible portrays such prophets as false—true prophets would always prophesy the truth, even if it meant disaster for Israel and the king. The court prophet Zedekiah predicts military victory for the kings of Israel and Judah, but Micaiah prophesies defeat (see 1 Kgs 22:6–28). The court prophet Hananiah predicts that Judah will overthrow their Babylonian rulers, but Jeremiah insists they will not (see Jer, ch. 28).

The prophets often challenged kings and ruling authorities. Nathan confronted King David about his adultery and murder (see 2 Sm 12:1–12). The Word of the Lord that the prophet had to speak was often unpopular, and prophets had to be ready to suffer persecution for their messages (see Ez 2:6). Micaiah (see 1 Kgs 22:26–27) and Jeremiah (see Jer 32:2–3) were imprisoned by the kings for their prophecies against Israel and Judah.

The prophets came from all walks of society. Ezekiel was a priest (see Ez

1:3); Jeremiah was from a priestly family (see Jer 1:1). Amos, in contrast, was a shepherd and tended fruit trees (see Am 7:14).

The Old Testament has several references to women prophets. Miriam, the sister of Moses, is called a prophetess as she sings a song of victory over the Egyptians (see Ex 15:20). The priest Hilkiah as well as other royal officials delivered the message of the prophetess Huldah to King Josiah: she spoke of God's threats but also of God's mercy for those who repent (see 2 Kgs 22:14–20; 2 Chr 34:22–28). Nehemiah mentions the prophetess Noadiah with disapproval (see Neh 6:14). The judge Deborah is also called a prophetess (Jgs 4:4).

Symbolic Actions of the Prophets

The old saying "Actions speak louder than words" applies to the biblical prophets, as they often, at the Lord's command, performed symbolic actions. Isaiah was told to walk naked and barefoot, symbolizing the status of a prisoner of war (see Is 20:2–5). Jeremiah was told to purchase a potter's flask and then smash it as a symbol of the coming destruction of Jerusalem (see Jer, ch. 19). He was also to wear a yoke as a symbol of the coming conquest and bondage of the Judean people (see 27:1–2). Ezekiel was told to draw the city of Jerusalem on a clay tablet and build model towers and battering rams to signify the coming siege of Jerusalem by its enemies (see Ez 4:1–3).

According to Josephus, a certain Theudas (who lived shortly after the time of Jesus) claimed to be a prophet and announced that he would divide the Jordan River so that the people could cross it (see Acts 5:36).

Message of the Prophets

What kind of messages from the Lord did the various prophets announce? There are several common themes.

First, the prophets threatened God's punishment on Israel for her sins, especially her abandonment of the Lord to worship other gods. Jeremiah foretold that God would allow Jerusalem to be conquered and her leading people taken into exile (see 25:1–14). Amos warned that on the "Day of the Lord" (the day of God's judgment), Israel would not be rewarded (the common expectation of the Israelites) but rather would suffer God's punishment: "Will not the day of the LORD be darkness and not light, gloom without any brightness?" (5:20). He also recorded the Lord's words: "I will send fire upon Judah, / to devour the castles of Jerusalem" (2:5). Warnings of God's judgment on other nations and on the Israelites on the Day of the Lord are a constant theme throughout Joel, Zephaniah, Obadiah (see v. 15), and Malachi (see 3:19).

Second, the prophets often criticized the people's habit of offering empty sacrifices that did not reflect changed hearts. Isaiah recorded the Lord's words: "What care I for the number of your sacrifices? / . . . I have had enough of whole-burnt rams / and fat of fatlings. / . . . Make justice your aim: redress the wronged, / hear the orphan's plea, defend the widow" (1:11–17).

Third, the prophets called for justice for the poor and oppressed in Israel. Amos verbally attacked the comfortable and wealthy, those "who trample upon the needy / and destroy the poor of the land" (8:4); Jeremiah criticized those who "oppress the resident alien, the orphan, and the widow" (7:6).

Finally, the prophets also held out hope that God would bless Israel by sending a messiah to defeat evil and establish the reign of peace. "The spirit of the LORD shall rest upon him. / . . . He shall judge the poor with justice / . . . with the breath of his lips he shall slay the wicked. / . . . Then the wolf shall be a guest of the lamb / . . . the cow and the bear shall be neighbors" (Is 11:2–9). "The days are coming, says the LORD, when I will make a new covenant with the house of Israel and the house of Judah. . . . I will place my law within them, and write it upon their hearts" (Jer 31:31–34). "They shall beat their swords into plowshares / and their spears into pruning hooks; / One nation shall not raise the sword against another, / nor shall they train for war again" (Is 2:4).

Early Christians believed that these prophecies were fulfilled by Jesus and the Church that he established (see Mt 1:22, 2:5).

Christian Prophets

The Apostle Paul lists prophecy as one of the spiritual gifts (see 1 Cor 12:10) and assumes that a prophet has a recognized role as a church leader (see v. 28). The prophet delivers his message from God to the other church members "for their building up, encouragement, and solace" (14:3). Apparently, God spoke to these prophets frequently, as Paul shows in his description of a typical church assembly: "Two or three prophets should speak, and the others discern. But if a revelation is given to another person sitting there, the first one should be silent" (vv. 29–30). The prophet Agabus foretold a famine (see Acts 11:28) and also Paul's arrest in Jerusalem (see 21:11). Agabus followed the tradition of symbolic actions, taking Paul's belt and binding his own feet and hands, saying, "This is the way the Jews will bind the owner of this belt in Jerusalem" (21:11).

The early Christian writing, the *Didache,* written around the year 100, provides several rules for how to distinguish between a true prophet and a false prophet (see 11:3–12). For example, if the prophet asks for money for himself, he is a false prophet, but not if he asks for money for others in need.

Christian prophecy was not limited to males. Already at Jesus' presentation in the Temple, Anna is called "prophetess" (see Lk 2:36). Paul taught that a woman should keep her head covered when she was praying or prophesying (see 1 Cor 11:5). The four daughters of Philip the evangelist had the gift of prophecy (see Acts 21:9).

Prophecy Today

At times a modern figure such as Martin Luther King Jr. is called a prophet. Like the biblical prophets, King boldly spoke God's message of truth, even when it was unpopular. Like the prophets, King suffered persecution for his message and eventually gave his life for it. Like the prophets, King spoke up for the poor and oppressed.

King often quoted from the biblical prophets. In his famous "I Have a Dream" speech, he quoted Amos: ". . . then let justice surge like water, / and goodness like an unfailing stream" (5:24).

Does God still reveal direct messages to prophets today? Many Christian churches, especially in the charismatic or Pentecostal tradition, do in fact recognize a continuing gift of prophecy. Within the Catholic Church, there is a charismatic movement that emphasizes the role of spiritual gifts such as prophecy.

Related Passages

Major prophets: Isaiah, Jeremiah, Ezekiel, Daniel. *Minor prophets:* Hosea, Joel, Amos, Obadiah, Jonah, Micah, Nahum, Habakkuk, Zephaniah, Haggai, Zechariah, Malachi. *Elijah and Elisha:* 1 Kgs, ch. 17—2 Kgs, ch. 9. *Prophetic visions:* Is 1:1, Hab 1:1, Ez 1:1. *Prophetic state:* 1 Sm 10:5–6. *Court prophets:* 1 Kgs 22:6–28. *Challenges to kings:* 2 Sm 12:1–12. *Woman prophets:* Ex 15:20, Jgs 4:4, 2 Kgs 22:14–20. *Symbolic actions:* Is 20:2–5; Jer, ch. 19, 28; Ez 4:1–3. *Prophetic judgment on Israel and the Day of the Lord:* Jer 25:1–14; Amos 5:18–20; Joel, Zephaniah, Mal 3:19. *Criticism of hypocritical sacrifices:* Is 1:11–17. *Concern for the poor and oppressed:* Is 1:11–16; Jer 7:6, 22:3; Ez 22:7; Zech 7:9–10; Mal 3:5. *Prophecies of the messiah and the messianic age:* Is 2:2–5, 9:1–6, 11:2–9; Jer 31:31–34; Zec 9:9–17. *Christian prophecy:* Acts 11:28, 21:9–11; 1 Cor 11:5, 12:10, 14:1–5.

Punishment

"Let the punishment fit the crime." This saying reflects one key aspect of our sense of justice today—that an action should receive an appropriate reward or punishment.

You may be aware that biblical punishments (such as stoning) were harsher than modern Western punishments. Let's try to get a better sense of how the biblical mind thinks about this central aspect of justice.

Restitution and Justice

Biblical culture shared the basic sense that a transgressor must make restitution: a person must pay for any damage or loss he or she caused, along with an extra amount as a punishment if the damage or loss was intentional. Compare "When a man steals an ox or a sheep and slaughters or sells it, he shall restore five oxen for the one ox, and four sheep for the one sheep" (Ex 21:37) with "When a man is burning over a field or a vineyard, if he lets the fires spread so that it burns in another's field, he must make restitution" (22:4).

The well-known biblical law of "eye for an eye, tooth for a tooth" (21:24) is an example of the concept of restitution. The version in Leviticus explains that "whoever takes the life of an animal shall make restitution of another animal. A life for a life! Anyone who inflicts an injury on his neighbor shall receive the same in return. Limb for limb, eye for eye, tooth for tooth!" (24:18–20). One purpose of this law may have been to *limit* revenge: If someone kills another person, for example, the person's family may not take revenge on the killer's family by killing even more people. The law provided a limitation on blood feuds between families.

In addition, the biblical concept of justice also included equal treatment of all parties. "You shall not act dishonestly in rendering judgment. Show neither partiality to the weak nor deference to the mighty, but judge your fellow men justly" (Lv 19:15; see Dt 16:18–20). It is true, nevertheless, that not all people were equal under Israelite law. If a man struck and killed a fellow Israelite, he would be put to death; yet if the same man killed his slave, he would receive a lighter punishment (see Ex 21:12–21).

In the New Testament, however, Jesus gives his own radical interpretation of the law: "You have heard that it was said, 'An eye for an eye and a tooth for a tooth.' But I say to you, offer no resistance to one who is evil. When someone strikes you on [your] right cheek, turn the other one to him as well" (Mt 5:38–42). Jesus' followers, then, were not to insist on their own rights and were not to seek revenge.

Does Jesus' teaching apply to nations as well? If a nation is attacked, for example, should that nation refuse to fight back? These questions are too complex to cover here. We will note that only some Christians (such as the Quakers and the Amish) do understand Jesus to mean that a Christian must never fight in a war, while Catholic and most Protestant traditions teach that war can be justified if the cause is just (such as self-defense), if it is a last resort, and if the damage caused by the war does not clearly outweigh the injustice against which the war is waged.

Death Penalty

The Old Testament proclaims the death penalty for a strikingly large number of offenses. Following are just a few of the crimes punishable by death:

- practicing sorcery or fortune-telling (see Ex 22:17, Lv 20:27)
- Israelites' worshiping other gods (Ex 22:19, Nm, ch. 25; Dt, ch. 13)
- having sexual relations with a close relative (see Lv 20:11–12)
- committing adultery (see Lv 20:10, Dt 22:22; same penalty for both the man and woman)
- having homosexual relations (see Lv 20:13)
- having sexual relations during menstruation (see Lv 20:18)
- a girl's not being a virgin before her before betrothal (see Dt 22:20–21)
- committing murder: "If anyone sheds the blood of man, / by man shall his

blood be shed; / For in the image of God / has man been made" (Gn 9:6; see also Ex 21:12, Lv 24:21).
- working on the Sabbath (see Ex 35:2; see also Nm 15:32–36)
- eating leavened bread during the Passover week (see Ex 12:15)
- a non-priest's going into the Dwelling or Temple (see Nm 1:51, 3:10)
- eating blood (see Lv 17:10)
- eating holy food while impure (see Lv 7:20)
- using blasphemy against God's name (see Lv 24:16)
- hitting or cursing one's own parents (see Ex 21:15,17; Lv 20:9)
- refusing to obey parents (see Dt 21:18–21)

Some people were executed by being burnt to death (see Lv 20:14); the most common method seems to have been stoning (see v. 27). The guilty person would be taken out of the city gates (outside the order and "cleanness" of the community) to be stoned to death (see Dt 17:2–5). Golgotha, the place of Jesus' execution, was outside the walls of Jerusalem (see Mk 15:22).

Notice that many capital crimes involve breaking purity laws. An underlying concept is that the criminal is impure and that her or his impurity will contaminate the whole body of the community. Thus, the person needs to be "cut off" from the community by execution. According to many laws, in fact, the whole community should take part in stoning the criminal (see Lv 24:16, Nm 15:36). A common statement connected with executing a transgressor is, "Purge the evil from your midst" (Dt 17:7, 21:21).

This purity concept carries over into the New Testament thought world. When a church member is involved in an incestuous relationship, Paul insists that the member be expelled from the

Church (see 1 Cor 5:2). Paul makes the analogy that even a small amount of yeast affects the whole batch of dough, and then quotes Deuteronomy: "Purge the evil person from your midst" (v. 13).

New Testament thought no longer calls explicitly for the death penalty, but it does require that offending members be expelled from the community so that the entire community can be protected. Jesus instructs his followers that if a member of the church sins (the sin is not specified), then someone should confront the person's sin privately. If the person does not change his behavior, other church members should become involved. If the person still persists in the sinful behavior, "then treat him as you would a Gentile or a tax collector" (Mt 18:15–18). In other words, members of the church should no longer associate with that person (see also 2 Thes 3:14–15).

Judges

Any society needs to have a system that interprets the law in controversial cases. In the Palestinian villages, judges who decided such cases were priests, Levites, or respected elders (see Ex 18:13–27; Dt 17:8–9, 22:15). (These local authorities differed from the judges described in the Book of Judges, who were more like military leaders.) Local judges would typically gather at the city gate to hear a case. When Boaz wishes to settle a legal matter regarding the inheritance of Naomi's property, he calls ten elders to the city gate to act as witness (see Ru 4:1–2).

Related Passages

"Eye for an Eye": Ex 21:24, Lv 24:18–20. *Jesus' interpretation:* Mt 5:38–42. *Death penalty:* Ex 22:17–19, Lv 20:1–18. *Methods of execution:* Lv 20:14–16,27. *Execution as cleansing of community:* Dt 17:7, 21:21. *New Testament expulsion of unrepentant sinners from community:* Mt 18:15–18, 1 Cor 5:1–13. *Judges:* Ex 18:13–27, Dt 17:8–9, Ru 4:1–2.

See Also

- "Priests and Levites"
- "Purity"
- "Torah"

Purity

The concept of purity is central to the biblical way of thinking, especially to the Old Testament thought world. Essentially, it is a way of looking at the world that divides reality into pure and impure categories.

The Israelite viewpoint that distinguishes between pure and impure, however, cannot be summed up by those two words in English. We need to bring in several other pairs of words in order to grasp the wider meaning of the Israelite concept: holy / ordinary (or profane), life / death, clean / unclean, and order / disorder.

The concept of purity is connected in an especially close way with the concept of holiness (see the "Holiness" article). Essentially, any person or object that comes into contact with the holy must be in a state of purity.

Uncleanness

As a noun, the Hebrew root word *tm'*, is translated as "uncleanness"; as a verb, it is translated as "to defile." To get a better sense of this word's meaning, let's consider how it is used in a range of different situations:

- Uncleanness is identified with sores or blotches on the skin (see Lv, ch. 13).
- Certain animals are unclean (see Lv, ch. 11).
- Uncleanness is due to contact with a dead body (see Nm 19:11, Ez 44:25) or with the carcass of an unclean animal (see Lv 11:24).
- Females are unclean from menstruation or another flow of blood (see Lv 15:19–30), as well as after childbirth (see Lv, ch. 12).
- Males are unclean from any kind of unusual emission from the penis or emission of semen (see Lv 15:1–17).
- Uncleanness is due to sexual intercourse (see Lv 15:18) and especially due to sexual relations outside of marriage (see Gn 34:5, Lv 18:20).
- Uncleanness is due to worshiping other gods or associating with other religions. This sense of uncleanness seems to be connected with the concept that worshiping other gods was similar to committing adultery against the Lord (see Lv 19:31, Ez 22:3, Hos 5:3, Jer 2:7).
- Uncleanness is used as a metaphor for sin or wickedness in general (see Is 6:5–7, Eccl 9:2).

Uncleanness could be transmitted by touch. When an unclean person touched furniture or another object, that object would also become unclean (see Lv 15:4–12,26–27). A person with an unclean skin disease was required to shout out, "Unclean! Unclean!" in order to warn other people of his approach (see 13:45).

Depending on the case, cleansing from impurity involved ritual bathing (see 15:21; Nm, ch. 19) and offering sacrifices (see Lv, ch. 12).

The opposite of the concept of uncleanness (tm') is, of course, "cleanness" (taher, in Hebrew). When Naaman washes, he becomes "clean" (taher) from his skin ailment (see 2 Kgs 5:10, Lv 14:1).

Purity, the Temple, and Symbolism

Uncleanness could be associated with moral sinfulness (such as adultery), but its fundamental meaning is not moral. Notice that many of the restrictions are associated with conception and giving birth (childbirth, sexual fluids) or with death (impurity of corpses or of spilled blood).

Scholars such as E. P. Sanders point out that impurity is associated with the changeable realm of the ordinary (birth and death) in contrast to the unchangeable realm of the holy. An essential goal of the purity laws, therefore, is to draw clear boundaries between the realm of the ordinary and the realm of the holy (especially the most holy place on earth, the Temple). The "unclean" thus symbolizes not so much evil as it does the changeable and fleeting nature of ordinary life.

Anthropologists such as Mary Douglas see a related symbolism in the human body itself. In many cultures, the individual body of a community member symbolizes the religious community as a whole. (Paul uses this general concept when he describes individual members of the Corinthian Church as members of the Body of Christ in 1 Cor, ch. 12.) The skin of the body, then, symbolizes the border between the sacred community and the ordinary, or profane, world outside of the community (see the "Holiness" article). Thus, a blemish on the skin, or the flow of a fluid (sexual fluid, blood) from the inside of the body to the outside symbolizes the danger of the "unclean" outside world's "infecting" or "contaminating" the holy community.

The symbolism of impurity cannot be separated from the symbolism of the Temple. Most impurities restricted a person's access to the Temple or the holy things associated with the Temple (such as meat that had been offered as a sacrifice). "Everyone who fails to purify himself after touching the body of any deceased person, defiles the Dwelling of the LORD and shall be cut off from Israel" (Nm 19:13; see Lv 12:4, 15:31).

Purity is also closely connected with the concept of order. Cleanness is associated with the concern to keep all things in their proper places or categories: an unclean animal is one that blurs the distinction between two distinct categories (see the "Food Laws" and "Holiness" articles). In the Genesis Creation story, chaos is the result of blurring the distinctions between light and darkness, or between the waters and the dry land. This same concern to draw clear boundaries may also be symbolized in the bodily fluids that cross the boundaries of the skin, or the idea that periods of transition and change (especially birth and death) cross boundaries.

The seriousness of maintaining purity and thus protecting the holiness of the Temple and the proper worship of God is shown in the fact that certain violations of purity were punishable by a sentence of death (being "cut off from the people"; see the "Punishment" article). One who was unclean must be kept apart from the holy; serious uncleanness must be kept completely apart from the holy community (see the "Chosen People" article).

Methods of Purification from Uncleanness

Water was the main means of purifying a person or object from uncleanness. Immersion pools were characteristic of Second Temple Palestine. They have been found in Herod's palaces, the houses of ordinary people in Jerusalem, and at the Qumran community. They were usually 6 to 9 feet in width and length, and often 7 feet deep. The pools were cut into bedrock, and had to be filled naturally, either by rainwater or spring water. Steps led down to the bottom of the pool.

Other purification methods were used, however, especially in the Diaspora, where ritual hand washing was practiced. An Egyptian text refers to Jews' washing their hands while praying. This may explain why Diaspora synagogues are often located by rivers or by the sea. Paul expects to find a Jewish "place of prayer" by a river in Philippi (see Acts 16:13).

Purity and Ordinary Life

Biblical commandments require ordinary people to be pure when going to the Temple or when eating food associated with the Temple sacrifices. But the location of immersion pools in remote areas show that people were concerned to be pure more often. It is probable, for example, that women commonly immersed after childbirth and menstruation. Men would also have to immerse themselves if they touched anything that the menstruating woman had touched.

Women, however, were not excluded from everyday life because of menstruation. A menstruating woman would continue her daily routine of cooking, household work, and caring for children. Jesus encounters a woman with a "flow of blood" in an ordinary crowd—there is no indication that she was socially isolated (see Mk 5:25–34).

Priests did follow special rules of purity. They most likely immersed themselves every day, as their food was food offered in sacrifice and they had to be in a state of purity to eat it.

Pharisees and Essenes also had their own special purity rules. Essenes, for example, immersed themselves before every evening meal. The Pharisees washed their hands frequently (see Mt 15:1–2) before eating.

Early Christians and Purity Laws

In our discussion of the food laws, we saw that Jesus himself did not reject the validity of the food laws, nor did he reject the purity laws in general. When Jesus healed a man with leprosy, for example, he told him, "Go, show yourself to the priest and offer for your cleansing what Moses prescribed; that will be proof for them" (Mk 1:40–45).

When Gentiles began to join early Christian Churches (considered to be holy communities), the leaders of the Jerusalem Church made the following ruling regarding their level of purity: The Gentiles should "abstain from meat sacrificed to idols, from blood, from meats of strangled animals, and from unlawful marriage" (Acts 15:29; see also 21:25). All of these actions are associated with purity laws; a strangled animal was one that had not been slaughtered in a kosher manner.

Early Christianity and the Metaphorical Sense of Purity

Early Christians, because of their roots in Judaism, understood their church communities as holy places and, in fact, could describe themselves as God's Temple: "Do you not know that you are the temple of God?" (1 Cor 3:16); "For we are the temple of the living God" (2 Cor 6:16; see also Eph 2:21–22). Supporting Mary Douglas's insight that the individual body of the community member symbolizes the body of the whole community, Paul says, "Do you not know that your body is a temple of the holy Spirit within you" (1 Cor 6:19).

To live in the holy community, Christians needed to maintain a level of purity. Paul's language, for example, often reflects the basic distinctions of clean and unclean: "Let us cleanse ourselves from every defilement of the flesh and spirit, making holiness perfect in the fear of God" (2 Cor 7:1). James says, "Religion that is pure and undefiled before God and the Father is this: to care for orphans and widows in their affliction and to keep oneself unstained by the world" (1:27). Paul insists that the sin of incestuous behavior will infect the holiness of the whole Corinthian Church community if the sinner is allowed to remain in the community: "Purge the evil person from your midst" (1 Cor 5:13).

Christian Purity Today

Christians today of course do not follow the purity laws (with the exception of groups such as the Seventh-day Adventists). Yet the more metaphorical aspects of purity and holiness remain essential to the Christian view of the world. Christians are called to live a lifestyle that is distinct from the values of "the world" (mainstream society). This purity still includes watching what we eat (avoiding overeating or drinking too much), keeping sexually pure, and keeping our thoughts pure from the many temptations of modern life, including gossip, pornography, jealousy, and greed.

Related Passages

Purity laws: Lv, ch. 11–15. *Cleansing from impurity:* Lv, ch. 12; 15:21; Nm, ch. 19. *Jesus and purity:* Mt 15:1–20; Mk 1:40–45, 5:25–34. *Impurities' effect on the Temple:* Nm 19:13. *Special purity rules of the Pharisees:* Mk 7:1–4. *Early Church and purity:* Acts 15:1–35. *Metaphorical purity of Christian communities:* 1 Cor 3:16, ch. 5–6; 2 Cor 6:14–18.

See Also

- "Chosen People"
- "Food Laws"
- "Holiness"
- "Temple"

Resurrection

Just as the Old Testament in general has no conception of the Christian idea of heaven and hell, so it also, with some exceptions, has no conception of a resurrection from the dead. When a person dies, the person simply descends to the shadowy existence of Sheol (see the "Afterlife" article).

The belief in resurrection does appear in later Old Testament writings. Daniel says, "Many of those who sleep / in the dust of the earth shall awake; / some shall live forever, / others shall be an everlasting horror and disgrace" (12:2). The same hope is evident in Second Maccabees, where some young Jewish men refused to deny their faith even under torture. When one young man is threatened with having his tongue and hands cut off, he responds, "It was from Heaven that I received these; for the sake of his laws I disdain them; from him I hope to receive them again." Another says, "The King of the world will raise us up to live again forever" (2 Mc 7:9–11).

Not all Jews in Jesus' time accepted these changing ideas. The Sadducees, in keeping with the main Old Testament teaching, taught that there was no resurrection of the dead (see Mk 12:18–27). In a debate with Jesus, they tried to prove that the belief was not logical: If a woman had seven husbands when she was alive, whose wife would she be in the resurrection? Jesus replied, "When they rise from the dead, they neither marry nor are given in marriage, but they are like the angels in heaven" (v. 25). In other words, Jesus was saying that our standards and ideas concerning this world do not necessarily apply to the afterlife—life in the next world is of a different kind.

The Pharisees, however, did believe in the resurrection (as well as in angels and spirits). At Paul's trial before the Jewish religious authorities, Paul claims, "My brothers, I am a Pharisee, the son of Pharisees; I am on trial for hope in the resurrection of the dead" (Acts 23:6). He realized that this would cause a controversy, and sure enough, a dispute broke out between the Pharisees and the Sadducees (see vv. 7–10).

Bodily Resurrection

When Paul was teaching the early churches about the resurrection, again confusion and debate arose. Members of the church at Corinth (in Greece) were puzzled when Paul taught them that the body would be raised from the dead (see 1 Cor 15:35). Many people could accept the idea that the spirit or soul might live on after their death; Greek philosophers such as Plato taught that a person's soul was eternal. But it was obvious that the physical body died and then decayed and decomposed.

Paul tries to make his point with an analogy. A seed does not sprout into a plant unless it first "dies" and is buried in the ground. So too the physical body dies, but in the resurrection, it will be raised as a "spiritual body" (vv. 36–44). Paul's phrase means that this renewed body will not be animated by a "natural soul" *(psyche)* but by the spirit *(pneuma)* (see the "Human Nature" article).

Gospel narratives of Jesus' Resurrection also insist that Jesus did not just rise as a spirit: he rose *body* and spirit. Jesus' tomb was found *empty* (see Mk 16:1–8, Lk 24:1–3). The risen Jesus says plainly: "Look at my hands and my feet, that it is I myself. Touch me and see, because a ghost does not have flesh and bones as you can see I have" (Lk 24:39). He even eats a piece of fish, again emphasizing his bodily nature (see vv. 41–43; see also Jn 20:27).

On the other hand, it is also clear that Jesus' risen body is no ordinary physical body. Jesus appears and disappears suddenly (see Lk 24:31, Jn 20:19) and his followers do not recognize him at first (see Lk 24:16, Jn 20:15). This is a kind of existence that is neither strictly spiritual nor strictly physical but seems to have characteristics of each.

The Significance of the Resurrection of the Body

The biblical teaching on the resurrection of the body is a holistic view of the human. It sees as valuable not only the spiritual and intellectual aspects of the human but also the physical. It sees the spiritual, mental, and physical aspects of the human as a harmony. This Christian view is in line with some recent holistic trends in the medical and health fields. The basic insight is that humans are a unified whole; a person's health involves all aspects of that person.

Our physical body is not just something we *have;* it is part of who we *are.* If we were pure spirits, we would be angels, not humans. It is through our body that we express emotions, relate with other people, and experience reality through our five senses. Christians believe that this essential relationship between body, mind, and spirit cannot be separated, even in death.

Related Passages

Late Old Testament belief in resurrection: Dn 12:2, 2 Mc 7:9–11. *Jesus' debate with the Sadducees:* Mk 12:18–27. *Pharisee-Sadducee debate on resurrection:* Acts 23:6–10. *Paul's view of the "spiritual body":* 1 Cor 15:35–58. *Jesus' risen body:* Lk 24:36–43, Jn 20:19–28.

See Also

- "Afterlife"
- "Death and Burial Customs"
- "Human Nature"
- "Jewish Sects"

Sabbath

Sabbath refers to the Jewish custom of dedicating one day a week to the worship of God and to rest from work; a custom later adapted by Christians. In the Jewish tradition, the holy day of rest and worship is Saturday; in the Christian tradition, it is Sunday. For Jews the Sabbath actually begins Friday evening at sundown, as each day begins in the evening in the Jewish reckoning.

The commandment to observe the Sabbath is one of the Ten Commandments: Remember to keep holy the Sabbath day. On this day, no work was to be done by the Israelite family, their slaves, non-Israelites living with them, or even by their animals (see Ex 20:8–11). The version in Exodus connects the Sabbath with God's rest after Creation; the version in Deuteronomy connects it with the liberation of the Israelites from Egypt (see 5:12–15). The two major, interrelated purposes of the Sabbath are (1) to rest from ordinary, profane work and (2) to focus the mind and heart on an active worship of God and a study of his commandments.

The Sabbath is closely connected with the holiness of the people. "Take care to keep my sabbaths, for that is to be the token between you and me throughout the generations, to show that it is I, the LORD, who make you holy" (Ex 31:13; see Lv 19:3). This holiness was considered to be so profound that a person deliberately violating the Sabbath was to be executed (see Ex 31:14, 35:2). Numbers recounts how a man found gathering sticks on the Sabbath was stoned to death by the community (see 15:32–36). The people as a whole will be blessed if they keep the Sabbath holy, and cursed if they fail to observe it properly (see Is 58:13–14, Jer 17:19–27).

Sabbatical Year and Jubilee

Closely related to the rest and holiness of the seventh day are commandments regarding rest and holiness in seven-year cycles. Every seventh year, the land was to have a complete rest, with no planting or harvesting (see Lv 25:1–7); the poor were free to gather the unharvested crops (see Ex 23:10–11). During this year, creditors were supposed to "relax" their claims against Israelite debtors and lend freely to the needy, and all Israelite slaves were to be freed (see Dt 15:1–18). Every seventh cycle of seven years (every forty-nine years) was the Jubilee year. This time was to be made holy by "proclaiming liberty": each person was to return to his own family property to prevent ownership of land by only a wealthy few (see Lv 25:10–23).

Sabbath observation and its concern for holiness, then, are closely tied to concerns for equality and justice in Israelite society.

Active Worship and Prayer on the Sabbath

On the Sabbath, the Israelites were to gather together in a "sacred assembly" (Lv 23:3). The Bible itself does not command study of Scripture on the Sabbath, but in New Testament times, both Philo and Josephus assume that Jews should gather in synagogues on the Sabbath in order to study the Torah; the Acts of the Apostles supports this assumption (see 13:14,27; 17:1–2). The Sabbath service included praying and singing hymns; the Sabbath would be celebrated with a festive meal.

Sabbath Restrictions

The Jewish tradition took seriously the commandment "No work may be done" (Ex 20:10). But the commandment is quite general: What exactly is meant by *work*? Different Jewish groups answered this question in a variety of ways.

The Mishnah lists thirty-nine specific types of work that are forbidden on the Sabbath, including agricultural work (plowing, reaping; see Ex 34:21), preparing food (kneading, baking), spinning or weaving, cutting up a carcass, writing, building, or lighting a fire (see 35:3). Philo says that not even one branch, leaf, or piece of fruit could be cut or plucked on the Sabbath.

The writings found in the Dead Sea Scrolls show the strictest interpretation of Sabbath rest. If an animal should fall into a pit, for example, one should not take it out. If a person should fall into water, it was forbidden to help him or her with a rope or ladder.

A general rabbinic principle was that any work (such as preparing a meal) was forbidden if it could have been done prior to the Sabbath. A second principle was that in potentially life-threatening circumstances, the Sabbath rest could be violated. Thus, a midwife could be called to help a woman deliver a child on the Sabbath. But if the injury was not life-threatening, then the rules of the Sabbath still applied: a broken limb, for example, could not be set.

Some more specific passages attracted attention. Exodus 16:29 reads, "On the seventh day everyone is to stay home and no one is to go out." What exactly is meant by *going out*? Should a person literally not leave the house, not even to attend a worship service?

One interpretation focused on limiting travel. When we hear that Jesus' disciples returned to Jerusalem from the Mount of Olives, a "sabbath day's journey away" (Acts 1:12), this refers to the general rabbinic principle that a Jew could travel no more than 2,000 cubits, or a little over 1,000 yards, on the Sabbath. This distance seems to be based on the distance between the Ark of the Covenant and the rest of the Israelite camp in the wilderness times (see Jos 3:4).

Another specific prohibition was carrying any kind of burden or load on the Sabbath (see Jer 17:19–27). A man healed by Jesus is criticized for carrying his mat on the Sabbath (see Jn 5:10).

It seems that ancient Jews in general observed the Sabbath strictly because Greco-Roman authors often comment on the custom. But there were exceptions. Nehemiah recounts his efforts to enforce the Sabbath rest in Jerusalem when he found that the people were engaged in business activities and buying goods from Gentiles on the holy day (see 13:15–22).

Gospel Controversies over the Sabbath

Jesus himself observed the Sabbath: Luke reports that Jesus went to the Nazareth synagogue on the Sabbath "according to his custom" (Lk 4:16).

The Gospels, however, are filled with stories of conflicts between Jesus and other Jewish religious authorities regarding acceptable behavior on the Sabbath. These stories in no way imply that Jesus rejected Sabbath observation—they simply reflect the fact that different Jewish teachers had different interpretations of what was and what was not acceptable behavior on the Sabbath.

In one account, Jesus' disciples were plucking ears of grain on the Sabbath (see Mt 12:1–8). Some Pharisees complain to Jesus that this is unlawful, seeing it as a violation of the prohibition against harvesting (see Ex 34:21). Jesus responds with biblical examples of exceptions to rules (as when David ate bread that was authorized for priests only). Jesus' general point is that God is more concerned with broader values such as mercy rather than exact rules. His general principle was "The sabbath was made for man, not man for the sabbath" (Mk 2:27).

The major focus of Sabbath controversies in the Gospels, however, is over the specific question of healing on the Sabbath (see Mt 12:9–14, Lk 13:10–17, Jn 5:1–18). We have seen that the general rabbinic principle was that the Sabbath rest could be violated if a person's life was in danger. When Jesus heals a man with a withered hand (see Mk 3:1–6) or a crippled woman (see Lk 13:10–17), the complaint of the other religious authorities is that this healing could have waited: "There are six days when work should be done. Come on those days to be cured, not on the sabbath day" (Lk 13:14).

Jesus indeed could have waited in those cases. He seems, however, to have deliberately provoked confrontations to raise the deeper question of proper behavior on the Sabbath. Jesus asks, "Is it lawful to do good on the sabbath rather than to do evil, to save life rather than to destroy it?" (Mk 3:4). In this way, Jesus is clearly within the scriptural tradition of the sabbatical year and the Jubilee: seeing the Sabbath holiness as closely connected with helping the poor and oppressed of society.

From Sabbath to the Lord's Day

Christians very early on changed from observing the Sabbath on Saturday to observing it on Sunday in honor of Jesus' Resurrection on the first day of the week (see Mt 28:1). The community at Troas gathered to break bead on the first day of the week (see Acts 20:7). Paul possibly alludes to this practice (see 1 Cor 16:2). This day came to be known simply as the Lord's Day (see Rv 1:10).

Related Passages

Sabbath commandments: Ex 16:29, 20:8–10, 35:3; Dt 5:12–15. *Sabbath restrictions:* Ex 16:29, 34:21, 35:3; Jer 17:19–27. *Sabbath and the holiness of the people:* Ex 31:13. *Sabbatical year:* Lv, ch. 25; Dt 15:1–18. *Sabbath and Torah study:* Acts 13:14,27; 17:1–2. *Sabbath's day journey:* Acts 1:12. *Jesus' controversy with Pharisees on plucking grain:* Mt 12:1–8, Mk 2:23–28. *Jesus' controversies on healing on the Sabbath:* Mt 12:9–14, Lk 13:10–17, Jn 5:1–18. *Lord's Day:* Acts 20:7, Rv 1:10.

See Also

- "Festivals"
- "Holiness"
- "Jewish Sects"
- "Poverty and Wealth"
- "Synagogues and Prayer"
- "Torah"

Sacrifices and Offerings

For many of us today, the idea of killing an animal and offering it as a sacrifice to God seems bizarre, if not criminal. Yet offering such sacrifices was essential

to virtually all religions throughout the ancient Mediterranean world. Animal sacrifices, as well as food or drink offerings, were practiced by the ancient

Greeks, Romans, Egyptians, and Babylonians. In the Bible, sacrifices are described already in the days of Cain and Abel (see Gn 4:3–4); detailed instructions on how, when, and where to sacrifice are given in several parts of the Torah (see, for example, Lev, ch. 1–7; Nm 15:1–30).

Even if killing an animal on an altar seems bizarre to us today, the general idea of sacrifice is still very much with us. We speak of soldiers' sacrificing for their country. We say that a soldier killed in action has made the ultimate sacrifice. At times we speak of parents' sacrificing for their children, meaning that parents have given up something (perhaps some vacation or leisure time, perhaps some material comforts they might have had) for the benefit of their children. We understand that sacrifice involves the willingness to give up something that is precious, even to the point of giving up one's life.

The basic biblical idea is the same. The people of Israel were called on to give up, to sacrifice, something that was precious and valuable to them. The animals—sheep, goats, cattle, birds—as well as the grain offerings, were basic necessities for survival. The Israelites offered the very best of what they had— the sacrificed animals had to be without any blemish (see Lv 3:1). Sacrifices involved giving up something precious for God.

The Torah allows exceptions for families too poor to afford a sacrifice. If a person could not afford a lamb or goat for a sin offering, he was allowed to bring two turtledoves or two pigeons. If he could not afford the birds, then he was allowed to offer fine flour (see 5:7–11). Joseph and Mary, for example, offered the sacrifice of the birds after Mary had given birth to Jesus (see Lk 2:24).

To get a more concrete idea of biblical sacrifice and its meaning, let's consider some details.

Offering the Sacrifice

Only clean animals (see Lv, ch. 11) that were without blemish (see 3:1) were sacrificed. This included sheep, cattle, and goats, as well as birds. Offerings of flour, oil, and wine were also made (see Lv, ch. 2; Nm 15:1–12).

In the days before the Torah was given to Moses, patriarchs such as Noah (see Gn 8:20) and Abraham offered sacrifices (see 15:7–12), but by Second Temple times, only priests did so.

The offering of sacrifices is closely associated with the holy places, especially the Tent of the Meeting, and later the Jerusalem Temple. Israelites did offer sacrifices at other holy sites. Bethel, for example, was a sacred site (Jacob had built an altar there; see Gn 35:1, 1 Kgs 12:26–30, 2 Kgs 17:28). The Samaritans built a temple at Mount Gerizim, apparently as a rival to the Second Temple in Jerusalem (see Jn 4:20).

The authors of biblical books such as Deuteronomy and Kings, however, understood the Jerusalem Temple as the only legitimate place to offer sacrifices and worship God (see, for example, Dt 12:4–6). King Josiah ordered the destruction of all other places of worship in Israel, associating them with the worship of false gods (see 2 Kgs 23:1–24).

In a typical sin offering sacrifice, the father of a family would bring an animal into the outer court of the Temple, confess the sin to a priest, lay his hands on the animal's head, and slaughter it (see Lv 4:27–31, Nm 5:7). The priest would take the blood and put in on the altar, either in the outer Court of the Priests or in the Holy of Holies.

Besides sacrifices offered by individuals, daily sacrifices were offered for the entire community at the Temple. A lamb was sacrificed in the morning and another in the evening (see Ex 29:38–39). Additional sacrifices were offered on Sabbaths and festival days. These daily offerings were paid for with the half-shekel Temple tax charged to adult male Jews both in Palestine and in the Diaspora (see Mt 17:24–27).

Types of Sacrificial Offerings

Peace Offering

The peace offering was a general category that could include thanksgiving, votive (a sacrifice to fulfill a vow), or a free-will offering (see Lv 7:12–16). In the peace offering, the meat of the slaughtered animal was shared between the priests and the person offering the sacrifice (see vv. 29–34; see also Nm 18:8–20).

Sin Offering and Guilt Offering

The essential purpose of a sin offering was to make atonement for a sin. In sin offerings, the priests received the meat of the slaughtered animal.

The term *sin offering* is misleading for modern readers, as we usually think of sin as intentionally doing something ethically wrong. A sin offering, however, would also be made even if a person unknowingly broke a commandment but later discovered the infraction (see Lv, ch. 4). A sin offering was also made for impurities. For example, a woman would have to make a sin offering after giving birth to a child (see 12:6) or to purify a person from skin disease (see 14:18–20). Guilt offerings (see 5:14–26, 7:1–10) are similar to sin offerings;

they make atonement for both intentional (such as stealing from a neighbor) and unintentional "sins" against Torah commandments.

First Fruits Offering

The people were to offer the "first fruits" of their grain, wine, and oil (see Dt 18:4). Every firstborn, either of animals, or of humans, was also to be offered to the Lord. Clean animals were to be sacrificed, but humans and unclean animals could be redeemed (see Nm 18:15–17; see also Ex 13:12–16)—a certain amount of money could be paid for them instead. Luke understood Jesus' presentation in the Temple as a fulfillment of the Exodus commandment (see Lk 2:22–23).

Holocausts

In a holocaust (or "whole burnt offering"), the sacrificed animal is burnt completely on the altar (see Lv 1:3–17). Philo says that the holocaust offering was a way of honoring God, as the entire offering was burnt up.

Meaning of Sacrifice

Sacrifices may have originated with the idea of offering food to feed the gods. Several passages mention the Lord's smelling the sacrifice as a "sweet odor" (see Gn 8:21). But other passages clarify that the people of Israel should not understand it in this way: "Were I hungry, / I would not tell you, / for mine is the world and all that fills it. / Do I eat the flesh of bulls / or drink the blood of goats?" (Ps 50:12–13).

One essential meaning of a sacrifice was as a remembrance of God. In offering the first portion of a harvest to God, or offering the firstborn of an animal, the Israelites were reminded that God had provided this food for them in the first place by his creation. Philo says that offerings were a way of honoring and giving thanks to God.

A second major meaning, applying to sin and guilt offerings, involved making atonement. This basically involves making up for some kind of sin by offering something of value to God (see the "Atonement" article). The blood of an animal was essential for purification from sin, because it represents life (see Lv 17:11). The life blood of the person's animal seems to have been a substitute of the life of the person making the offering.

Offering a sacrifice was not a substitute for personal responsibility. If someone stole from or cheated another person, he or she must first repay the victim (plus one fifth extra) and *then* offer a sacrifice (see Nm 5:5–8).

Sacrifices were closely associated with the concept of purity. Sin defiled (made "unclean") not only the person who committed the sin, but the whole community, including the holy places. With the sacrifice of a goat on the Day of Atonement, the high priest would "make atonement for the sanctuary be-

cause of the sinful defilements and faults of the Israelites" (Lv 16:16). The blood of the sacrifices cleansed the holy places, thus allowing all of Israel to worship God properly.

Spiritual Sacrifice

The prophets and Old Testament writers accepted the system of sacrifices, but they insisted that these sacrifices were worthless if the person offering a sacrifice did not also sincerely and personally repent.

The psalmist says: "For you do not desire sacrifice; / a burnt offering you would not accept. / My sacrifice, God, is a broken spirit; / God, do not spurn a broken, humbled heart" (Ps 51:18–19). Isaiah records the Lord's words: "In the blood of calves, lambs and goats / I find no pleasure. / . . . Wash yourselves clean! / Put way your misdeeds before my eyes; / cease doing evil; learn to do good" (1:11–17). Jesus himself followed in this tradition, approving of the scribe's words, "And 'to love him with all your heart, with all your understanding, and with all your strength, and to love your neighbor as yourself' is worth more than all burnt offerings and sacrifices" (Mk 12:32–34). Paul too calls on Christians "to offer your bodies as a living sacrifice, holy and pleasing to God, your spiritual worship" (Rom 12:1).

On the Day of Atonement, a goat was sacrificed for the people's sins. Then the high priest laid his hands on a second goat—symbolically transferring the people's guilt—and that goat would be abandoned in the desert.

Jesus' Sacrifice on the Cross

The early Christians understood the death of God's Son, Jesus, as the ultimate sacrifice that made atonement for sins. Paul said, "For our paschal lamb, Christ, has been sacrificed" (1 Cor 5:7) and taught that God put Jesus forth "as an expiation, through faith, by his blood" (Rom 3:25). The Letter to the Hebrews understands Jesus' sacrifice as an atonement that took away the need to offer sacrifices: "We have been consecrated through the offering of the body of Jesus Christ once for all. . . . For by one offering he has made perfect forever those who are being consecrated" (Heb 10:10,14). Jesus, the perfect high priest, offers himself as the perfect sacrifice (see 7:26—9:28).

Related Passages

Ritual sacrifices: Lv, ch. 1–7, 17; Nm 15:1–30. *Alternative sacrifices for the poor:* Lv 5:7–11, Lk 2:24. *Restriction of sacrifices to the Jerusalem Temple:* Dt 12:4–6. *Daily sacrifices:* Ex 29:38–39. *Sin offering:* Lv, ch. 4; 12:6. *First fruit offering:* Dt 18:4. *Holocaust:* Lv 1:3–7. *Spiritual sacrifice:* Ps 51, Is 1:11–17, Mk 12:32–34, Rom 12:1. *Atonement:* Lv 17:11. *Cleansing the Temple:* Lv 16:1. *Jesus' atoning sacrifice:* Rom 3:25, Heb 10:1–18.

See Also

- "Atonement"
- "Priests and Levites"
- "Purity"
- "Sin"
- "Taxes and Tithes"
- "Temple"

Sexuality

Many people believe the Bible has a negative attitude toward human sexuality, portraying it as something shameful or dirty. Yet the reality is quite different: the Bible's basic understanding is that sexuality is a great gift of intimacy, pleasure, and fruitfulness, given by God.

This positive view of sexuality is part of the Bible's overall positive view of the physical body. The biblical view of human nature is holistic: the body is not a weight that drags down the spirit; rather body and spirit form an essential unity. The body is valued so highly that it will be raised and transformed in the resurrection (see the "Human Nature" and "Resurrection" articles).

So the physical expression of love is not considered inferior to a more spiritual love. Sexual love forms an essential part of a holistic, mutually healthy relationship of love between a husband and wife (see 1 Cor 7:3–5).

Our Sexuality: An Image of Divine Love

Our male or female sexuality is not something arbitrary but is an essential aspect of human nature. Both versions of the Genesis Creation story emphasize this aspect: "God created man in his image; / in the divine image he created him; / male and female he created them" (1:27). In the second version, the male is incomplete, lonely, until he is made complete by the creation of his partner, Eve (see 2:18–25).

Genesis 1:27 shows the close connection between our sexuality and the fact that humans are made in God's image. This does not mean that God is male or female—because God is eternal Spirit, God is beyond those categories. Rather, as Pope John Paul II pointed out, it means that our sexuality is a physical sign or image of God's nature. Our physical bodies show us that we are incomplete by ourselves and can find completion only in loving relationships with others—our bodies are images of the truth that it is God's very nature to, in a sense, reach beyond himself in love.

The Song of Songs: A Celebration of Physical Love

If a person believes the Bible has a negative view of sexuality, she or he only has to read the Song of Songs to change that belief. The Song of Songs is a poetic dialogue between a bride and her groom. The two lovers praise one another's beauty, going into intimate detail:

> *His head is pure gold. . . .*
> *His eyes are like doves. . . .*
> *His lips are red blossoms. . . .*
>
> *His body is a work of ivory*
> *covered with sapphires. . . .*
> *His mouth is sweetness itself;*
> *he is all delight.*
> *Such is my lover, and such my friend.*
> *(Song 5:11–16)*
>
> *Your rounded thighs are like jewels.*
> *. . .*
> *Your navel is a round bowl. . . .*
> *Your breasts are like twin fawns.*
> *(Song 7:2–4)*

The Song does not shy away from expressing physical desire:

> *Let him kiss me with the kisses of*
> *his mouth!*
> *More delightful is your love than*
> *wine!*
> *(Song 1:2)*
>
> *Your very figure is like a palm tree,*
> *your breasts are like clusters.*

> *I said: I will climb the palm tree,*
> *I will take hold of its branches.*
> *Now let your breasts be like clusters*
> *of the vine*
> *and the fragrance of your*
> *breath like apples.*
> *(Song 7:8–9)*

Through the centuries, many Jews have interpreted the Song of Songs as a symbolic poem representing God's love of Israel, and many Christians have interpreted it as representing Christ's love for the Church. Within its context in the whole Bible, where the marital relationship is often used as a symbol for God's relationship with God's people, this is certainly one legitimate understanding.

But this interpretation should not negate the obvious meaning: a very human celebration of sexual attraction and love. Those who put the books of the Bible together saw no contradiction between the two meanings.

Sexuality as Symbolic of God's Relation with God's People

In the prophetic writings, the Lord is portrayed as the husband of Israel; thus, Israel's worship of other gods is portrayed as adultery (see Hos, ch. 1–3; Jer 3:1–13; Ez, ch. 16, 23).

Comparing the relationship between husband and wife with the love between Christ and the Church, Paul quotes Genesis 2:24: "For this reason a man shall leave [his] father and [his] mother / and be joined to his wife, / and the two shall become one flesh." Paul comments, "This is a great mystery, but I speak in reference to Christ and the church" (Eph 5:31–32). Again, this passage suggests a connection between the intimacy of sexual union and the intimacy of the divine-human relationship of love.

Becoming One in a Sexual Relationship

The Genesis Creation story ends with a reflection on the relationship between man and woman: "That is why a man leaves his father and mother and clings to his wife, and the two of them become one body. The man and his wife were both naked, yet they felt no shame" (2:24–25). Again, we see the holistic biblical view: The relationship between husband and wife makes them "one" at many different levels, including the "oneness" of sexual intercourse.

Jesus refers back to Genesis 1:27 ("God made them male and female") and 2:24 in his teaching on marriage and divorce. Because the two have become one by joining their lives in marriage and their bodies in sexual union, the two cannot be separated by divorce (see the "Marriage" article). "What God has joined together, no human being must separate" (Mk 10:1–12).

The biblical assumption is that sexual union will occur within a committed relationship only. If a young woman was found to not be a virgin before her marriage, she was to be stoned to death (see Dt 22:13–21). Both man and woman in an adulterous relationship were to be stoned (see v. 22).

Paul also refers to Genesis 2:24 in his teaching on sexual relations. In condemning prostitution, he comments: "[Or] do you not know that anyone who joins himself to a prostitute becomes one body with her? For 'the two,' it says, 'will become one flesh'" (1 Cor 6:16). Paul explains further, "Every other sin a person commits is outside the body, but the immoral person sins

against his own body" (v. 18). The great sin of uncommitted sex is that it denies the natural meaning of sexual intercourse—the deep unity between two people.

In its holistic view, the Bible teaches that the union of sexual intercourse cannot be separated from a spiritual and emotional union. Even if a couple agrees to a one-night stand with no commitment, they are lying to each other with their bodies. The body has its own language, as Pope John Paul II taught, and the physical union of sexual intercourse means that a couple has joined themselves in a trusting, intimate bond. If they deny the natural meaning of this action, the natural result can only be hurt feelings, confusion, and hardened hearts.

The Biblical View of Homosexuality

Our society today is more and more accepting of homosexual relations as a legitimate way for a same-sex couple to express their love for each other. Though we cannot do full justice to this sensitive issue in this brief article, we can briefly sum up the overall biblical attitude toward homosexual relations.

The purity laws in Leviticus condemn homosexual activity: "You shall not lie with a male as with a woman; such a thing is an abomination" (Lv 18:22), even prescribing the death penalty for this action (see 20:13). The Bible gives no reason for this condemnation; it is likely that homosexuality was seen as a blurring of the boundaries between male and female, and thus as "unclean" (see the "Purity" article).

The key New Testament passage on homosexuality is Romans 1:26–28. Paul argues that although all people (including Gentiles) can have true knowledge about God from nature, many have turned away from this knowledge. Paul sees homosexual relations as a result of ignoring God's will as it is revealed in nature, because our physical sexuality is a sign of God's intention that sexual union should be between male and female. Paul's letters also have two further condemnations of homosexual behavior as sinful (see 1 Cor 6:9, 1 Tm 1:10).

Catholic teaching follows this biblical tradition by teaching that homosexual activity is contrary to God's will as seen in creation, and is therefore sinful. Unlike the Bible, however, Catholic teaching distinguishes between homosexual activity and a homosexual orientation. If a person is naturally sexually attracted to people of his or her own sex, this attraction, if it is not acted upon, is not sinful. But the Church still calls upon people with this same-sex attraction to remain celibate, even if this is difficult. People who have a homosexual orientation must be accepted with respect and compassion, yet the Church cannot accept homosexual actions, because they contradict God's natural order and lead to a confused sexuality.

Related Passages

Role of sexuality in God's creation: Gn 1:26–27, 2:18–25. *Praise of physical beauty and love:* Song of Songs. *Analogy of God's relationship with humans with marital relationship:* Jer 3:1–13; Ez, ch. 16, 23; Hos, ch. 1–3. *Analogy of Christ's relationship with the Church with marital relationship:* 1 Cor 6:12–20, Eph 5:21–32. *Jesus' teaching on marriage and divorce:* Mk 10:1–12. *Biblical view on homosexuality:* Lv 18:22, 20:13; Rom 1:26–28; 1 Cor 6:9–10; 1 Tm 1:10.

See Also

- "Human Nature"
- "Marriage"
- "Purity"
- "Resurrection"
- "Women"

Sheep, Goats, and Shepherds

Sheep and goats were essential to life in biblical Palestine. "The lambs will provide you with clothing, / and the goats will bring the price of a field. / And there will be ample goat's milk to supply you" (Prv 27:26–27).

Sheep and goats provided essential products, such as milk and cheese. Goat's hair was used in making tents, and the wool of the sheep was essential in making clothing. This wool was often bleached to a pure white, leading to the comparison "as white as wool" (Is 1:18, Dn 7:9, Rv 1:14).

The meat of a young goat was prepared for special occasions, such as entertaining a guest or for a special feast (see Jgs 6:19, Lk 15:29). For religious purposes, both sheep and goats were essential to the sacrificial system.

Shepherds

The youngest boy of a family often watched the sheep, as did David, the youngest son of Jesse (see 1 Sm 16:11). At times, however, girls also watched over sheep, as did Rachel (see Gn 29:9; see also Ex 2:16). (The name Rachel in Hebrew means "ewe," a female sheep.)

Shepherds led the sheep out to pasture, making sure that no sheep went astray and became lost. They also defended the sheep from wild animals or robbers. Shepherds often carried a bag filled with food; David used this bag to hold the stones with which he fought Goliath (see 1 Sm 17:40). Shepherds also carried a rod and a staff (see Ps 23:4). The rod was often made of hard wood such as oak, and could be used as a weapon to protect the sheep from wild animals. The same Hebrew word can also refer to a king's scepter (see Gn 49:10).

The shepherd's staff sometimes had a crook at the end of it. The shepherd could use it as a walking stick, as well as for handling the sheep. Such a staff was also commonly used by anyone, such as the elderly, who needed assistance in walking (see Zec 8:4).

Shepherds also used a slingshot to throw pebbles to catch the sheep's attention. David used his slingshot in his battle with Goliath (see 1 Sm 17:40).

In addition to finding good pastureland for the flock, shepherds also needed to find a reliable water source. Because sheep can be frightened by swiftly moving streams, the source must be relatively calm. Thus, the Psalmist compares the Lord to a good shepherd: "The LORD is my shepherd; / there is nothing I lack. / In green pastures you let me graze; / to safe waters you lead me" (Ps 23:1–2).

Shelters were sometimes built for the sheep on mountainous terrain or for protection against storms. Sometimes caves were used (see 1 Sm 24:4). Jesus describes a more elaborate structure: a space enclosed by stone walls with a gate guarded by a watchman: "The gatekeeper opens it for him, and the sheep hear his voice, as he calls his own sheep by name and leads them out" (Jn 10:3).

Flocks were often mixed together. Jacob saw three flocks huddled together at a well (see Gn 29:2). When the time came to separate the sheep, each shepherd made a distinctive call, and they followed him. "When he has driven out all his own, he walks ahead of them, and the sheep follow him, because they recognize his voice" (Jn 10:4).

Symbolism of the Sheep and Shepherd

The people of Israel are often portrayed as defenseless sheep, and the leaders of the people as shepherds. Isaiah says, "We had all gone astray like sheep, / each following his own way" (53:6).

Ezekiel condemns Israel's leaders for pasturing themselves, instead of acting as good shepherds by strengthening the weak, healing the sick, binding up the injured, and seeking the stray sheep (see Ez 34:2–4). The people without good rulers are like wandering sheep (see v. 5; Zec 10:2).

A common biblical image is of the Lord himself as the true shepherd of Israel (Ps 23:1: "The LORD is my shepherd"). Isaiah describes God's care for his people: "Like a shepherd he feeds his flock; / in his arms he gathers the lambs, / Carrying them in his bosom, / and leading the ewes with care" (40:11). Jesus compares God's joy over one repentant sinner with a shepherd's seeking a stray sheep: "And when he does find it, he sets it on his shoulders with great joy" and celebrates with friends and neighbors (Lk 15:4–7).

For large flocks, extra people would be hired to help watch the sheep. Jesus notes that a hired man may not truly care for the sheep and may run away when a wolf comes (see Jn 10:12–13). But the good shepherd will not abandon his flock. Jesus says: "I am the good shepherd. A good shepherd lays down his life for the sheep" (Jn 10:11). When

A common biblical image is of the Lord himself as the true shepherd, seeking out the lost sheep of Israel.

Jesus saw a vast crowd, "his heart was moved with pity for them, because they were like sheep without a shepherd, and he began to teach them many things" (Mk 6:34).

Use of Sheep in Worship

For some sacrifices, the Torah allowed the use of either a goat or a sheep (see Lv 1:10, Ex 12:5). Male lambs were used for thanksgiving offering, atonement, or redemption sacrifices; the Passover lamb was an especially important sacrifice (see Ex 12:1–5, Lv 23:12). Solomon was said to have sacrificed 120,000 sheep when he dedicated the Temple (see 1 Kgs 8:63).

Early Christians understood Jesus' death as an atoning sacrifice; because Jesus' death occurred at Passover, Paul refers to Jesus as the Passover lamb that was sacrificed (see 1 Cor 5:7). This same imagery explains John's reference to Jesus as the "Lamb of God" (1:36) and the references in Revelation to Jesus as

"a Lamb that seemed to have been slain" (5:6).

The prophet Isaiah describes God's suffering servant: "Like a lamb led to the slaughter / or a sheep before the shearers, / he was silent and opened not his mouth" (53:7). Luke applies this prophecy to Jesus (see Acts 8:32–35), perhaps thinking of how Jesus remained silent when questioned by the Roman governor Pontius Pilate (see Mt 27:11–14). First Peter also sees this passage as a symbol of Jesus' gentleness and willingness to suffer in silence (2:21–25).

Rams

A ram, an adult male sheep, was sacrificed on important occasions. A ram was sacrificed to marking the covenant between the Lord and Abraham (see Gn 15:9), to replace Isaac as a sacrifice (see 22:13), and on Pentecost (see Lv 23:18).

Rams' horns were also significant in biblical society. Samuel had a horn filled with olive oil that he used to anoint David as king (see 1 Sm 16:1). The ram's horn was also used as a kind of trumpet, the *shofar,* which was blown on the Day of Atonement to announce the Jubilee year (see Lv 25:9). When the priests blew on the rams' horns outside Jericho, the walls of the city collapsed (see Jos, ch. 6).

Goats

Goats were also offered as sacrifices, and goat's blood could even be brought into the Holy of Holies (see Lv 16:15). On the Day of Atonement, one goat was sacrificed. The priest confessed the sins of the people over the head of another goat, and the goat was then driven off into the wilderness (see vv. 20–28). This custom led to the English term *scapegoat*, referring to an innocent person who is blamed for the wrongs of another.

Goats' hair in Palestine is long and black and is spun and woven into a heavy cloth used to make tents (see Song 1:5). The covering over the Dwelling was made of goats' hair (see Ex 26:7). Bedouins in the Middle East still use goats' hair for their tents today.

Goats could also have a negative connotation in the biblical world. Goats are generally more troublesome for a shepherd than sheep. They are more difficult to control and more likely to stray into a farmer's fields. Because several male goats will mate with a flock (in contrast, only one ram typically mates with a flock of ewes), goats were also symbolic of sexual promiscuity. In ancient religions, goats were often associated with wild, unrestrained behavior (such as the Greek god Pan, who was half man and half goat).

Sheep and Goats on the Day of Judgment

In Jesus' parable of the Last Judgment, there is a separation of the sheep and goats. Those who are condemned are placed on the left hand of the Son of Man and are symbolized by goats; those who enter eternal life are on the right hand of the Son of Man, and are symbolized by sheep (see Mt 25:31–46).

In biblical cultures, the right hand is associated with honor and strength. Expressions referring to God's honor and power always refer to the right hand: "The LORD's right hand strikes with power" (Ps 118:15); the Messiah will be seated at the right hand of God (see 110:1). At the human level, the right hand also symbolizes honor and trustworthiness. The leaders of the Jerusalem Church gave Paul and Barnabas "their right hands in partnership" (Gal 2:9).

Biblical commentators offer different explanations for why sheep are separated from goats. Sometimes the animals are sheltered together but then separated for grazing, as sheep and goats do not graze well together. Ezekiel also refers to judgment as a separation between sheep (see 34:17–24).

As noted earlier, goats at times have negative connotations in biblical cultures—this connotation is clearly behind the association of goats with those who are condemned.

Related Passages

Sheep and shepherding in ordinary life: Gn 29:9, Prv 27:26–27, 1 Sm 16:11. *Goats on the Day of Atonement:* Lv, ch. 16. *God as shepherd:* Ps 23, Lk 15:4–7. *Leaders as shepherds, people as sheep:* Is 53:6; Ez, ch. 34; Zec, ch. 10–11. *Jesus as the Good Shepherd:* Jn 10:1–18, 1 Pt 2:21–25. *Passover lamb:* Ex 12:1–5. *Jesus and the imagery of the lamb:* Acts 8:32–35, 1 Cor 5:7, 1 Pt 2:21–25, Rev 5:6. *Judgment between sheep and goats:* Mt 25:31–46.

See Also

- "Agriculture"
- "Atonement"
- "Food and Drink"
- "Sacrifices and Offerings"

Sickness and Health

Biblical ideas concerning illness and disability cannot be separated from biblical concepts of holiness and purity. In this view of reality, illness and disability are associated with impurity, sin, death, division, and the profane. Health, on the other hand, is associated with purity, forgiveness of sin, life, wholeness, and holiness.

Major goals of the Israelite purity laws were to prevent contact of the impure with the holiness of the Temple and to cleanse the Temple from any impurity that it had suffered. Thus, any animal that was not "whole" could not be offered as a Temple sacrifice—the animal could have no defect (see, for example, Lv 4:3,28). A priest with any physical defect (for example, blindness or a crippled hand or foot) could not approach the altar (see Lv 21:17–23). A person with a skin disease had to live outside the community because this impurity would contaminate the holiness of the Temple as well as the holiness of the people (see 13:45–46).

Yet this does not imply that the physically disabled were simply cast out of Israelite society. In fact, mistreating those with disabilities was a itself a violation of holiness: "You shall not curse the deaf, or put a stumbling block in front of the blind, but you shall fear your God. I am the LORD" (19:14). A disabled priest was still allowed his share of eating the Temple sacrifices (see 21:22).

Causes of Illness: Natural and Supernatural Causes

What causes illness? In our culture today, we generally look for a natural cause. If we catch a cold or the flu, we know that it was caused by some kind of virus. When someone contracts cancer, medical science looks to why cancerous cells are reproducing themselves; at times we can point to a specific direct cause, such as the effects of smoking. But notice that at times even our culture looks for supernatural causes. When a close friend becomes seriously ill, we might ask: "Why did God allow this person to get sick at such a young age?" Or we comfort ourselves with the thought that everything happens for a reason, again assuming that illnesses have supernatural causes.

Some ancients did investigate the natural causes of disease. The Greek Hippocratic tradition is the most notable in the ancient Mediterranean world. Biblical societies, in contrast, focused almost exclusively on supernatural causes of illness. They typically attributed illness either to God or to demonic forces.

Some biblical statements attribute illness directly to God, "Come, let us return to the LORD, / For it is he who has rent, but he will heal us; / he has struck us, but he will bind our wounds" (Hos 6:1). "Who gives one man speech and makes another deaf and dumb? Or who gives sight to one and makes another go blind? Is it not I, the LORD?" (Ex 4:11). This view emphasizes that all events are ultimately under God's control because God is the all-powerful Creator.

A related belief is that illness is God's punishment of sin. According to the theology of many biblical writers, if the Israelites follow the laws of the Covenant, they will be blessed with good health; if they do not, they will be cursed with diseases (see Ex 15:26; Dt 7:15, 28:15–22). Jesus' disciples illustrate this widespread cultural assumption when they ask, "Rabbi, who sinned, this man or his parents, that he was born blind?" (Jn 9:2). Job's friends also assume that Job must have sinned to earn his suffering (see Jb 4:7).

In Jesus' time, the belief that disability and illness were caused by demonic forces was widespread. "And a woman was there who for eighteen years had been crippled by a spirit" (Lk 13:11). Jesus' own activity included many exorcisms, or driving out of demons. One spirit was a "mute and deaf" spirit (see Mk 9:25), another is an "unclean spirit" associated with a man who "was always crying out and bruising himself with stones" (5:5). The first-century Jewish writing called the Testament of Solomon connects specific demons with specific illnesses, such as headaches or eye diseases.

Finally, we should note the general belief that illness and death are simply the result of humanity's fall into sin. "God did not make death, / nor does he rejoice in the destruction of the living" (Wis 1:13). Illness, disability, and death are not part of God's original plan for humans, as Genesis, chapters 1–2, shows us. These negative conditions arose only after the first sin of Adam and Eve—they are the distortion of an originally good creation. In the eschatological age, all suffering will cease: "There shall be no more death or mourning, wailing or pain, [for] the old order has passed away" (Rv 21:4).

Healers in Biblical Society

As we noted, Israelite society, with its focus on supernatural causes of illness, did not develop traditions of natural medicine like the Hippocratic tradition. Physicians, however, were known

in Israel and in the early Christian communities (see 2 Chr 16:12, Mk 5:26). Midwives were also well established (see Ex 1:15–22).

Israel focused on what we may call charismatic healers—those who healed with supernatural power. Prophets are associated with healing. Elisha, for example, heals Naaman of his skin disease (see 2 Kgs, ch. 5). Isaiah is connected with King Hezekiah's healing (see Is, ch. 38). Hanina ben Dosa, a rabbi who lived around the time of Jesus, was known as a charismatic healer. Josephus refers to the secret healing knowledge possessed by the Essenes.

Jesus and his followers were charismatic healers as well: healing various illnesses, casting out demons, and even raising the dead, relying on touch, verbal commands, and the faith of the sick person only (see Mk 6:13; Acts 3:1–10, 8:7, 9:32–43, 20:7–12). Paul speaks of the supernatural gift of healing possessed by some members of his church (see 1 Cor 12:9,28,30). In James the elders (presbyters) of the church have a charismatic healing power (see 5:14–15).

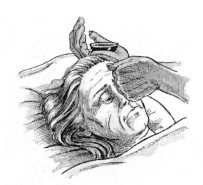

In the early Christian church, the presbyters prayed for the sick, anointing them with oil in the name of the Lord.

Holistic Healing

The Book of Sirach combines faith in God's healing power with trust in human medicinal skill. "My son, when you are ill, delay not, / but pray to God, who will heal you. / . . . Then give the doctor his place / lest he leave; for you need him too" (38:9–12). In Sirach's view, God established the physician's profession and gave the doctor his wisdom (see vv. 1–2).

We see this combination of natural and supernatural healing elsewhere. The Lord promises to heal Hezekiah in response to his prayers (see Is 38:5), but Isaiah also orders "a poultice of figs to be taken and applied to the boil, that he might recover" (v. 21). Jesus' disciples use olive oil in their healings (see Mk 6:13, Jas 5:14). Olive oil was well known in ancient times as a medicine. It is possible that Jesus' use of saliva is connected with the ancient belief in the healing properties of saliva (see Mk 7:33, 8:23; Jn 9:6).

Challenges to the View That Illness Is Caused by Sin

The view that illness is God's direct punishment of sin is questioned in the Book of Job. Job denies that his illness and related suffering are due to his sins: "God has dealt unfairly with me. / . . . I cry out 'Injustice!' I am not heard" (19:6–7). Even though Job eventually repents of his accusations and admits that final answers are beyond him (see 42:1–6), his story still serves as a powerful challenge to overly simplistic explanations of human suffering.

Jesus himself denies that suffering is a direct punishment of sin. Those who suffer oppression or accident are no worse sinners than those who do not (see Lk 13:1–5). A man was born blind not because of his own sins or the sins of his parents, but rather so that "the works of God might be made visible through him" (Jn 9:3).

Though Jesus denies a direct relationship of cause and effect between sin and illness, he assumes there is a relationship. When a paralyzed man is brought to him for healing, Jesus says, "Courage, child, your sins are forgiven" (Mt 9:2) and then heals the man physically. In the Letter of James, the physical healing of a person is closely connected with forgiveness of sin: "Confess your sins to one another and pray for one another, that you may be healed" (5:14–16).

Healing and Salvation

When questioned whether he was the Messiah who would bring in the eschatological age, Jesus responded with a list of signs that featured his healings prominently: "The blind regain their sight, the lame walk, lepers are cleansed, the deaf hear, the dead are raised" (Mt 11:5). Jesus' healings in this world were a sign of the ultimate healing brought about by the Kingdom of God, inaugurated with the coming of Christ, where "there shall me no more death or mourning, wailing or pain, [for] the old order has passed away" (Rv 21:4).

Related Passages

Holiness, purity, and disability: Lv 13:45–46, 19:14, 21:17–23. *God as the ultimate cause of illness and health:* Ex 4:11, Hos 6:1. *Illness as punishment for sin:* Dt 28:15–22, Jb 4:7, Jn 9:2. *Demons as the cause of illness:* Mk 5:1–20, 9:14–32; Lk 13:10–17.

References to physicians: 2 Chr 16:12, Mk 5:26. *Charismatic healing:* 2 Kgs, ch. 5; Mk 6:13; Acts 3:1–10; 1 Cor 12:9,28,30. *Holistic healing:* Sir 38:1–5. *Challenges to the direct connection between illness and sin:* Jb 19:6–7, Mt 9:1–8, Lk 13:1–5, Jn 9:1–3. *General connection of illness and sin:* Mt 9:2–8, Jas 5:14–16. *Healing and salvation:* Mt 11:5, Jas 5:14–18, Rv 21:4.

See Also

- "Covenant"
- "Holiness"
- "Purity"
- "Sacrifices and Offerings"
- "Sin"
- "Temple"

Sin

Most people today would define the word *sin* in either one or both of the following ways: (1) as an offense against God or a violation of God's law, and (2) as an action an individual knows is wrong but chooses to do anyway. We find both views in Scripture, along with a rich variety of other views that both complement and challenge one another. Views on sin changed and developed over the centuries.

Old Testament Concepts of Sin

In the Old Testament, the Hebrew word most commonly translated as "sin" is *het*. Its most basic meaning is "to miss the mark, to go astray from the right path." It often means failing to do one's social duty to another person. King Hezekiah uses the word when he fails to pay tribute to the Assyrian king: "I have done wrong" (2 Kgs 18:14). Reuben uses the word to chastise his brothers for selling Joseph into slavery: "Didn't I tell you . . . not to do wrong to [to sin against] the boy?" (Gn 42:22). If a person steals from or lies to a neighbor, he sins (see Lv 5:1,20–26).

This word also applies to missing out on one's duty to God. The Lord tells Joshua, "Israel has sinned: they have violated the covenant which I enjoined on them" (Jos 7:11).

Sin is also closely associated with the purity laws. If a Nazarite (a person who makes a special vow to dedicate him or herself to God) comes into contact with a dead body, he or she "sins" (see Nm 6:9–11). To purify herself from uncleanness after childbirth, a woman should offer a sin offering (see Lv 12:6). A person who unintentionally violates God's commandment still sins (see 5:17, Nm 15:22–29).

The basic concept in the Old Testament is that any violation of the Torah is a sin, even if it was done unintentionally, and even if it involved a strictly natural process, such as giving birth to a child.

Sin seems to be understood as almost a physical presence that causes people and things to become unclean. The sin of touching a dead body "defiles the Dwelling of the Lord"; if the unclean person has not been ritually purified, "his uncleanness still clings to him" (Nm 19:13). The physical application of the blood of the sacrificed animal was necessary to cleanse the defiled altar; the physical application of special water was necessary to cleanse the person (see Lv 4:30, Nm 19:12).

Paul's Teaching and Original Sin

Paul's teaching that "just as through one person sin entered the world, and through sin, death, and thus death came to all, inasmuch as all sinned" (Rom 5:12) forms the basis for the Christian understanding of Original Sin. There is much confusion on this topic, so we need to consider carefully what Paul says here.

Sin entered the world through one person—Adam. In Paul's thought, Adam simply represents all humans—the story of Adam and Eve symbolizes how all humans make the choice to sin—"inasmuch as all sinned." This choice to sin, this "missing the mark" in one's relationship with God and others, results in an existence that is marked by sickness, suffering, and ultimately death. Paul conceives of sin as a kind of a power that has distorted human nature: all people are "under the domination of sin" (Rom 3:9); sin is a negative power that "dwells in me" (7:17).

The Christian teaching that a baby is born with Original Sin does not mean that babies are personally sinful—after all, a baby simply does not have the cognitive or physical ability to know that an action is wrong and yet do it anyway. The point is rather that the baby is born with a human nature that has been distorted by sin. As the child grows up, he or she, at some point, will inevitably be drawn toward negative or destructive behaviors—our very human nature has become distorted by the power of sin.

The Power of Sin and Need for Atonement

One theme uniting the diverse senses of sin in Old and New Testaments is the power of sin and the inability of a person to overcome that power on her own. In the Old Testament, sin is a quasi-physical power that clings to objects and requires the intervention of a blood sacrifice in order to cleanse it. In Paul's thought, sin is a power that almost takes on a life of its own within the individual person. The person is powerless to free herself or himself from the domination of sin. It is only through uniting herself or himself to the atoning death of Christ that the "slavery to sin" might be overcome (see Rom 6:1–11). So just as the sacrifice of an animal may have substituted for a person's own death as payment for sin (see the "Sacrifices and Offerings" article), so too uniting oneself with Christ's death in Baptism (see Rom 6:3–4) is an alternative way of offering one's own life in payment for sin.

Sin in Honor-Shame Societies

From a social scientific perspective, sin can be defined as missing the mark by failing to meet culturally expected duties towards another person. In Israel these cultural expectations are enshrined in the Torah. In an honor-shame society, to sin against another person involves shaming that person.

In Jesus' parable of the prodigal son, a son breaks social expectations by demanding his share of his father's inheritance while the father is still alive—in effect saying that he wished his father was dead (see Lk 15:11–12). After squandering his inheritance, he finally repents and returns to his father, saying, "Father, I have sinned against heaven and against you" (v. 18). As a consequence of his sin, he expects to be shamed by having his social status lowered: "I no longer deserve to be called your son; treat me as you would treat one of your hired workers" (v. 19). The

127

father, however, also breaks social expectations by welcoming him back as a son, choosing not to regain his own social status (honor) by punishing his son.

Sin as a Debt

In the Lord's Prayer, Jesus teaches his disciples to pray "Forgive us our debts, / as we forgive our debtors" (Mt 6:12); Luke's version reads "Forgive us our sins / as for we ourselves forgive everyone in debt to us" (11:4). The cultural metaphor thus imagines sin as a debt or obligation owed to God: God is perhaps imagined as a patron to whom the client is deeply in debt. The debt or obligation is so large or difficult that it cannot be paid or fulfilled; thus, the only solution is to ask the patron to forgive the debt. This understanding is reflected in Jesus' parable of a servant whose huge debt is forgiven by the master until the servant himself refuses to forgive a fellow servant (see Mt 18:23–35).

Jesus' point seems to be that a person's obligations to God are so great that he or she must rely on God's forgiveness only. But God's forgiveness is contingent on the person's own treatment of other people—if the person is willing to overlook the money or obligations owed by his or her own client, then God too is willing to overlook the debt.

Developing Beliefs Regarding the Consequences of Sin

As with many cultural beliefs, biblical ideas on the consequences of sin changed and developed over time. In the Ten Commandments, we read, "For I, the LORD, your God, am a jealous God, inflicting punishment for their fathers' wickedness on the children of those who hate me, down to the third and fourth generation" (Ex 20:5). The passage clearly reflects a group-oriented perspective—the individual identity of the child is so closely tied with the family group that the child naturally shares in the punishment of the father's sin. Later biblical texts reject this group-oriented view in favor of individual responsibility: "The son shall not be charged with the guilt of his father, nor shall the father be charged with the guilt of his son" (Ez 18:20).

The cultural view that disease or disability is a direct punishment for sin (see Dt 28:15–22, Jn 9:2) is challenged in the Book of Job and in Jesus' teaching (see Lk 13:1–5, Jn 9:3; see also the "Sickness and Health" article).

Related Passages

Sin as failing a social duty to another: 2 Kgs 18:14. *Sin as failing a duty to God:* Jos 7:11. *Sin as impurity:* Lv, ch. 12. *Unintentional sin:* Lv 5:17. *Quasi-physical nature of sin:* Nm 19:13. *Blood as atoning:* Lv 17:11. *Effect of Adam's sin:* Rom 5:12–14. *Power of sin:* Rom 3:9, 7:17. *Freedom from sin and dying with Christ:* Rom 6:1–11. *Parable of the prodigal son (sin as shaming):* Lk 15:11–32. *The Lord's Prayer (sin as debt):* Mt 6:9–15, Lk 11:2–4. *Parable of the unforgiving servant:* Mt 18:23–35. *Sin and group-oriented perspective:* Ex 20:5; Ez, ch. 18.

See Also

- "Atonement"
- "Family"
- "Honor and Shame"
- "Human Nature"
- "Sacrifices and Offerings"
- "Sickness and Health"
- "Taxes and Tithes"

Slavery

In the ancient Mediterranean world, virtually all societies had slaves. Greeks and Romans had slaves, as did Babylonians and Egyptians. Slavery was simply accepted as a natural and normal part of everyday life.

Today we take it for granted that all people are created equal. But people in ancient world had the opposite assumption. Greek and Roman philosophers, for example, taught that because some people are naturally not very intelligent or responsible, nature had made them to be slaves.

Prisoners captured in war and debtors who could not pay off debts were two common sources of slaves. In the ancient Near East in general, slaves were understood as their master's property and had few or no human rights. They were often branded, for example, to identify whom they belonged to.

Slavery in the Old Testament

Israelites owned both Israelite and non-Israelite slaves. Most often the Israelites were enslaved because they could not pay their debts. In such a situation, a man would either sell himself or his wife and children as slaves (see Neh 5:5). One of Jesus' parables relates, "Since he had no way of paying it back, his master ordered him to be sold, along with his wife, his children, and all his property, in payment of the debt" (Mt 18:25).

The great patriarchs of Israelite history, such as Abraham (see Gn 12:16), Isaac (see 24:35), and Jacob (see 32:6), owned slaves. Even the Judeans returning from the Babylonian Exile owned slaves (see Ezr 2:64–65).

Slaves in Israel were regarded as property. Consider the following rule: "When a man strikes his male or female slave with a rod so hard that the slave dies under his hand, he shall be punished. If, however, the slave survives for a day or two, he is not to be punished, since the slave is his own property" (Ex 21:20–21).

Slaves are often listed as part of a person's property. Abraham "received flocks and herds, male and female slaves, male and female asses, and camels" (Gn 12:16; see also 24:35).

There was some recognition of human rights, however. If a master "knocks out a tooth of his male or female slave, he shall let the slave go free in compensation for the tooth" (Ex 21:27). All slaves, including foreign-born slaves, were to be circumcised, as a sign that they too were part of the people's Covenant with God (see Gn 17:12–13); they could even share in the Passover meal (see Ex 12:44). Slaves did not have to work on the Sabbath (see Dt 5:14). The humane treatment of slaves is frequently justified by recalling the Hebrews' own experience of slavery: "Your male and female slave should rest as you do. For remember that you too were once slaves in Egypt, and the LORD, your God, brought you from there with his strong hand and outstretched arm" (vv. 14–15).

An Israelite male slave would be set free after six years (see Ex 21:2). The Book of Leviticus goes further, arguing that Israelites should not be considered slaves at all, only hired workers, for God had said, "Since those whom I brought out of the land of Egypt are servants of mine, they shall not be sold as slaves to any man" (Lv 25:42; see also Dt 15:12–15).

Slavery in Greco-Roman Times

Though slavery did exist in ancient Israelite society, it was not essential to Israelite economics. In contrast, ancient Greco-Roman economies were based on slavery. In large cities, up to a third of the population was slaves.

Yet slavery in ancient Greco-Roman societies was quite different from the slavery that was practiced in the United States until the nineteenth century. First, it was in no way based on race. In addition, certain slaves were highly educated and played important roles in managing the household or business affairs of their masters. We see this in one of Jesus' parables:

> Who, then, is the faithful and prudent servant, whom the master has put in charge of his household to distribute to them their food at the proper time? Blessed is that servant whom his master on his arrival finds doing so. Amen, I say to you, he will put him in charge of all his property. (Mt 24:45–47)

The Greek word translated as "servant" in this passage is *doulos*. It is probably better translated as "slave," because a *doulos* was regarded as the property of his master.

The status of slave was usually not a lifelong status; many slaves were freed when they became older. A freed slave in the Roman Empire generally was given Roman citizenship.

Many slaves, however, were forced to work in brutal and dehumanizing conditions in agricultural work or in mines. Others were forced to work in the Roman galleys or to "entertain" Romans by fighting to death as gladiators.

According to the Roman poet Juvenal, a Roman matron justified her decision to crucify a slave with the words: "This is my will and my command. If you are looking for a reason, it is simply that I want it." According to another Roman poet, Horace, one master had his slave crucified for tasting the soup while bringing it from the kitchen.

In addition to prisoners of war and debtors unable to pay their debts, children born to slave women were also a significant source of slaves (see Mt 18:25).

Acceptance of Slavery

Just as slaves in Hebrew society were regarded as part of the household (and thus were circumcised and shared in meals such as the Passover meal), so too Greco-Roman slaves were considered part of the extended household.

It is very likely that when a master became a Christian, his or her slaves also became Christian. After Lydia was convinced by Paul's preaching, "she and her household" were baptized (Acts 16:15). Paul and Silas tell the Philippian jailer, "Believe in the Lord Jesus and you and your household will be saved" (16:31).

Early Christians took slavery for granted as a normal institution of society. No early Christian advocated abolishing slavery but merely advised that slaves obey their masters and that masters treat their slaves well. The Pauline tradition taught, "Slaves be obedient to your human masters with fear and trembling, in sincerity of heart, as to Christ" (Eph 6:5). Slaves should be obedient even to cruel masters:

> Slaves, be subject to your masters with all reverence, not only to those who are good and equitable but also to those who are perverse. For whenever anyone bears the

pain of unjust suffering because of consciousness of God, that is a grace. (1 Pt 2:18–19)

Christian masters also had obligations: "Masters, act in the same way toward them, and stop bullying, knowing that both they and you have a Master in heaven and that with him there is no partiality" (Eph 6:9; see also Col 4:1). These passages from Ephesians and Colossians are part of what are sometimes called household codes, which lay out rules for how husbands and wives, parents and children, and masters and slaves within a household should relate to each other. Husbands, parents, and masters are clearly the leaders, but they should lead in a fair and considerate way. Wives, children, and slaves should accept the authority of their leaders. In the honor-shame–based biblical societies, adhering to these assigned social roles brought honor to the household.

Biblically-Based Criticism of Slavery

Like all ancient Christians, the Apostle Paul did not call for abolishing slavery. Yet in his letters, Paul insists that Christians who are free and those who are slaves are not essentially different.

Paul's Letter to Philemon deals with a slave, Onesimus, who apparently had escaped from his master Philemon and had come to stay with Paul. Paul sends him back to Philemon, but urges Philemon to receive Onesimus back "no longer as a slave but more than a slave, a brother, beloved especially to me, but even more so to you, as a man and in the Lord" (Phlm, v. 16).

Paul also insists, "For the slave called in the Lord is a freed person in the Lord, just as the free person who has been called is a slave of Christ" (1 Cor 7:22). Paul calls himself a "slave of Christ Jesus" (Rom 1:1, Phil 1:1). In a famous passage Paul describes the Christian community in this way: "There is neither Jew nor Greek, there is neither slave nor free person, there is not male or female; for you are all one in Christ Jesus" (Gal 3:28).

Paul did not take what to us would seem to be the next logical step: if all people are equal in Christ, and if slaves should be treated not as slaves but as brothers, and if a slave called in Christ is truly a free person, then it makes sense that slavery as an institution is evil and should be abolished. But Paul did not take this step, no doubt because slavery simply seemed so natural to his culture.

But when later Christians did in fact declare that slavery itself is evil, and that no person has the right to own another, they used biblical teachings to justify this step. They could refer to Paul's teachings, or to the original teaching of Genesis that all people (including slaves) were created in the image of God (see 1:26–27).

Slavery as an institution nearly disappeared in Europe in the early centuries after Christianity began. When the slave trade was revived after the European discovery of the Americas, the Catholic Church rather quickly stated its opposition. In 1527 Pope Paul III officially pronounced that no Indian in the Americas should be enslaved; statements by popes in the 1600s also insisted that no Indians or blacks should be enslaved.

Related Passages

Prevalence of slavery in the Old Testament: Gn 12:16, 24:35, 32:6; Ezr 2:64–65.; *Torah on the limited rights of slaves:* Ex 21:1–11,20–21; Dt 5:14–16, 15:12–18. *Household slaves:*

Dt 5:14, Mt 24:45–51. *Debt slavery:* Neh 5:5, Mt 18:25. *Household codes on slavery:* Eph 6:5–9, Col 3:22—4:1, Philemon, 1 Pt 2:18–25. *Paul's view on slavery and freedom:* 1 Cor 7:22, Gal 3:28, Philemon.

See Also

- "Family"
- "Honor and Shame"
- "Poverty and Wealth"

Spiritual Powers

Popular television shows and movies portray angels as people who have died and are now angels in heaven. The Bible, however, never portrays angels as humans who have died; rather, they are understood as spiritual powers who are intermediaries between the earthly realm and the spiritual realm.

Imagining Angels

Because angels are invisible spiritual powers, the Bible often uses concrete images to imagine them. They are pictured with wings (see Is 6:2), or as taking on human form (see Dn 8:15–17). Because every culture imagines spiritual realities in terms familiar to that culture, God is often pictured in biblical cultures as a king on this throne, surrounded by spiritual powers that form a court or council. God is also imaged as a military commander and the angels as his armies.

God's Heavenly Council

Just as a Near Eastern king would be surrounded by his advisors, assistants, or military officers, so too the Bible pictures the Lord on his heavenly throne as surrounded by a heavenly council or court. This image was common in other Near Eastern religions as well: Canaanites also imagined the high god El surrounded by his divine court: it is in fact likely that the biblical authors originally borrowed this image from the Canaanites.

Members of the heavenly court are known by a variety of names: "the assembly of the holy ones" (Ps 89:6), "the sons of God" (Jb 1:6), "heavenly beings" (Ps 29:1) and even "gods" (*elohim*; Ps 82:1; 89:7)—"gods" in the sense of divine beings. In Psalm 82, the divine council is composed of the gods of the other nations: God convicts them of neglecting the rights of the poor and needy, and demotes them to the status of mortals.

In Isaiah's vision, God's throne is surrounded by winged creatures known as "seraphim" (see 6:1–2). Daniel sees that "thousands upon thousands were ministering to him, / and myriads upon myriads attended him" (7:10). In Revelation, God's court is composed of twenty-four elders, crowned and dressed in white (see 4:4).

Four Living Creatures, Cherubim, and Archangels

A variation of the heavenly council image depicts God's throne surrounded by four living creatures. The classic description of the creatures is found in Ezekiel, chapter 1. The prophet describes the four creatures as human in form, but each with four wings and four faces: that of a man, a lion, an ox, and an eagle (later Christian tradition associated each of the creatures with one of the four Gospel writers). John's vision in

Revelation 4:6–9 combines elements of Ezekiel's four creatures with characteristics of the seraphim from Isaiah's vision (see 6:2–4).

These four creatures are identified with the cherubim associated with the Jerusalem Temple (see Ez 10:20–22). The cherubim are familiar in much Near Eastern art and mythology. They are divine figures, made up of a combination of various human and animal parts. Cherubim are portrayed on both ends of the lid of the Ark of the Covenant, the place where God's presence was believed to rest (see Ex 25:17–22, 37:7–9). Images of cherubim were also woven into the curtain of the Holy of Holies (see Ex 26:1; see also 1 Kgs 6:29).

The cherubim are thus pictured as divine beings supporting the throne of the Lord (the Ark, as the resting place of God, is closely identified with God's throne): "your throne upon the cherubim" (Ps 80:2). In biblical cultures, the number four is associated with completeness (see the "Number Symbolism" article). Ezekiel's image implies that all spiritual powers support, and are subordinate to, the Lord.

The four creatures are apparently the basis for later traditions' identifying four archangels who are in God's presence. Qumran, Second Temple, and rabbinic sources speak of four angels before God's throne. Three are consistently identified as Michael, Gabriel, and Raphael; the fourth name varies (Sariel, Phanuel, Uriel). Other sources sometimes speak of seven angels before God's throne (see Tb 12:15; see also the reference to "seven spirits" before God's throne in Rv 1:7, 4:5). Seven, like four, signifies completeness.

Only Gabriel (see Dn, ch. 8–9; Lk, ch. 1), Michael (see Dn, ch. 10, 12; Jude; Rv, ch. 12), and Raphael (only in Tobit) are mentioned directly in the Bible.

The Hosts

Angels are often understood as a heavenly army. The title Lord of Hosts (*Sabbaoth,* in Hebrew), which occurs 285 times in the Bible (for example, Zec 8:1, Jas 5:4) means "Lord of the armies." Joshua encounters an angel with a sword, who tells him, "I am the captain of the host of the Lord" (Jos 5:14). We see occasional glimpses of this army: "a flaming chariot and flaming horses" carry Elijah to heaven (2 Kgs 2:11), and spiritual horses and "fiery chariots" protect Elisha (6:17). One function of the heavenly army is to patrol the earth and report back to the Lord (see Zec 6:1–8). Jesus uses a Roman military term in referring to "legions of angels" (Mt 26:53).

The stars were sometimes identified with the heavenly host of angels, as it was a common assumption in the ancient world that stars were living beings (see Neh 9:6, Ps 33:6). Judges reports, "From the heavens the stars, too, fought" (5:20). A star falling from the sky to the earth is identified as an angel (see Rv 9:1).

Stars are also associated with spiritual forces opposed to God. Jude alludes to rebellious stars who are punished (see v. 13). Isaiah records that on "that day the Lord will punish / the host of the heavens" (24:21).

Spiritual Powers' Ruling the Nations

Just as the Lord had a special relationship with the people of Israel, so too the Bible often associates each nation with a certain spiritual power (see Dt 32:8–9, especially the Septuagint version; see also Ps 82). Daniel refers to spiritual representatives of Persia (the "prince of the kingdom of Persia"; see 10:13) and of Greece (see 10:20). The archangel Michael is said to be the great prince, the guardian of the Jewish nation (see Dn 12:1).

In apocalyptic visions, political power and spiritual power are closely identified. In Daniel the political and military power of empires is symbolized by beasts that rise from the sea but whose power and authority are determined by events in the heavenly court (see 7:1–12). In Revelation the power of the Roman Empire is closely associated with the power of Satan (represented by a dragon; see Rv 13:1–4).

Biblical terms such as *principalities, powers,* and *authorities* (see 1 Cor 15:24, Eph 1:21, Col 1:16, 1 Pt 3:22) also reflect the belief in spiritual powers closely associated with human rulers.

In general, these conceptions form part of the biblical belief that events on earth are a reflection of heavenly events. The slaying of a beast in the heavenly court (see Dn 7:11) indicates that the power of corresponding earthly empire is at an end.

What Angels Do

The primary role of the biblical angel is as God's messenger. The basic meaning of the biblical words most commonly translated as "angel" (*malach,* in Hebrew; *aggelos,* in Greek) is "messenger." The angel Gabriel announces to Mary that she will give birth (see Lk 1:26–38; see also Gn 16:7–12), and an angel announces the actual birth to the shepherds (see Lk 2:9–14). An angel warns Abraham not to sacrifice his son (see Gn 22:11–12).

The message may also be in the form of a vision. God sends his angel to reveal to John the prophecies of Revelation (see Rv 1:1). If the vision requires an interpretation, angels provide that as well (see Dn 8:15–26; see also Zec 1:9).

Besides bringing God's messages, angels also carry out God's will. An angel leads the Israelites through the wilderness (see Ex 14:19). At the Last Judgment, angels will separate the righteous from evildoers (see Mt 13:39–42). When angels blow trumpets (see Rv 8:2) or pour out bowls (see 16:1), God's punishments are released on earth.

At times the "angel of the Lord" is so closely identified with God that it is difficult to distinguish between the two (see Gn 16:7–13, Ex 3:1–5). In these cases, apparently, the biblical authors are trying to communicate two beliefs: (1) that God truly is in communication and contact with his people, and (2) that God is so holy that humans cannot come into *direct* contact with God; the contact must be mediated through an angel.

Angels also present prayers before God. The archangel Raphael tells Tobit and Sarah that it was "I who presented and read the record of your prayer before the Glory of the Lord" (Tb 12:12). In Revelation an angel offers "the prayers of all the holy ones" at a heavenly altar (8:3–4).

In a related sense, angels serve as advocates for people on earth. One belief is that each person has a "guardian angel" who intercedes for them in heaven. Jesus refers to the angels of the "little ones" who "always look upon the face of my heavenly father" (Mt 18:10; see Jb 33:23–26).

Angels praise God. The seraphim cry out, "Holy, holy, holy is the LORD of hosts!" (Is 6:3). At the birth of Christ, a multitude of the heavenly host praise

God, saying, "Glory to God in the highest" (Lk 2:14). In the Catholic understanding, when we worship God in Mass, we join our praise to that of the angels.

Evil Spiritual Powers

The Bible has various terms for evil spiritual powers: "the devil and his angels" (Mt 25:41); evil or unclean spirits (see Mk 3:11), and demons (see Lk 8:2). Occasionally the evil spirits are associated with illnesses or disabilities (Mk 9:25: a "mute and deaf spirit"), but other times a clear differentiation is made between illnesses and demon possession: "They drove out many demons, and they anointed with oil many who were sick and cured them" (6:13).

The belief was that an evil spirit took complete possession of a person. When Jesus interacts with those possessed by a demon, he addresses the demon only (see Mk 1:23–25). Demons are associated with the gods worshiped by other nations (see 1 Cor 10:14–22). The name Beelzebul, used for Satan, is a variation on one of the titles of the Canaanite god Baal. Satan is the "prince of demons" (Mk 3:22–23).

The concept of evil spirits opposed to God seems to have arisen only during Second Temple times. Many scholars attribute this development to the influence of Persian religious beliefs on Jews after the time of the Babylonian Exile.

The Hebrew verb *satan* means basically "to accuse," and at first a *satan* served as a sort of prosecuting attorney in God's divine council. In one of Zechariah's visions, he is shown "Joshua the high priest standing before the angel of the LORD, while Satan stood at his right hand to accuse him" (Zec 3:1). Satan has this same function in Job, where he appears with the "sons of God" in the divine council in order to accuse Job of having a weak faith in the Lord (see Jb 1:6–11; see also 1 Chr 21:1). It is only in Second Temple literature and the in New Testament that we find the developed idea of Satan and his evil angels fighting a spiritual warfare against God and his angels.

The common Christian belief that Satan was originally a good angel who rebelled against God is not found directly in the Bible. The account is found in Second Temple works, such as *Life of Adam and Eve.* This story is reflected in Revelation, however, when Michael and his angels battle the dragon and his angels, and the dragon (identified as the devil) and his allies are cast out of heaven (see Rv 12:7–9; see also Is 14:12–21, Lk 10:18).

Demonic Powers Today

In our world today, we usually hear little about demons or demonic possession. Some people think the belief in demons is part of an outdated view of the world. Now that we have scientific explanations for physical or mental illnesses, according to this view, we no longer have to attribute such occurrences to demons.

There is some truth to this view. As noted in the "Sickness and Health" article, biblical societies generally had little grasp of natural causes of disease, thus attributing them to spiritual powers. What the Bible describes as demonic possession, we today might describe as a natural physical or mental illness.

Yet the Catholic Church continues to teach that evil spirits do in fact exist. Their influence in the vast majority of cases, however, is quite subtle, and cannot easily be distinguished from natural causes. Yet when we consider the depths of evil to which humans often sink (think of the Nazi death camps or the twisted mind of a sadistic serial killer), it is hard to simply attribute such evil to natural causes. It seems that in such cases, a person or a group of people have, through their own choices, opened themselves to the influence of demonic forces.

Related Passages

Visions of the God enthroned and the heavenly court: 1 Kgs 22:19–23; Ps 82; Is, ch. 6; Ez, ch. 1; Dn, ch. 7; Rv, ch. 4. *Cherubim:* Ex 25:17–22, Ez 10:20–22. *Archangels:* Tobit; Dn, ch. 8–10; 1 Thes 4:16; Rv, ch. 12. *Angelic armies:* Jos 5:14, Mt 26:53. *Stars as spiritual powers:* Jude, v. 13; Rv 9:1. *Spiritual powers and nations:* Dt 32:8–9; Ps 82; Dn, ch. 7, 10:14, 12:1, ch. 20; Eph 1:21; Col 1:16; Rv 13:1–4. *Angels as messengers:* Gn 16:7–12; Lk 1:26–38, 2:9–14. *Angels and God's judgment:* Mt 13:39–42, Rv 8:2. *Angel of the Lord:* Gn 16:7–13, Ex 3:1–5. *Intercessory angels:* Tb 12:12, Rv 8:3–4. *Guardian angels:* Mt 18:10. *Angelic worship of God:* Is 6:3, Lk 2:14. *Demons:* Mk 1:21–28, 3:23–30; 1 Cor 10:14–22. *Satan:* Jb, ch. 1; Zec, ch. 3; Lk 10:18; Rv 12:7–9.

See Also

- "Afterlife"
- "Canaanite Religion"
- "Cosmology"
- "Number Symbolism"

Synagogues and Prayer

The synagogue is the Jewish place of prayer and worship. Like the word *church, synagogue* can refer both to a building used for prayer and worship of God as well as the congregation of the faithful who gather at such a building.

The origin of synagogues is not clear. They may have arisen after the Babylonian Exile, for Jews who could not regularly worship at the Jerusalem Temple. The focus of the synagogue was on prayer and the reading and study of the Scriptures—but no ritual sacrifices were offered as at the Temple. The Acts of the Apostles mentions synagogues in major Mediterranean cities: Damascus (see 9:2), Salamis (see 13:5), Antioch in Pisidia (see v.14), Iconium (see 14:1), Thessalonica (see 17:1), Beroea (see v. 10), Athens (see v. 17), Corinth (see 18:4), Ephesus (see v. 26). In Jesus' time, there were synagogues in Palestine as well; Luke mentions one in Jesus' hometown of Nazareth (see Lk 4:16).

In addition to serving as centers of worship and study, the synagogues also functioned as community centers. A synagogue near Rome, for example, had an attached dining hall and baking facilities.

Two Greek terms are regularly translated as "synagogue" in the New Testament: *synagogue* (see Lk 4:16) literally meaning "a gathering of people," and *proseuche* literally meaning "(a place of) prayer" (see Acts 16:13). The later rabbinic term is *bet midrash,* meaning "house of study."

Archeological evidence from Diasopora synagogues shows that Jewish communities often had good relations with their Gentile neighbors. One synagogue at Rome was dedicated to the Emperor Augustus. A synagogue at Sardis (modern-day Turkey) stood next to a Roman bath and gymnasium in the heart of the city. Josephus records a decree of a Roman official allowing the Jews to have a building of their own for worship and the freedom to manage their own internal legal affairs.

Even before the Temple was destroyed in AD 70, there were synagogues in Palestine and even in Jerusalem itself (see Acts 6:9). An inscription from first-century AD Jerusalem refers to the head of a synagogue, Theodotus, a priest who was the son and grandson of the heads of the synagogue. Luke portrays Jesus' reading from a scroll and preaching in the Nazareth synagogue (see 4:16–30). Early synagogue services may have been held in large private houses rather than in separate buildings, a practice mirroring the early Christian house-church (see Rom 16:5).

Just as the Ark of the Covenant, kept in the Holy of Holies, was the center of the Jerusalem Temple, so the Torah scrolls were the heart of the synagogue. The scrolls were kept in an ark representative of the Ark of the Covenant, which in turn was housed in a wall niche facing Jerusalem. This orientation reflects the biblical custom of praying toward Jerusalem and the Temple (see 1 Kgs 8:44,48; 2 Chr 6:34,38; Dn 6:11). In early synagogues, the ark was portable (perhaps a wooden chest); later it became fixed into the wall. Synagogues also typically had a raised podium for proclaiming the Scriptures.

Josephus and Philo tell us that the Jewish communities met at the synagogue every Sabbath for the reading and studying of the Law. Jesus read from the scroll and preached in the Nazareth synagogue (see 4:16–30); we hear of "the reading of the law and the prophets" in the synagogue at Antioch of Pisidia (Acts 13:15; see also 13:27, 17:1–2). Philo speaks of priests' or elders' reading the laws and interpreting them.

Synagogues were sometimes elaborately decorated. A famous third-century

The menorah, or seven-branched candle stand, appeared in synagogue art and is used in modern synagogue worship.

AD synagogue at Dura Europos (Syria) has a series of fifty-eight panels that depict biblical scenes. Typical Jewish art symbols include the *lulav* (palm or other branches carried during the Feast of Booths), the *shofar* (ram's horn blown on the Day of Atonement), and the menorah (seven-branched candelabrum associated with the Temple lampstand).

Prayer in the Synagogue

The fact that a common Greek name for a synagogue is *proseuche*—"(a place of) prayer"—illustrates the centrality of prayer in the synagogue service.

The most important prayer in Judaism is the Shema—a prayer based on Deuteronomy 6:4–5: "Hear, O Israel! The Lord is our God, the Lord alone! Therefore, you shall love the Lord, your God, with all your heart, and with all your soul, and with all your strength." When Jesus was asked what the greatest command was, he named the Shema, adding, "The second is this: 'You shall love your neighbor as yourself'" (Mk 12:28–30). According to the Mishna, the Shema should be said twice a day— in the morning and evening. The prayers were said both at home and in the synagogue.

After citing the Ten Commandments and the Shema, Deuteronomy insists that these words must be memorized and taken to heart. "Bind them at your wrist as a sign and let them be as a pedant on your forehead. Write them on the doorposts of your houses and on your gates" (6:8–9).

From these passages, Jews developed the practices of wearing phylacteries (see Mt 23:5), or *tefillin,* during synagogue prayers. These are small boxes, containing the Ten Commandments, the Shema, and related biblical passages, that are literally bound to a person's wrists and forehead with leather straps.

There is some evidence of singing hymns and having communal meals in Second Temple synagogues, especially in the Diaspora.

In addition to the Shema, the rabbinic prayer the Eighteen Benedictions (also known as the *Amida*) was most likely recited in Second Temple synagogues. In many ways, the Eighteen Benedictions are similar to the Lord's Prayer in that they call on God to make his name holy ("hallowed") and ask God to establish his will on earth as it is established in heaven. The prayer thanks and praises God for healing the sick and raising the dead, and asks that God watch over his people and the Jerusalem Temple. It is said standing, facing Jerusalem.

Related Passages

Diaspora synagogues: Acts 9:2, 13:5,14. *Nazareth synagogue:* Lk 4:16–30. *Torah reading and study:* Lk 4:16–30, Acts 13:14–47. *Shema:* Dt 6:4–9, Mk 12:28–30. *Prayer facing Jerusalem:* Dn 6:11.

See Also

- "Festivals"
- "Sabbath"
- "Temple"

Taxes and Tithes

The old saying "The only sure things in life are death and taxes" held true for biblical societies also, where the populace was taxed by both government and religious authorities. Taxes were paid in three ways: as money, as a percentage of crops or animals, or as forced labor.

Taxes in Old Testament Times

In ancient Israel, government tax collection was unsystematic, varying from king to king. Taxes were levied in order to pay tribute to foreign kings (see 2 Kgs 15:20, 23:35); Solomon employed forced labor in building the Temple and other building projects (see 1 Kgs 5:27–32, 9:15—22). Samuel warned the people that a king would make them slaves and take 10 percent of their crops, vineyards, and flocks (see 8:15–17), but it is unclear to what extent the kings actually did these things. Taxes were also collected to maintain the priests and the Temple (see 2 Kgs 12:5).

Taxes in First-Century Palestine

The exact percentage of income that was taken in taxes by the Roman government in Jesus' time is not clear. One scholarly estimate puts it at around 12.5 percent. We know that shortly after the Maccabean revolt, a Syrian king referred to his right to collect "a third of the grain and half of the fruit of the trees" (1 Mc 10:30).

In addition to a tax on crops, the Herodian government also collected a "head tax." Every male over fourteen and every female over twelve in a family was assessed a tax of one *denarius* (approximately the daily wage of a laborer). A census would be taken in order to register each family for tax purposes (see Lk 2:1). This is the tax discussed by Jesus and the Pharisees when Jesus concluded, "Repay to Caesar what belongs to Caesar and to God what belongs to God" (Mk 12:17).

Besides these direct taxes, the Romans charged many indirect taxes, such as road tolls and port fees. The Roman military stationed in Palestine also had the legal right to force the native population to help them carry supplies for up to one mile; this right is reflected in Jesus' teaching, "Should anyone press you into service for one mile, go with him for two miles" (Mt 5:41). Roman soldiers exercised this right when they forced Simon of Cyrene to carry Jesus' cross when Jesus became too weak to carry it (see Mk 15:21).

The government regulated economic activity in other ways. Fishermen, for example, could not merely go out and fish in Palestinian lakes; rather, they had to obtain a contract from a tax collector, who might lend them money to buy boats and nets, in return for a percentage of their profits. This tax collector, in turn, had contracted with a chief tax collector who had been appointed by King Herod. Because his office was in the fishing village of Capernaum, Jesus' disciple Matthew was most likely a contractor of fishing rights (see Mt 9:9, Mk 2:14).

Religious Taxes or Tithes

The tithes collected by Jewish religious leaders were also a kind of tax. Tithes were 10 percent of a worker's produce, including both crops and flocks (see Lv 27:30–33). There were two main tithes. One tithe was to be taken to Jerusalem during the festival times, or sold and the money spent in Jerusalem (see Dt 14:22–29). Every third year, however, this tithe was put into a community storehouse, where people, including the "alien, orphan, and widow," could come and "eat their fill" (Dt 14:28–29). Another tithe was used to support the priests and Levites, who did not work their own land. This tithe was given to the Levites who, in turn, would give a tithe of this tithe to the priests (see Nm 18:21–32). This seems to have been a tithe on crops, not on animals.

Additionally, the people gave a first fruits offering from their crops or herds, which was brought either in kind or as a money payment to the Temple during the pilgrimage festivals (see vv. 15–19). The Torah also requires other offerings, such as a wave offering (v. 11) and a sin offering (see Lev 4:27–28). Tobit explains how he faithfully paid these various tithes and offerings (see 1:6–8).

The Torah does give options for a poor person's offering. If a person could not afford an animal, he could offer two birds; if he could not afford two birds, he could offer flour (see Lv 5:7–10; see also 12:8, 14:21–22).

Finally, the Temple tax, required annually of every adult Jewish male, was used for the general needs of the Temple. In Jesus' time, the Temple tax was a half shekel (or two *drachmas*), approximately the cost of two days' wages for a laborer. Jesus refers to this tax in his discussion with Peter (see Mt 17:24–27). This tax was collected not only in Palestine but also in Jewish communities throughout the Diaspora.

The Tax Collection System in Jesus' Time

Neither the Roman emperors nor the Hellenistic kings who ruled over Palestine collected taxes directly; rather, they operated through the client-patron system. Patrons were typically member of the elite class who had wealth or power and thus could offer protection or other benefits to a client in return for the client's loyalty, goods, or services. "Brokers" were people in the middle who would put patrons in touch with clients. Even rulers such as King Herod were essentially clients of the Roman emperor, governing with the emperor's approval.

At the top of this patronage system, the Roman emperor demanded a certain amount of tribute tax from his client King Herod. Herod in turn contracted with members of the elite who were designated as "chief tax collectors." At times the high priest was also involved in guaranteeing the delivery of a certain amount of taxes to the Romans. These chief tax collectors, in turn, hired a number of local tax collectors (brokers) who brought in the actual revenue. The tax collectors mentioned in the Gospels are all local Jews (see Mk 2:15; Lk 18:10–14, 19:1–10).

The right to collect taxes in a certain area (village or district) was auctioned off to the highest bidder. The chief tax collector contracted with the local tax collectors to bring in a certain amount of money; anything over that amount was kept by the local tax collector.

The local tax collectors were among the most despised members of the Jewish communities for several reasons: (1) they earned money by collecting other people's money, which was considered dishonorable in itself; (2) they had a reputation for dishonesty (the tax collector Zacchaeus promises Jesus he will repay four times over anything he has extorted [see Lk 19:8]); (3) they were actively cooperating with the Romans who were occupying the land of Israel. Thus, tax collectors were grouped together with prostitutes (see Mt 21:31) and sinners (see Mk 2:16) as the dregs of society.

Some farmers who were forced from their land by their inability to pay their debts formed gangs of outlaws who survived by raids on the wealthy elite. The "criminals" crucified on either side of Jesus (see Lk 23:33) and Barabbas, the prisoner who was released instead of Jesus (see vv. 18–25), were possibly outlaws of this type. They were popular among the people as "Robin Hoods" who resisted Roman elites and their clients; this may have been one factor in the crowd's decision to release Barabbas instead of Jesus (see Lk 23:25).

Jesus himself taught his followers to pay their taxes (see Mt 17:25–27 [Temple tax], Mk 12:13–17 [Roman tax]), as did Paul (see Rom 13:6–7).

Related Passages

Temple tax: Mt 17:24–27. *Tax collectors:* Mt 9:9–13; Lk 18:10–14, 19:1–10. *Forced labor:* 1 Kgs 5:27–32, 9:15–22; Mt 5:41; Mk 15:21. *Tithes:*

Dt 14:22–29, Nm 18:21–32. *Reduced offerings for the poor:* Lv 5:7–10, 12:8, 14:21–2. *"Social Bandits":* Lk 23:18–25. *Christian duty to obey government and pay taxes:* Mk 12:13–17, Rom 13:1–7.

See Also

- "Agriculture"
- "Fishing"
- "Money"
- "Poverty and Wealth"
- "Priests and Levites"
- "Temple"

Temple

Have you ever been particularly aware of God's presence? Perhaps it happened as you watched a beautiful sunset or as you prayed in church or at a time when a friend unexpectedly called as you were going through a rough time. Though we know theoretically that God is always present, we also experience God's presence more clearly at certain times and in certain places.

Biblical societies shared the common modern belief that God is present throughout the universe: "Do I not fill / both heaven and earth? says the LORD" (Jer 23:24). But just as we associate God's clearer presence with particular holy places (such as a church or a secluded spot in the mountains), so too did biblical societies. God's presence was understood to exist in a special way in the Jerusalem Temple, which is often simply called "the house of the LORD" (Ps 122:1) or the "house of God" (Neh 6:10). The Israelites realized that God could not be completely confined in a building, thus they tended to describe his presence in the Temple indirectly, referring, for example, to "the LORD's glory" (1 Kgs 8:11; see Ez 3:12) in the Temple.

The Temple was built on a hill, the Temple Mount, in east Jerusalem. Originally built in the time of King Solomon in the tenth century BC, it was destroyed during the Babylonian conquest (587 BC). Groups returning from the Babylonian Exile began building the Second Temple around 520 BC (see Ezr, ch. 3). Beginning in 20 BC, King Herod the Great remodeled and expanded it. This Herodian Temple was destroyed by the Romans in AD 70. Today the Temple Mount is occupied by the Dome of the Rock and the Al-Aqsa mosque, Islamic holy places built by Muslim rulers in the late 600s and early 700s. (You may be familiar with the golden dome of the Dome of the Rock in pictures of the Jerusalem skyline.)

Ark of the Covenant and the Dwelling (Tabernacle)

God's presence was associated in particular with the Ark of the Covenant. The Ark was essentially a wooden box or container, overlaid with gold, that contained the Ten Commandments (see Ex 25:16, 1 Kgs 8:9). (Hebrews 9:4 states that the Ark held "the gold jar containing the manna, the staff of Aaron that had sprouted, and the tablets of the covenant"). Two cherubim face one another, with their wings spread out toward each other (see Ex 37:1–9). The top of the Ark was known as the propitiatory (or "mercy seat").

Here God was thought to be present. The Lord says to Moses, "There I will meet you and there, from above the propitiatory, between the two cherubim on the ark of the commandments" (Ex

141

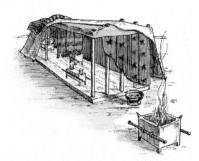

This is an artist's rendition of the sanctuary furnishings within the meeting tent.

25:22). The Ark in this sense can be understood as God's throne (see the "Spiritual Powers" and "Afterlife" articles).

The Ark was first made during the time when Israel was wandering in the wilderness after Moses led them out of Egypt. It was housed in a tent known as the Tent of the Meeting or the Dwelling (also called the Tabernacle in some translations). Eventually, the Ark was moved to the Jerusalem Temple built by Solomon (see 1 Kgs 8:1–12).

After the time of the Babylonian conquest, however, references to the Ark of the Covenant disappear. There are no references to its presence in the Second Temple. An account in Second Maccabees records that Jeremiah hid the Dwelling and the Ark in a cave at Mount Nebo (see 2:4–8).

Solomon's Temple

The structure of the Jerusalem Temple essentially paralleled the structure of the Dwelling. In Solomon's Temple, the sanctuary was divided into one area containing the incense altar, tables for the bread offering, lampstands, and one area known as the Holy of Holies, which housed the Ark of the Covenant. Two 10-foot-tall cherubim, carved from

olive wood and overlaid with gold, also stood in the inner chamber. A courtyard outside the sanctuary had a bronze altar for burnt offerings and a bronze container holding water for ritual purification (for more details on Solomon's Temple, see 1 Kgs, ch. 6–7; 2 Chr, ch. 3–4).

Throughout its history, however, Solomon's Temple was not always dedicated to the pure worship of the Lord alone. King Mannaseh, for example, set up an Asherah idol (a Canaanite fertility goddess) in the Temple (see 2 Kgs 21:7). The prophets condemned Israelites who worshiped at the Temple but were corrupt or immoral in other ways (see Jer, ch. 7). Attempts were regularly made to reform the Temple worship: the efforts of Hezekiah (see 2 Chr, ch. 31) and Josiah (see 2 Kgs, ch. 23) are notable.

The Second Temple, built during the time of Ezra and Nehemiah, also had its share of troubles. In 167 BC, Antioches IV Epiphanes set up an altar to (or image of) Zeus in the Temple (see 1 Mc 1:54). Later the Maccabees recaptured the Temple from the forces of Antiochus and rededicated it (see 4:36–59).

The Herodian Temple

Herod's Temple is not described directly in the Bible, but Josephus provides extensive descriptions, as does "Middoth," one of the tractates of the Mishnah.

The Temple complex was surrounded by a massive stone wall; many of its stones weighed several tons. Parts of this wall still stand today; the best-known section is the Western Wall, a sacred site where Jews still go to pray. This outer wall enclosed an outdoor courtyard known as the Court of the Gentiles.

An inner wall enclosed the main sanctuary space; signs on its gates warned Gentiles not to enter, under pain of death. The Court of the Priests surrounded the sanctuary; the altar for burnt offerings was located here. Because of the holiness of the altar, only priests were allowed in this area; not even Levites could enter. When the sanctuary was built, Josephus says that priests had to be specially trained in carpentry and masonry to work on it, for no one else was allowed access.

Outside of the Court of the Priests, separated by a low wall (about 1½ feet high), was the Court of the Israelites, open to all Jewish men.

At the eastern end of this court, separated by a higher wall, was the Court of the Women. The Mishnah records that the Women's Court had a balcony, from which the women could watch the sacrifices. The Mishnah also states that the fifteen steps leading up from the Court of the Women to the Court of the Israelites correspond to the fifteen Psalms of Ascent (see Ps 120–134). The Levites sang on these steps.

This is an artist's rendition of a lampstand and sprinkling bowl that would have been used in Temple worship.

The sanctuary itself was a roofed building divided into two chambers. The outer chamber held a gold-plated incense altar, a gold-plated table for the bread offering, and a seven-branched lampstand made of pure gold (see Ex 37:10–29). The inner chamber, separated by a curtain (said to have been torn in two when Jesus died [see Mk 15:38]), was the Holy of Holies. Only the high priest could enter this area, and he only one day a year, on the Day of Atonement (see Lv 16:1–19). Josephus tells us that the Holy of Holies was empty, as the Ark had not been recovered.

There were various other rooms in the Temple Mount area: treasury rooms, quarters where priests who offered the morning sacrifice slept, storerooms for wine and oil, rooms for baking bread. Josephus reports that the high priest's council also met in the Temple porticos (covered walkways supported by columns) that ran along the walls.

The Temple was richly decorated. Josephus reports that the front of the sanctuary was gold-plated and reflected the sun so brightly that it dazzled people's eyes. The Temple had richly embroidered curtains, lamps, intricately carved columns, and immensely valuable treasures in its storehouses.

In addition to the singing of the Levites, individuals also prayed at the Temple. The New Testament mentions that Anna (see Lk 2:37), a tax collector and a Pharisee (see 18:10), and Peter and John (see Acts 3:1) prayed there. Isaiah calls the Temple the "house of prayer" (56:7). Yet the Temple was essentially different from the synagogue: its reason for being was the fact that God was present in a special way in that place. Faithful Jews went there to acknowledge and worship God, mainly through sacrifice.

The Temple, Kinship, and Political Systems

The operation of the Temple was not purely "religious"; it was closely tied to Israelite kinship and political systems. King Solomon had built the First Temple, and King Herod rebuilt the Second Temple, motivated largely by his desire to increase his own honor and prestige among the people. The priests who served at the Temple were all males who could trace their descent from the tribe of Levi; chief priests were drawn from a few elite families. The Hasmonean rulers combined the roles of chief priest and king. Later King Herod appointed the high priests.

In New Testament times, the high priest and his associate chief priests were held responsible for maintaining order in the Temple and in Jerusalem as a whole, including seeing that taxes were collected to pay tribute to Rome. The Antonia Fortress, garrisoned by Roman troops in Jesus' time, stood at the northwest corner of the Temple Mount.

The Temple System and the Economy

The Temple system was tied up intricately with not only the economy of Jerusalem but the entire Jewish world.

The Temple was supported not by voluntary contributions but rather by the Temple tax collected from all adult male Jews (see Mt 17:24–27). Jews from Alexandria to Rome regularly sent this tax to Jerusalem.

The Temple had a vast storehouse of treasures. Sacred vessels used in the rituals were kept there as were expensive gifts sent by patrons or clients from all over the world, including gifts from the Roman Emperor Augustus. Israelite kings kept money there, as did private citizens, as the Temple served as a kind of bank. Certain priests administrated the treasury. Roman generals or governors and Israelite kings occasionally raided the treasury for their own purposes.

The economy of Jerusalem was dominated by the Temple activity. Certain families had monopolies in supplying material such as wood, incense, and bread. Others supplied animals, food for the animals, wine, oil, and salt. When Herod's rebuilding of the sanctuary ended in AD 62, Josephus says that eighteen thousand men (among them stonecutters, masons, and carpenters) lost their jobs.

Moneychangers most likely operated in the porticos along the outside Temple walls. As Jews were required to pay the Temple tax with a silver shekel minted at Tyre, moneychangers were needed for pilgrims who came from all over the Mediterranean world with a variety of coins. Sellers of birds for sacrifices also most likely operated in the outer porticos. This is the likely setting for Jesus' "cleansing of the Temple" (see Mk 11:15–19).

Some scholars have argued that the Temple system is an example of the elite exploiting the non-elite through a system of mandatory tithes and sacrifices (see the "Taxes and Tithes" article for details). Together with the taxes and other charges demanded by the Romans and their local patrons, these costs placed great pressure on the non-elite, forcing many into debts they could not repay (see the "Poverty and Wealth" article).

There is truth to this view. The interests of the priestly elite who ran the Temple and the political elite (Rome and its Herodian patrons, for example) were closely allied. Jesus himself criticizes the Jerusalem scribes (a group often closely allied with priestly interests; see Mk 11:27) who "devour the houses of widows and, as a pretext, recite lengthy prayers" (12:40).

Several other factors, however, must be considered to attain a balanced view. First, the Torah does allow options for the poor. If a person could not afford an animal, he could offer two birds; if he could not afford two birds, he could offer flour (see Lv 5:7–10, 12:8, 14:21–22). Second, one of the religious tithes was to be spent by the family itself in Jerusalem; every third year it was to be placed in a collection for the poor (see the "Taxes and Tithes" article). Third, the Israelite people themselves seem not to have regarded the sacrifices or tithes as a burden but rather as a duty toward God that they accepted with little or no question.

The Eschatological Temple

The Jerusalem Temple is at the heart of the prophets' vision of the end times. Ezekiel has a lengthy description of an ideal Temple to be rebuilt after the return from the Babylonian Exile (see Ez, ch. 40–48). Isaiah envisions a final day when all the nations on earth will stream toward Jerusalem to worship the Lord, when the "mountain of the LORD's house / shall be established as the highest mountain" (Is 2:2; see Mi 4:1). Even in the days of the Messiah, then, the Temple, renewed and reformed, would play a role.

Although Jesus' disciples continued to go to the Temple after Jesus' Ascen-

sion (see Acts 3:1), its primary meaning in the New Testament is a symbolic one. The Gospel of John associates it with Jesus' body (see 2:19). Paul calls the bodies of individual church members "the temple of the holy Spirit" (1 Cor 6:19). Much New Testament thought sees the church of Christ as the eschatological Temple (see 2 Cor 6:16, Eph 2:21–22, 1 Pt 2:4–10). Hebrews and Revelation follow the common ancient Jewish tradition of picturing heaven modeled on the Jerusalem Temple (see Is, ch. 6; Heb 8:5, 9:24; Rv 15:5—16:1).

Related Passages

Description of the Ark of the Covenant and the Dwelling: Ex, ch. 25–27, 36–40. *Description of Solomon's Temple:* 1 Kgs, ch. 6–7; 2 Chr, ch. 3–4. *Building of the Second Temple:* Ezr, ch. 3; Haggai. *Prayer at the Temple:* Is 56:7; Lk 2:37, 18:10; Acts 3:1. *Temple tax:* Mt 17:24–27. *Jesus' "cleansing" of the Temple:* Mk 11:15–19. *Eschatological temple:* Ez, ch. 40–48; Is 2:2–4; Mi 4:1–7. *Church as temple:* 2 Cor 6:16, Eph 2:21–2, 1 Pt 2:4–10. *Heaven as a temple:* Is, ch. 6; Heb 8:5, 9:24; Rv 15:5—16:1.

See Also

- "Afterlife"
- "Canaanite Religions"
- "Holiness"
- "Priests"
- "Sacrifices and Offerings"
- "Spiritual Powers"
- "Taxes and Tithes"

Torah

In modern American society, we value our freedom. We tend to dislike rules, seeing them as restrictions on our freedom of choice. But in ancient Israel, the rules of the Torah (usually translated as "Law") were understood in quite a different way. The lengthy Psalm 119, for example, is entirely dedicated to praising God's laws: "Your decrees are my delight; / they are my counselors" (v. 24). "How I love your teaching, Lord! / I study it all day long" (v. 97). "Your word is a lamp for my feet, / a light for my path" (v. 105).

Why the difference in attitudes? Let's take a closer look.

Covenant of the Torah

The word *Torah* is often translated as "Law," but many scholars believe that a better translation is "way of life," as the Torah's commandments and prohibitions cover all areas of human life. The term refers most directly to the commandments given by God to Moses as part of the Covenant between God and Israel (see Ex, ch. 20; Dt, ch. 5). The Talmud identifies 613 commandments; according to some authorities, these are divided into 365 prohibitions (for example, "You shall not kill") corresponding to each day of the year, and 248 positive commandments (for example, "Love your neighbor as yourself") corresponding to the number of bones or organs in the human body. The commandments are found in the first five books of the Bible (thus the five books themselves are sometimes called Torah).

The Covenant, an agreement that defines the relationship between a patron and client, is the essential context for properly understanding the Torah.

In the Covenant of the Torah, God, conceived as a patron, promises the people of Israel that he will be faithful to them and bless them. They, in turn, will follow the commandments of Torah (see the "Covenant" article).

If the people follow the commandments, thus staying within the Covenant, they will be blessed with health, prosperity, and peace; if they do not, they will be cursed with diseases and disasters (see Lv, ch. 26; Dt, ch. 27–28).

The Covenant of the Torah establishes the people of Israel as God's Chosen People (see the "Chosen People" article). Because of their relationship with God, the people are holy, as God is holy (see Lv 19:2: "Be holy, for I, the Lord, your God, am holy"). The commandments of Torah are a means for the people to maintain this holy status. Thus, the penalty for breaking a commandment of Torah is often described as being "cut off from his people" (v. 8). A person's self-identity is closely tied to following Torah; following the rules of Torah establish one as an Israelite.

Torah and Order in a Holy Society

The Israelite concept of holiness, in turn, is closely tied with concepts of order, purity, wholeness, health, and life (see the "Holiness" article). Let's consider first the concept of order.

A healthy society is an ordered society. In Israelite societies, order meant that each person would know his or her place in the hierarchical, patriarchal society. The Torah commands provide this order. Children should respect parents and the elderly (see Lv 19:3,32). Masters must respect the limited rights of their slaves (see Ex 21:1–32). Marriage and inheritance laws reinforced the patriarchal kinship systems (a man's brother was to marry his widow [see Dt 25:5–10]; daughters inherited only if there were no sons [Nm 27:8]; see the "Family" and "Marriage" articles).

Social order includes providing for the poor of society. Farmers shall not harvest all of their crops but must leave some for the poor (see Lv 19:9–10). Sabbatical laws sought to ensure that no family would be impoverished by debt and that each family would retain possession of its own land (see Dt 15:2; Lv, ch. 25; see the "Poverty and Wealth" article).

Social order presupposes honesty in people's relations: Do not lie or steal; be honest in business dealings (see Lv 19:11,35–36).

Torah and Purity

The primary purpose of the purity laws of the Torah is to establish order in the world by clearly separating the holy from the ordinary. In Israel holiness was manifested primarily in the Jerusalem Temple—the place where the glory of God was present (see the "Temple" article). Only clean animals, those who fit in orderly categories, could be eaten and offered as sacrifices in the holy Temple. Blood and sexual fluids, symbolizing dangerous crossing of proper boundaries, caused uncleanness and thus were clearly separated from the holiness of the Temple (see the "Food Laws" and "Purity" articles).

The laws of sacrifice in the Torah established order by purifying the holy Temple from the infection of sin (see the "Atonement" and "Sacrifices and Offerings" articles). At a social level, commandments to sacrifice and tithe functioned to support a class of priests in their holy duties (see the "Taxes and Tithes" article). At a symbolic and theological level, the sacrifices and tithes were a reminder to be thankful for God's blessings, and also to recall the realm of the sacred in the midst of ordinary, daily activity.

Laws concerning the festivals (for example, Passover, the Feast of Tabernacles, the Feast of Weeks) and the Sabbath created order by distinguishing between sacred and ordinary time (see the "Festivals" and "Holiness" articles).

Torah and Group Identity

A further function of the Torah is to distinguish between Israelites and non-Israelites (Gentiles). Certain practices reinforced the individual Israelites' identification with the "in-group"— food laws ensured that Israelites would normally not eat with non-Israelites; circumcision physically marked the Israelite as distinct; observance of the Sabbath rest distinguished Jews from all other groups.

As discussed in the "Chosen People" article, the Bible records quite distinct models by which Israelites related to the "out-group." Deuteronomy insists on strict separation to avoid "contamination" by foreign religious beliefs, to the extent of insisting that indigenous tribes of Canaan be exterminated (see Dt 7:2). Another model, however, presumes interaction with Gentiles, seeing the Israelites as a "light to the nations" who will draw Gentiles to the worship of God by their example (see Is 2:2, 49:6); we see a hint of Israel's vocation to the nations already in God's covenant with Abraham: "All the communities of the earth / shall find their blessing in you" (Gn 12:3).

This brief discussion shows how essential the Torah was in Israel. It brought order, and thus holiness, to every aspect of life. It is not surprising, then, that the Psalmist considers the Torah "a light to my path."

Related Passages

Love of Torah: Ps 119. ***Covenant of the Torah:*** Ex, ch. 20; Dt, ch. 5. ***Blessings and curses of following the Torah:*** Lv, ch. 26; Dt, ch. 27–28. ***Torah and holiness:*** Lv, ch. 19.

See Also

- "Atonement"
- "Chosen People"
- "Covenant"
- "Family"
- "Festivals"
- "Food Laws"
- "Holiness"
- "Marriage"
- "Poverty and Wealth"
- "Priests and Levites"
- "Punishment"
- "Purity"
- "Sacrifices and Offerings"
- "Taxes and Tithes"
- "Temple"

War

War in biblical societies is understood as a normal and expected aspect of human affairs. The Israelites were in regular military conflict with one another, with neighboring peoples in Canaan, and with the great empires of Egypt, Assyria, Babylonia, Greece, and eventually Rome. The Old Testament is filled with accounts of war, including guidelines for how the Israelites should conduct a war (see Dt, ch. 20–21).

Weapons of War

The typical Israelite soldier was armed with a sword, dagger, and shield. Swords were made of iron; blades were straight or sickle-shaped, and sometimes two-edged (see Heb 4:12, Rv 1:16).

Slings and stones were not just used by David in his battle with Goliath (see 1 Sm 17:40–51). Ancient Near Eastern soldiers used them regularly (see Jgs 20:16). Bows and arrows facilitated longer-range fighting (see 1 Chr 5:18). Arrows had heads of metal or stone; bows were made of wood or a combination of wood and

animals' horn. Flaming arrows were often shot in order to set an enemy city or camp on fire (see Eph 6:16). Other common weapons were spears, lances, javelins, and battle axes.

For protection, a soldier carried a shield, often made of a wooden or metal frame covered with leather, of various shapes and sizes (a small, round shield is sometimes translated as a "buckler"). A helmet was often made of wood covered in leather. Body armor included a coat of mail (often made of leather with metal scales sewn on it) or a breastplate.

Chariots were used as weapons of war by the Israelites and their enemies.

King Uzziah's standard issue to his soldiers includes "bucklers, lances, helmets, breastplates, bows and slingstones" (2 Chr 26:14).

To attack a walled city, armies would use battering rams and siege walls (see 2 Kgs 25:1). Horses, cavalry, and chariots were key elements in ancient warfare. Chariots could be two-wheeled or four-wheeled and hold up to four men. They were primary weapons of the feared Egyptian (see Ex 14:9, 15:1), Assyrian, and Babylonian armies, all of whom conquered the Israelites at some point. King Solomon had fourteen hundred chariots and built special chariot cities (see 1 Kgs 9:19, 10:26).

The Herodian Army

Herod the Great, ruler at the time of Jesus' birth, was an unpopular client-king of the Romans, holding on to power by using his own army to suppress and intimidate any opposition. Besides drafting his own subjects, Herod hired foreign mercenaries, including Gauls (from modern-day France) and Germans. He built fortresses throughout his kingdom to maintain control over his own subjects, including the Antonia Fortress in the northwest corner of the Temple Mount. Herodian soldiers appear often in the Gospels. Soldiers of Herod Antipas (son of Herod) executed John the Baptist (see Mk 6:27) and mocked Jesus (see Lk 23:11). Soldiers of Herod Agrippa I (Herod's grandson) arrested Peter in Jerusalem (see Acts 12:4). Sometime after King Herod's death, his troops were incorporated into the Roman army as auxiliaries.

The Roman Army

The basic unit of the Roman army was the legion; first-century Rome had twenty-five legions. Each legion had approximately five thousand infantry and 120 cavalry, and was divided into ten cohorts, each of approximately five hundred troops. Legions were formed from Roman citizens; non-citizens were used as auxiliary troops (see Acts 23:23). In the eastern Empire, however, the majority of legionnaires were non-Italians from the Roman provinces.

The word *legion* had entered into the daily speech in Jesus' time: When Jesus asks a demon for his name, he replies: "Legion is my name. There are many of us" (Mk 5:9). Jesus refers to his ability to call on twelve legions of angels (see Mt 26:53).

The weapons and armor of a Roman legionnaire in Jesus' time included a two-edged sword, a javelin, a belt with a short dagger, a large shield, light body armor, boots, and an iron helmet.

Under Emperor Augustus, four legions were stationed in Syria. Smaller Roman forces were stationed in Palestine; the centurion Cornelius was a member of the Italica cohort at Caesaria (see Acts 10:1). Additional troops were sent to Jerusalem at the time of the pilgrim festivals such as Passover, when the great number of pilgrims increased the chances for unrest. Roman soldiers patrolled the porticos on the outer Temple walls at these times.

The centurion was at the heart of Roman military leadership. He commanded an infantry unit composed of approximately eighty soldiers, despite his title's implication of one hundred men. The centurion was a veteran solider who was paid approximately sixteen times as much as a regular solider.

Jesus healed a centurion's servant at Capernaum. Jewish elders describe him thus: "He loves our nation and he built the synagogue for us" (Lk 7:5). It is possible that this centurion was Jewish. Officers in

Herod's army used the title centurion, and we have second-century inscriptional evidence of a Jew serving as a centurion in the Roman army. (In general, however, Jews were exempt from military service in the Roman army.) In Acts of the Apostles, the centurion Cornelius (clearly a Gentile) is reported as one who gave alms generously to the Jewish people (see 10:1–2).

We meet Roman soldiers often throughout the Gospels. They flog, mock, and crucify Jesus (see Mt 27:27–36). On the way to the execution, the soldiers force Simon of Cyrene to carry Jesus' cross, exercising their legal right to require local residents to carry their gear (in this case, the military property is a cross) for one Roman mile (see Mt 5:41, 27:32). At Jesus' Crucifixion, a centurion declares, "Truly this man was the Son of God" (Mk 15:39).

In Acts of the Apostles, a cohort is sent to restore order when rioting breaks out over rumors that Paul had defiled the Temple (see 21:31–40). The centurion Julius, commander of the Augusta cohort, had custody of Paul and other prisoners on their journey to Rome (see 27:1).

Ideology of the Holy War

Many biblical passages reflect what some scholars refer to as a holy war ideology. The essential belief is that God himself fights in wars in support of his Chosen People, the Israelites (see Ex 14:14, Dt 20:1–4). God is also said to deliver the enemy into the power of the Israelites (see Jos 6:2,16, 1 Sm 23:4). The frequent title Lord of Hosts pictures God as the leader of an angelic army (see the "Spiritual Powers" article); some passages explicitly say, "The LORD is a warrior" (Ex 15:3). A basic assumption

was that if the people were faithful to the Lord and his commandments, they would be victorious in war; if they were not, they would be defeated (see Lv 26:24–34). At its extreme, the holy war ideology justified the Israelites' complete extermination of the Canaanite tribes in order to prevent them from leading the Israelites astray into the worship of their gods (see Dt 20:16–18).

In the writings of the prophets, however, the ideology of holy war is reversed. Because of the sins of Israel, the Lord is pictured as attacking the Israelites: "I will send fire upon Judah, / to devour the castles of Jerusalem" (Am 2:5). Here the Lord is understood as working not through the Israelite forces but through foreign powers such as the Assyrians and Babylonians. The prophets declare that these foreign conquests are God's punishment of the people's sins (see Jer 7:8–15). Foreign powers, however, could also benefit Israel: the Persian King Cyrus is called the Lord's "anointed" because he allowed the Judeans to return home from exile (see Is 45:1).

Eschatological War and Peace

The common Jewish understanding in Jesus' time was that at the fulfillment of history, all strife, suffering, and evil would be eliminated, and the messianic reign of peace and justice would be established on earth: "They shall beat their swords into plowshares / and their spears into pruning hooks; / One nation shall not raise the sword against another, / nor shall they train for war again" (Is 2:4, Mi 4:3, Zec 9:10).

In some descriptions, however, the establishment of this messianic peace is preceded by the violent destruction of forces of evil. God's messiah would first "strike the ruthless with the rod of his mouth, / and with the breath of his lips he shall slay the wicked" (Is 11:4). The Book of Revelation describes the ultimate battle between the Messiah and his armies of angels against "the beast [symbol of the demonic political powers] and the kings of the earth and their armies" (19:14–19; see also 20:8–9). Jesus also assumes that in the last days, people will "hear of wars and reports of wars. . . . Nation will rise against nation and kingdom against kingdom" (Mk 13:7–8).

Because of the symbolic nature of apocalyptic language, it is unclear whether such passages refer to actual earthly wars or to struggles between spiritual powers.

Jesus' Attitude Toward War

Jesus taught his disciples: "Offer no resistance to one who is evil. When someone strikes you on [your] right cheek, turn the other one to him as well" (Mt 5:39). The "evil" ones clearly include the Romans, as one of Jesus' examples refers to the Roman right to force native peoples to carry burdens: "Should anyone press you into service for one mile, go with him for two miles" (v. 41). Jesus further teaches, "Love your enemies, and pray for those who persecute you" (v. 44).

Christians continue to debate the precise meaning of these passages. Should they apply only to the individual, or to nations? Is a Christian ever justified in serving as a soldier? Would Jesus accept the possibility of a just war in order to oppose a tyrant such as Hitler? We cannot enter into these debates here but only note that the debate continues.

Related Passages

Typical Israelite weapons and armor: 2 Chr 26:14. *Rules of war:* Dt, ch. 20–21. *Holy war ideology:* Ex 15:3; Dt 20:1–4,16–18. *Prophetic reversal of holy war ideology:* Jer 7:8–15, Am 2:5. *David and Goliath:* 1 Sm 17:40–51. *Jesus' Crucifixion and Roman soldiers:* Mt 27:26–38. *Forced labor to help carry military supplies:* Mt 5:41, 27:32. *Herodian soldiers:* Lk 23:11, Acts 12:4. *Centurions:* Lk 7:1–10; Acts, ch. 10. *Jerusalem cohort and Paul:* Acts 21:31–40, 22:24–29. *Eschatological war and peace:* Is 11:1–9; Rv, ch. 19–20. *Jesus and nonviolence:* Mt 5:38–48. *Spiritual warfare:* Eph 6:10–17.

See Also

- "Spiritual Powers"

Women

Biblical societies were patriarchal—males controlled the political, religious, family, and economic systems in all biblical societies.

Patriarchal Societies

In Israelite society, lineage is traced through the father. Lists of ancestors (genealogies) typically mention only fathers and sons (see Lk 3:23–24; Mt 1:1–16 is an interesting exception in mentioning four women ancestors). The father was the undisputed head of the household.

Men typically held political power as patriarchs, judges, and kings in Israel, while local councils and elders were also male. Occasionally, however, women were leaders. Deborah was a judge of Israel (see Jgs, ch. 4–6). Queen Athaliah ruled Judah alone for a time (see 2 Kgs, ch. 11). Other queens, such as Jezebel, powerfully influenced their royal husbands' policies (see 1 Kgs 16:31, 18:13, ch. 21). Judith and Queen Esther are also remembered as strong leaders of their people—each has an entire biblical book devoted to her story.

The Israelite priesthood was restricted to men. Yet some women are called prophetesses, messengers of God's Word: Miriam (see Ex 15:20), Huldah (see 2 Kgs 22:14–20), and Deborah (see Jgs 4:4; see also Neh 6:14, Lk 2:36, Acts 21:9, 1 Cor 11:5).

Men dominated the public economy in biblical societies. Women typically worked inside the home, caring for the family and managing the household, and thus typically did not earn an income. An unmarried woman was in a vulnerable position. The Bible frequently refers to widows and orphans as the most vulnerable and oppressed people in society (see Is 10:2, Jas 1:27). The story of Ruth relates how a poor widow escaped her poverty by marrying a wealthy man. Conversely, a widow who had some of her own means could hold a relatively independent role outside regular patriarchal structures (see Judith, 1 Tm 5:3–16).

Women's Role as Wife and Mother

The primary social role of a woman in biblical societies was to be a wife and mother. Women who could not bear children were subject to mockery by other women (see Gn 16:4, 1 Sm 1:6) and social stigma. When Rachel finally bears a child, she says, "God has removed my disgrace" (Gn 30:23). Women put great effort into bearing children. Hannah goes to the Temple to plead with God for a child (see 1 Sm 1:9–19). Women also sought out roots or plants that they believed would increase their fertility (see Gn 30:14–24). The theme of the woman who cannot bear a child but then is miraculously helped by God is standard in the Bible (see Gn, ch. 16–21; Jgs, ch. 13; 2 Kgs 4:14–17).

Many women died in childbirth, however (see Gn 35:16–20), and rates of infant mortality were high (up to 50 percent). Women thus prayed for protection for themselves and their infants. In addition to prayers to the Lord, Israelite women might also seek other sources of help. Archaeologists have discovered many amulets and figurines that were apparently used as magical protection against demons who sought to harm the infants, or to help barren women conceive. The Canaanite goddess Asherah and the Egyptian god Bes were sometimes invoked.

The role of a mother was highly respected in Israel, as children were to honor both parents equally: "Honor your father and your mother, that you may have a long life in the land which the LORD, your God, is giving you" (Ex 20:12). A mother taught both daughters and sons: "Hear, my son, your father's instruction, / and reject not your mother's teaching" (Prv 1:8, 6:20). The heading of one collection in the Book of Proverbs is "Lemuel, king of Massa: The advice which his mother gave him" (31:1). Mothers were also remembered among the people's ancestors: "Look to Abraham, your father, / and to Sarah, who gave you birth" (Is 51:2).

The great respect given to mothers carried over to the symbolic realm also. God is compared to a mother (see 42:14, 49:15, 66:13). Jesus compares himself to a mother hen (see Mt 23:37); Paul compares himself to a woman in labor (see Gal 4:19).

Women's Dependence on Fathers and Husbands

In Israelite society, a woman was not independent. The Mishnah states plainly that a woman remained under the control of her father until she entered into the control of her husband at marriage. If a woman made a vow and her husband or father disapproved, she was not bound (see Nm, ch. 30).

The unequal relationship in marriage is illustrated by the fact that one of the words for husband in Hebrew is *baal,* meaning "lord" or "master." Abraham is called the *baal* of Sarah (see Gn 20:3, 1 Pt 3:6).

In biblical societies, a marriage was typically arranged by a woman's father

(see the "Marriage" article). In Jewish society, a man could divorce his wife, but she could not divorce him. A man could have more than one wife, but a woman could have only one husband. A daughter could inherit property only if there were no sons (see Nm 27:1–11).

Women's Management of the Household

According to Philo, women should run the economy of the home, while men should run the affairs of the state. A woman's primary task was to provide food and clothing for the household, which included not only husband and children but also often extended family (including grandparents and married children) and (if the family was wealthy) servants or slaves.

Making bread was a central task in Palestine. A woman would grind flour at a hand mill and bake daily; this task alone took an estimated three to four hours (see Mt 24:41). The Torah commands that no one should take a hand mill as a pledge to repay a debt, because the family relies on it for its survival (see Dt 24:6).

Spinning and weaving in order to make clothes was also essential. These activities were not restricted to the poor. The daughter of the Roman emperor Caesar Augustus was taught to weave; the Mishnah says that a woman should work with wool, even if she is wealthy enough to afford servants. Skillful work was highly respected. When the disciple Tabitha dies, the believers show Peter tunics and cloaks that she had made (see Acts 9:39).

Another significant task was to draw water from a spring or well to supply the household. In the Bible, the watering place is often the site of encounters between men and women. Abraham's servant encounters Isaac's future wife Rebekah at a spring (see Gn 24:15–27), Jacob meets his future wife Rachel at a well (see 29:9–14), and Moses meets his future wife Zipporah at a well (see Ex 2:15–22). Jesus speaks with the Samaritan woman at a well (see Jn 4:4–42).

Work Outside the Household

Women would typically not work in the fields. Ruth gleans grain in the fields (see Ru 2:1–9) because she is a poor widow and has no other means of support. A woman's brothers make her work in a vineyard as a sort of punishment (see Song 1:6). Girls, however, would sometimes tend sheep. Rachel tended her father's sheep (see Gn 29:9; see also Song 1:8).

Women would sometimes work with their husbands or fathers at their trade. Both Priscilla and her husband Aquila are described as tentmakers (see Acts 18:2–3). Women sometimes sold their household products outside the home (see Prv 31:24). In the Diaspora, we read of Lydia, a woman who traded purple cloth (a luxury item) and hosted Paul and his companions in her home (see Acts 16:14–15).

Women and Purity

Many of the Torah's purity laws applied specifically to women. A woman was impure after childbirth and at the time of her menstruation (see Lev, ch. 12; 15:19–30). Anyone who touched her or any furniture on which she sat or lay would be unclean. We should not conclude from this, however, that women were excluded from their homes during their time of menstruation. This would have been quite impractical, as the woman was essential to the proper functioning of the home. The primary

restriction of these laws was to prevent impure women from going to the Temple. Women in a state of purity were allowed within the Temple but were restricted to the Court of the Women, which was outside of the Court of the Israelites, open to Israelite men.

Jesus and Women

Although women are not listed among Jesus' Twelve Apostles, the Gospels tell us that women did travel with Jesus in his journeys from village to village and accompanied him to his death in Jerusalem (see Mk 15:40–41, Lk 8:1–3).

Jesus was open to interaction with women. When he speaks with a Samaritan woman at a well, his disciples "were amazed that he was talking with a woman" (Jn 4:27). We can contrast Jesus' attitude with a saying from the Mishnah that criticizes a man who speaks too much with women, because he will neglect the study of the Torah and end up in Gehenna! When Jesus visits the home of Martha and Mary, Mary "sat beside the Lord at his feet listening to him speak" (Lk 10:39). Such a posture is a sign of a student or disciple: Paul sits "at the feet" of the learned Pharisee Gamaliel for his education (Acts 22:3).

Women in Early Christianity

Women had a significant role in the spread of early Christianity. They are the first witnesses to Jesus' Resurrection (see Mt 28:10, Jn 20:18). Mary, mother of John Mark, held church gatherings in her home in Jerusalem (see Acts 12:12); the "brothers" gathered at Lydia's home (see 16:40).

Priscilla and her husband, Aquila, traveled with Paul on his missionary journeys (see 18:18). Both husband and wife were involved in teaching the faith "more accurately" to the learned preacher Apollos (see v. 26), and they hosted church gatherings in their house (see 1 Cor 16:19). Paul calls them "co-workers in Christ Jesus, who risked their necks for my life" (Rom 16:3–4; see also Phil 4:2–3).

In a lengthy list of greetings at the end of his Letter to the Romans, Paul includes several references to women. He speaks of Mary, who "has worked hard for you," (16:6), Junia, who is "prominent among the apostles" (v. 7), and Tryphaena and Tryphosa, identified as "workers in the Lord" (v. 12). Paul also commends Phoebe to his Roman audience, "a minister of the church of Cenchreae" (Rom 16:1). The word translated as "minister" here is *diakonos,* a word that ranges in meaning from a servant or helper to a preacher of the Gospel. Because Paul refers to himself as a *diakonos* (see 1 Cor 3:5) and to church leaders at Philipi as *diakonoi,* it is likely that Phoebe is some kind of church leader, although her precise duties remain unclear.

Within the family, the early Christians continued a patriarchal model with the husband as head of the family and the wife as subordinate to her husband (see 1 Cor 11:3–12, Eph 5:21–32). Yet in these passages, the patriarchal model is qualified: the husband should love his wife in the self-sacrificing manner of Christ; husband and wife should become "one flesh" (Eph 5:25,31). And in First Corinthians Paul insists that "woman is not independent of man or man of woman in the Lord" (11:11).

The Controversial Role of Women in the Early Church

The role of women leaders is controversial even within the New Testament. In one passage, Paul teaches that women should be silent in the churches (see 1 Cor 14:33–35). This statement cannot mean that women should be completely silent, because in the same letter he assumes that women prophesy in church (see 11:5). A later passage in the Pauline tradition explicitly links women's silence to the authority to teach: "I do not permit a woman to teach or to have authority over a man. She must be quiet" (1 Tm 2:12).

The very fact that these passages forbid women speaking and teaching in the church indicates that some early Christian women were in fact speaking and teaching, and that this activity sparked controversy.

The role of women in Christianity today remains controversial. In the Catholic Tradition, the Church continues to affirm that only men may be ordained as priests. Women, however, have long taken leadership roles in their own communities of sisters, and recently many women are serving as lay ministers and in other leadership positions in the churches.

Related Passages

Patriarchal structure of society: Nm 27:1–11, ch. 30; Lk 3:23–38. *Women leaders in the Old Testament:* Jgs, ch. 4–6 (Deborah); Judith; Esther. *Women prophets:* Ex 15:20, 2 Kgs 22:14–20, Acts 21:9. *Women and childbearing:* Gn, ch. 16–21, 30:1–23; Jgs, ch. 13; 1 Sm, ch. 1. *Honored role of the mother:* Ex 20:12, Prv 1:8. *Female metaphors for the divine:* Is 42:14, 49:15, 66:13; Mt 23:37. *Women's work outside the home:* Prv 31:24; Acts 16:14–15, 18:2–3. *Women and purity:* Lv, ch. 12; 15:19–30. *Ideal wife:* Prv 31:10–31. *Jesus and women:* Lk 8:1–3, 10:38–42; Jn 4:4–42. *Women in the early*

Church: Mt 28:10; Acts 16:13–15,40; Rom 16:1–12. **Christian wives and husbands:** Eph 5:21–32, Col 3:18–19, 1 Pt 3:1–2. **Controversy over women's roles:** 1 Cor 14:34–36, 1 Tm 2:9–15.

- "Dress and Hair"
- "Dwellings"
- "Family"
- "Food and Drink"
- "Marriage"
- "Purity"

See Also
- "Canaanite Religion"
- "Dance and Music"

Bibliography

Primary Sources (Translations)
Charlesworth, James H.
The Old Testament Pseudepigrapha.
2 vols. New York: Doubleday, 1983.
Danby, Herbert.
The Mishnah. London: Oxford University Press, 1933.

Secondary Sources
Douglas, Mary.
Purity and Danger: An Analysis of the Concept of Pollution and Taboo, 2nd ed. London: Routledge, 2000.
Freedman, David Noel.
The Anchor Bible Dictionary. 6 vols. New York: Doubleday, 1992.
Hanson, K. C., and Douglas E. Oakman.
Palestine in the Time of Jesus: Social Structures and Social Conflicts, 2nd ed. Minneapolis: Fortress Press, 2008.
Lockyer, Herbert, ed.
Nelson's Illustrated Bible Dictionary. Carmel, NY: Guideposts, 1986.
Malina, Bruce J.
The New Testament World: Insights from Cultural Anthropology, 3rd ed. Louisville, KY: Westminster / John Knox Press, 2001.
Malina, Bruce J., and Richard L. Rohrbaugh.
Social Science Commentary on the Synoptic Gospels, 2nd ed. Minneapolis: Fortress Press, 2003.
Otto, Rudolf.
The Idea of the Holy: An Inquiry into the

Whiston, William, trans.
The Works of Josephus, updated ed. Peabody, MA: Hendrickson Publishers, 1987.
Yonge, C. D., trans.
The Works of Philo, updated ed. Peabody, MA: Hendrickson Publishers, 1993.

Pilch, John J.
The Cultural Dictionary of the Bible. Collegeville, MN: Liturgical Press, 1999.
Pilch, John J., and Bruce J. Malina.
Handbook of Biblical Social Values. Peabody, MA: Hendrickson Publishers, 2000.
Sanders, E. P.
Judaism: Practice and Belief 63 BCE–66 CE. London: SCM Press; Philadelphia: Trinity Press International, 1992.
Stegemann, Ekkehard, and Wolfgang Stegemann.
The Jesus Movement: A Social History of Its First Century. Minneapolis: Fortress, 1999.
Vamosh, Miriam Feinberg.
Women at the Time of the Bible. Herzlia, Israel: Palphot, 2007.
Wight, Fred H.
Manners and Customs of Bible Lands. Chicago: Moody Press, 1953.
Wigoder, Geoffrey.
Illustrated Dictionary and Concordance of the Bible. Jerusalem: G. G. The Jerusalem Publishing House, Ltd., 1986.

Scriptural Index

6:1–3	Dance and Music: Heavenly hymns and praises
6:1	Afterlife: God's throne and heavenly Temple
6:3	Spiritual Powers: Angelic worship of God
7:11	Cosmology: Covenant
9:1–6	Prophets: Prophecies of the messiah and the messianic age
11:1–9	Anointing: Age of the messiah
11:1–9	War: Eschatological war and peace
11:2–9	Prophets: Prophecies of the messiah and the messianic age
15:2	Death and Burial Customs: Mourning customs
20:2–5	Prophets: Symbolic actions
25:6	Food and Drink: Eschatological wine
25:6	Meals: Messianic feast
27:1	Creation: New Covenant
27:2–4	Agriculture: Vineyard and vines
40:6–7	Human Nature: Fragility of the human (basar)
42:14	Women: Female metaphors for the divine
49:6	Chosen People: God's choices
49:6	Chosen People: Openness to the Gentiles
49:6	Holiness: Holiness and the Chosen People
49:15	Women: Female metaphors for the divine
51:9–10	Creation: Covenant as bringing order to chaos
52:13—53:12	Atonement: Atoning death in the Old Testament
53:6	Sheep, Goats, and Shepherds: Leaders as shepherds, people as sheep
56:7	Temple: Prayer at the Temple
63:6	Agriculture: Vineyard and vines
66:13	Women: Female metaphors for the divine

JEREMIAH (Jer)
	Prophets: Major prophets
1:5	Chosen People: God's choice of the weak
2:8	Canaanite Religion: References to Canaanite worship
3:1–13	Sexuality: Analogy of God's relationship with humans with marital relationships
7:6	Prophets: Concern for the poor and oppressed
7:8–15	War: Prophetic reversal of holy war ideology
7:31	Canaanite Religion: Child sacrifices to Molech
8:13	Agriculture: Olive trees and fig trees
9:16–17	Dance and Music: Professional mourners
9:16–17	Death and Burial Customs: Professional lamenters
16:7	Food and Drink: Centrality of bread
17:19–27	Sabbath: Sabbath restrictions
ch.19	Prophets: Symbolic actions
19:6	Afterlife: Gehenna
22:3	Prophets: Concern for the poor and oppressed
23:13	Canaanite Religion: References to Canaanite worship
25:1–14	Prophets: Prophetic judgment on Israel and the Day of the Lord
ch.28	Prophets: Symbolic actions
31:31–34	Prophets: Prophecies of the messiah and the messianic age
31:31–33	Covenant: New Cosmology
32:35	Canaanite Religion: Child sacrifices to Molech

LAMENTATIONS (Lam)
	Dance and Music: Biblical books of songs

EZEKIEL (Ez)
	Prophets: Major prophets
ch.1	Afterlife: God's throne and heavenly Temple
ch.1	Spiritual Powers: Visions of the God enthroned and the heavenly court
1:1	Prophets: Prophetic visions
4:1–3	Prophets: Symbolic actions
ch.9–10	Chosen People: Separation from the Gentiles
ch.10	Afterlife: God's throne and heavenly Temple
10:20–22	Spiritual Powers: Cherubim
ch.16	Honor and Shame: Honor and gender roles
ch.16	Sexuality: Analogy of God's relationship with humans with marital relationship
16:4	Food and Drink: Salt
16:11–12	Dress and Hair: Women's jewelry
16:20–21	Canaanite Religion: Child sacrifices to Molech
ch.18	Sin: Sin and group–oriented perspective
22:7	Prophets: Concern for the poor and oppressed
ch.23	Sexuality: Analogy of God's relationship with humans with marital relationship
ch.34	Sheep, Goats, and Shepherds: Leaders as shepherds, people as sheep
ch.40–48	Temple: Eschatological temple

DANIEL (Dn)
	Prophets: Major Prophets
6:11	Synagogues and Prayers: Prayer facing Jerusalem
ch.7	Spiritual Powers: Spiritual powers and nations
7:9	Afterlife: God's throne and heavenly Temple
ch.8–10	Spiritual Powers: Archangels
10:14	Spiritual Powers: Spiritual powers and nations
12:1	Spiritual Powers: Spiritual powers and nations
12:2	Resurrection: Late Old Testament belief in resurrection
ch.20	Spiritual Powers: Spiritual powers and nations

HOSEA (Hos)
	Prophets: Minor prophets
ch.1–3	Sexuality: Analogy of God's relationship with humans with marital relationship
ch.1–2	Honor and Shame: Honor and gender roles
2:15	Canaanite Religion: References to Canaanite worship
6:1	Sickness and Health: God as the ultimate cause of illness and health
9:10	Agriculture: Olive trees and fig trees

JOEL (Jl)
	Prophets: Minor prophets
	Prophets: Prophetic judgment on Israel and the Day of the Lord
1:7	Agriculture: Olive trees and fig trees
2:1	Dance and Music: Trumpets and horns

AMOS (Am)
	Prophets: Minor prophets
2:5	War: Prophetic reversal of holy war ideology

MARK (Mk)

1:16–20	Fishing: Fishing families and cooperatives
1:16–20	Poverty and Wealth: Economic status of Jesus' followers
1:21–28	Spiritual Powers: Demons
1:22	Priests and Levites: Scribes
1:29–35	Hospitality: Christian hospitality networks
1:40–45	Purity: Jesus and purity
2:1–12	Dwellings: The roof
2:13–17	Meals: Jesus' eating with social outcasts
2:13–14	Fishing: Fishing and the patronage system
2:18–3:6	Jewish Sects: Pharisaic conflicts with Jesus
2:21–22	Food and Drink: Storing wine
2:22	Agriculture: Vineyard and vines
2:23–28	Sabbath: Jesus' controversy with Pharisees on plucking grain
3:16–19	Number Symbolism: Jesus' Twelve Apostles
3:20–35	Family: Family and Kingdom values
3:23–30	Spiritual Powers: Demons
3:31–35	Honor and Shame: Honor and family
4:3–20	Agriculture: Sowing and harvesting
4:30–32	Afterlife: Kingdom of God
4:31–32	Agriculture: Sowing and harvesting
4:35–41	Fishing: Fishing boats
5:1–20	Sickness and Health: Demons as the cause of illness
5:25–34	Purity: Jesus and purity
5:26	Sickness and Health: References to physicians
5:41	Languages: Aramaic phrases
6:1–6	Honor and Shame: Honor and family
6:6–13	Hospitality: Christian hospitality networks
6:13	Anointing: Anointing and health
6:13	Sickness and Health: Charismatic healing
6:34–44	Food and Drink: Feeding miracles
6:34–44	Meals: Jesus' feeding the crowds
6:38	Fishing: Eating fish
7:1–23	Food Laws: New Testament discussion of food laws
7:1–23	Jewish Sects: Pharisaic traditions
7:1–4	Purity: Special purity rules of the Pharisees
7:1	Priests and Levites: Scribes
7:34	Languages: Aramaic phrases
8:1–10	Food and Drink: Feeding miracles
8:1–10	Meals: Jesus' feeding the crowds
8:14–21	Jewish Sects: Pharisaic conflicts with Jesus
8:27–30	Anointing: Jesus the Messiah
8:34–35	Crucifixion: Symbolism of the cross
8:35	Human Nature: Psyche as natural life
9:2–8	Holiness: Holy places
9:11	Priests and Levites: Scribes
9:14–32	Sickness and Health: Demons as the cause of illness
9:47	Afterlife: Kingdom of God
9:48	Afterlife: Gehenna
9:49–50	Food and Drink: Salt
10:1–12	Honor and Shame: Honor and challenge and response
10:1–12	Jewish Sects: Pharisaic conflicts with Jesus
10:1–12	Sexuality: Jesus' teaching on marriage and divorce
10:2–12	Marriage: Divorce
10:17–31	Poverty and Wealth: Jesus' criticism of the elites
10:42–45	Family: Family and Kingdom values
10:45	Human Nature: Psyche as natural life
11:12–25	Agriculture: Olive trees and fig trees
11:15–19	Temple: Jesus' "cleansing" of the Temple
11:27–33	Honor and Shame: Honor and challenge and response
12:1–12	Agriculture: Vineyard and vines
12:1–12	Poverty and Wealth: Tenant farmers
12:13–17	Honor and Shame: Honor and challenge and response
12:13–17	Jewish Sects: Pharisaic conflicts with Jesus
12:13–17	Money: Paying taxes to the emperor
12:13–17	Taxes and Tithes: Christian duty to obey government and pay taxes
12:18–27	Jewish Sects: Sadducees
12:18–27	Resurrection: Jesus' debate with the Sadducees
12:28–30	Synagogues and Prayers: Shema
12:32–34	Sacrifice: Spiritual sacrifice
12:42–44	Money: Poor widow's contribution
13:21	Food and Drink: Making bread
14:1	Priests and Levites: Scribes
14:12–26	Festivals: Passover
14:26	Dance and Music: New Testament hymns
14:36	Languages: Aramaic phrases
14:38	Human Nature: Flesh (sarx) and spirit (pneuma)
14:53–64	Priests and Levites: Sanhedrin
14:61	Anointing: Jesus the Messiah
15:21	Taxes and Tithes: Forced labor

LUKE (Lk)

1:26–38	Spiritual Powers: Angels as messengers
2:9–14	Spiritual Powers: Angels as messengers
2:14	Spiritual Powers: Angelic worship of God
2:24	Sacrifices: Alternative sacrifices for the poor
2:37	Temple: Prayer at the Temple
2:45–55	Dance and Music: Women's songs of praise
3:23–38	Family: Patriarchal descent
3:23–38	Honor and Shame: Honor and family
3:23–38	Women: Patriarchal structure of society
4:16–30	Synagogues and Prayers: Nazareth synagogue
4:16–30	Synagogues and Prayers: Torah reading and study
5:1–11	Fishing: Fishing families and cooperatives
5:1–11	Holiness: The sacred and holy fear
6:20–26	Poverty and Wealth: Jesus' criticism of the elites
7:1–10	War: Centurions
7:11–14	Death and Burial Customs: Burial customs
7:41–43	Poverty and Wealth: Inability to repay debt
8:1–3	Poverty and Wealth: Economic status of Jesus' followers
8:1–3	Women: Jesus and women
9:59–62	Family: Family and Kingdom values
9:59–62	Honor and Shame: Honor and family
10:17	Names: Names and authority
10:18	Spiritual Powers: Satan
10:25–37	Jewish Sects: Samaritans
10:34	Anointing: Anointing and health
10:34	Food and Drink: Medicinal properties of wine
10:38–42	Women: Jesus and women
11:2–4	Sin: The Lord's Prayer (sin as debt)
12:57–59	Poverty and Wealth: Inability to repay debt

Subject Index